John Cullen Gruesser, Hanna Wallinger (Eds.)

Loopholes and Retreats: African American Writers and the Nineteenth Century

FORECAAST

(Forum for European Contributions
to African American Studies)

Volume 17

LIT

Loopholes and Retreats: African American Writers and the Nineteenth Century

edited by

John Cullen Gruesser and Hanna Wallinger

LIT

Bibliographic information published by the Deutsche Nationalbibliothek
The Deutsche Nationalbibliothek lists this publication in the Deutsche Nationalbibliografie; detailed bibliographic data are available in the Internet at http://dnb.d-nb.de.

ISBN 978-3-7000-0928-3 (Austria)
ISBN 978-3-8258-1892-0 (Germany)

A catalogue record for this book is available from the British Library

® LIT VERLAG GmbH & Co. KG Wien 2009
Krotenthallergasse 10/8
A-1080 Wien
Tel. +43 (0) 1-409 56 61
Fax +43 (0) 1-409 56 97
e-Mail: wien@lit-verlag.at
http://www.lit-verlag.at

LIT VERLAG Dr. W. Hopf
Berlin 2009
Fresnostr. 2
D-48159 Münster
Tel. +49 (0) 2 51-620 32 22
Fax +49 (0) 2 51-922 60 99
e-Mail: lit@lit-verlag.de
http://www.lit-verlag.de

Distribution:

In Germany: LIT Verlag Fresnostr. 2, D-48159 Münster
Tel. +49 (0) 2 51-620 32 22, Fax +49 (0) 2 51-922 60 99, e-Mail: vertrieb@lit-verlag.de

In Austria: Medienlogistik Pichler-ÖBZ GmbH & Co KG
IZ-NÖ, Süd, Straße 1, Objekt 34, A-2355 Wiener Neudorf
Tel. +43 (0) 22 36-63 53 52 90, Fax +43 (0) 22 36-63 53 52 43, e-Mail: mlo@medien-logistik.at

In Switzerland: B + M Buch- und Medienvertriebs AG
Hochstr. 357, CH-8200 Schaffhausen
Tel. +41 (0) 52-643 54 85, Fax +41 (0) 52-643 54 35, e-Mail: order@buch-medien.ch

Distributed in the UK by: Global Book Marketing, 99B Wallis Rd, London, E9 5LN
Phone: +44 (0) 20 8533 5800 – Fax: +44 (0) 1600 775 663
http://www.centralbooks.co.uk/html

Distributed in North America by:

Transaction Publishers
New Brunswick (U.S.A.) and London (U.K.)

Transaction Publishers
Rutgers University
35 Berrue Circle
Piscataway, NJ 08854

Phone: +1 (732) 445 - 2280
Fax: + 1 (732) 445 - 3138
for orders (U. S. only):
toll free (888) 999 - 6778
e-mail: orders@transactionpub.com

Acknowledgments

The editors wish to acknowledge the financial support of the University of Tours. In particular, we wish to thank the organizer of the 2005 Conference of the Collegium for African American Research, Professor Claude Julien, for his great help in securing funds for this conference and hence this volume.

We are also grateful for the many discussions of African American writers and the nineteenth century at several CAAR conferences. The scholarly exchanges before, during, and after our CAAR workshops were extremely helpful, and we hope that the conversation will continue.

We thank Alan Robbins for permission to use the photo on the cover of the volume.

The editors are also grateful for the help and support of Lit Verlag, especially Richard Kisling in the Vienna office.

Special thanks go to Johannes Peschek as well for his fine editorial help.

September 2008
John Cullen Gruesser, Kean University
Hanna Wallinger, Salzburg University

Contents

Introduction: Loopholes and Retreats in Nineteenth-Century African American Literature and Culture

John Cullen Gruesser

> My grandmother's house had seven rooms – two upper rooms, and five on the lower floor: on the west side there was a piazza. On the east side there were two rooms, with a lobby leading to the centre of the house. The room on the left on entering the lobby was used as a storeroom; the ceiling of this room was of boards, the roof was shingled; the space between the roof and the ceiling was from three and a half to four feet in height, running off to a point. My uncle made a cupboard in one corner of this room, with the top attached to the ceiling. The part of the board that covered the top of the cupboard was cut and made into a trap-door; the whole of it was so small and neatly done that no one would have believed it to be what it was – the entrance to her hiding-place. [...] She remained in that strange place of concealment six years and eleven months before she could get away!
>
> John S. Jacobs: *A True Tale of Slavery*

The remarkable espionage work of Mary Elizabeth Bowser provides a stunning example of a "loophole of retreat," the phrase used so powerfully by Harriet Jacobs in *Incidents in the Life of a Slave Girl* to describe a place of seeming limitation, danger, and weakness that becomes a site of possibility, safety, and empowerment. Bowser was born the slave of John Van Lew in Richmond, Virginia in 1839. When he died in 1851, his daughter, Elizabeth Van Lew, a staunch abolitionist, freed Bowser, bought and liberated her enslaved family members, and sent her to a Quaker school in Philadelphia where she was studying when the Civil War began. Van Lew had a reputation for dressing and acting eccentrically, which earned her the nickname "Crazy Bet" and made her the unlikeliest of Union spymasters. In 1863, she arranged for Bowser to work in the home of Jefferson Davis, where she was regarded as an unlettered and dimwitted but diligent bondwoman. In reality, she was not only free and well educated but also had a photographic memory, which she put to good use in examining the documents that crossed the desk of the President of the Confederate States of America. To transmit the intelligence she gathered to Van Lew and Thomas McNiven, a Union spy who disguised himself as a baker, she availed herself of everyday materials within the household, hiding military plans in empty egg shells, conveying messages by means of a food tray with a false bottom, and even using the clothes she hung up to dry to send coded messages. Perhaps because her real identity was suspected, Bowser fled Richmond in January 1865, attempting, unsuccessfully, to burn down the Confederate White House as she left, and no one knows what became of her afterward. So valuable was the information that she and Van Lew provided from the heart of enemy territory that General Grant called it the best intelligence he received from Richmond during the Civil War. "One of the highest-placed and most productive espionage agents of the Civil War," Bowser was inducted in 1995 into the United States Army Military Intelligence Hall of Fame, which noted in its citation that "Jefferson Davis never discovered the leak in his household staff [. . .] although he knew the Union somehow kept discovering Confederate plans" (Grosvenor, Williams, "Mary Bowser," "Mary Elizabeth Bowser"). Exploiting white assumptions about her mental abilities and slave status to make invaluable contributions to her people's struggle for freedom, Mary Bowser, astoundingly, managed to convert the headquarters of the Confederate war effort into a loophole of retreat.

The essays in this collection explore the loopholes and retreats employed and exploited by African American polemicists, poets, novelists, slave narrators, playwrights, short story writers, essayists, editors, educators, historians, clubwomen, and autobiographers during the nineteenth century. Jacobs derived the phrase "loophole of retreat" from William Cowper, perhaps via Lydia Maria Child; however, she makes it completely and uniquely her own in *Incidents*. Jacobs uses it as the name for the cramped crawl space, at once grave-like and womb-like, in which Linda Brent spends nearly seven years and as the title of a chapter she places dead center in the narrative (Warner 219, Burnham 278). As Michelle Burnham explains, "loophole" has both a military/spatial and a legal/textual denotation (281-85); in other words, the term has both a literal meaning – an actual hole – and a figurative one. Legal or textual loopholes, as Burnham suggests, are inherent in all laws (284). They provide the means by which to evade responsibility, penalty, or punishment. (Discovered reading the bible, W. C. Fields is said to have quipped that he was "looking for loopholes.")

Within a fortress a loophole is a small aperture through which to observe or shoot at an enemy without being observed or vulnerable to return fire. This type of loophole functions as both a defensive and an offensive space, something which is clearly reflected in *Incidents*. Linda often describes her struggle against Dr. Flint, in which her crawlspace plays a pivotal role, in military terms. After failing to escape to the North, she enters the loophole to avoid being returned to slavery and her master's control. Once there, however, she uses it to spy on Flint, gather intelligence about his movements, and send him phony messages so convincing that they spur him to journey to the North in search of her.

Prior to, throughout, and beyond the nineteenth century, legal loopholes were used to deny rights to African Americans. The United States Constitution's designation of a slave as three-fifths of a person did not confer even the most limited legal status on enslaved persons; rather, it served only to give slaveholders increased voting power – so much so, in fact, that it resulted in Thomas Jefferson's defeat of John Adams in the 1800 election (Wills 45). The United States Supreme Court, in its 1857 ruling in the *Dred Scott v. Sanford* case, declared that no person of African descent, slave or free, was a citizen of the United States ("Dred Scott"). In the post-Reconstruction era, legal loopholes were used to deny African Americans the citizenship and voting rights guaranteed to them by the Fourteenth and Fifteenth Amendment to the Constitution. Sutton E. Griggs includes an episode in his first novel *Imperium in Imperio (*1899) that clearly refers to late nineteenth-century legalistic maneuvers to deny civil rights to blacks. When the dark-skinned Belton Piedmont resoundingly defeats Bernard Belgrave in a public speaking competition on commencement day, the white Southern judges, in collusion with boys' white teacher, nevertheless award the prize to the lighter-skinned Bernard:

> They said: "That black nigger has beat the yellow one all to pieces this time, but we don't like to see nigger blood triumph over any Anglo-Saxon blood. Ain't there any loop-hole where we can give it to Bernard, anyhow?"
>
> "Well, yes," said the teacher eagerly, "on the ground of good behavior."
>
> "There you hit it," said the Mayor. "So we all decide." (29)

Despite such actions designed to deny rights to African Americans, during and after slavery, many blacks were able to find, create, and exploit loopholes to both the written and unwritten laws of white society.

"Retreat," too, is used in both military and non-military senses. The martial meaning of the word "retreat" – a pulling back of an armed force in a battle situation – aptly describes Linda's decision to enter the crawlspace. Yet the word's other definition – the act of withdrawing or retiring to a place of seclusion or refuge – has spiritual and artistic senses that are also applicable to *Incidents*. People make or go on retreats, often at retreat houses, in order to commune with God or nature or to seek or regain a state of peace or equilibrium. Similarly, writers and other artists withdraw to isolated locations, known as retreats, often in the company of people like themselves, to pursue their creative endeavors. While in the loophole of retreat, Linda spends considerable time thinking about her fate, questioning God's will, and reading scripture. She also becomes a strategically creative writer in her loophole when she composes letters to Flint about her fictional life in the North. To make them credible, she incorporates realistic details, such as New York City street names culled from copies of pro-slavery newspapers that have come into her possession.

As Jean Fagan Yellin and other critics have noted, in writing *Incidents* Jacobs draws upon the African American male slave narrative and the white, female sentimental novel to create a hybrid text that critiques and revises both traditions. Confronted with the black-white and slave-free oppositions dominating antebellum America, Jacobs uses gender as a loophole, asserting the common womanhood of Northern white free women and Southern black slave women. Frequently using direct addresses to her white, female readers, Linda asserts in the first nine chapters that all women should be entitled to chastity, love, marriage, children, a home, and a hearth but that slavery makes this impossible for black women. In Chapter 10, she radically departs from the sentimental novel and risks alienating the most rigidly moralistic members of her target audience by describing her deliberate choice to engage in a sexual relationship with Mr. Sands to thwart Flint's elaborate plot to set her up as his concubine. Linda's liaison with Sands not only results in two children, whose births transform *Incidents* from a story about a slave girl's struggle against sexual exploitation to one about a slave mother's efforts to protect her children from the horrors of the peculiar institution, but also results in a drastic falling off of direct addresses to her readers.

Just as *Incidents* diverges from the sentimental tradition, it differs from most slave narratives by not ending shortly after Linda reaches the North. Instead, it continues because what she finds there is not freedom. This shift in subject matter results in another alteration in Linda's relationship with her readers. In the earlier chapters, her goal is to gain the sympathy of her target audience by depicting the moral outrages faced by slave girls and slave mothers so that readers will agitate publicly for the abolition of slavery. In Chapters 29 through 41, however, Linda no longer describes injustices of which her audience can claim ignorance. Her readers may, in fact, participate in the prejudice, discrimination, and segregation to which blacks are subjected in the North. As Linda indicates in Chapter 37, it is only in departing the country of her birth and traveling to England that she experiences true freedom and undergoes a profound religious experience. The book's altered tone grows even more condemnatory in the final two chapters. Having endured numerous insults, survived "Hairbreadth Escapes" from slave catchers as a consequence of the Fugitive Slave Law, and witnessed her daughter's near-chattel status in the household of Mr. Sands's relations in Brooklyn, Linda sees little difference between North and South, describing herself as "a slave in New York" (655). It is left to the second Mrs. Bruce to articulate the message that is implicit in the final chapters of the narrative. Commenting on the penalty for aiding a fugitive slave, she states, "Shame on my country that it *is* so!" (656).

After having suspended the practice for a considerable period, Linda uses a direct address to her readers in the next to last paragraph, but without the previous intimacy. Reminding her audience that her work is a slave narrative and not a sentimental novel, Linda states that her "story ends in freedom" rather than in marriage, and then in an extraordinary passage she not only questions the legitimacy of her own newly acquired freedom but also points out a loophole in the freedom of the white people in the North: "I and my children are now free! We are as free from the power of slaveholders as are the white people of the north; and though that, according to my ideas, is not saying a great deal, it is a vast improvement in *my* condition" (664). No longer poignantly writing, as she did earlier, to those "happy free women" who form her target audience, she instead writes about them, powerfully and startlingly using her own experiences among them to expose the limitations of their freedom.[1]

Younger than Jacobs by two generations, James Weldon Johnson illustrates different aspects and ironies of the concepts of "loophole" and "retreat" in connection with late nineteenth-century and early twentieth-century United States race relations. After witnessing a lynching, the unnamed protagonist of his 1912 novel *The Autobiography of an Ex-Colored Man* sells his birthright for "a mess of pottage" by using his light skin as a loophole to retreat from the burden of being black in white America. Two decades later, in his memoir *Along This Way*, the Florida native Johnson recounts a pair of occasions in which his facility in Spanish and knowledge of a foreign culture provided him with a loophole to the Jim Crow policies on Southern trains, summing up each experience with the observation: "in such situations any kind of a Negro will do; provided he is not one who is an American citizen" (65, 89). Johnson repeats the passage to underscore the cruel joke that was African American citizenship in the era of disenfranchisement, peonage, lynching, and segregation. Despite their centuries-long presence in and significant contributions to the nation and in spite of changes to the Constitution following the Civil War, United States blacks were denied, by means of legal loopholes and mob violence, the rights white citizens took for granted. In addition, by custom and by law they were subjected to a caste system from which non-citizens, even non-citizens of color, were typically exempt.

Unlike the main character of his novel, Johnson did not abandon his people or the struggle against white intolerance. With the Democratic victory in the 1912 election, Johnson retired from the diplomatic corps after serving in Venezuela and Nicaragua to write editorials for the *New York Age* and work for and later lead the NAACP. Shortly after returning from Central America, he delivered an address in New York City entitled "Why Latin-America Dislikes the United States," which in many ways serves as the flipside to the paired train episodes detailed in *Along This Way*. In the speech, Johnson asserts that the true cause for resentment toward the United States is "our national and local Negro problem" (196). Noting that newspapers throughout the hemisphere highlight the acts of racial discrimination and anti-black violence that occur in the United States, Johnson contends that Latin Americans fear "not that southern republics will lose their independence to the United States, but that they will fall under the bane of American prejudice, a process which [they have] without a doubt, observed going on slowly but surely in Cuba, Puerto Rico and Panama" (197). Thus, he believes that efforts to foster friendly feelings among people north and south of the Rio Grande will not bear fruit "so long as there is in this country a Negro problem" (197). Although the United States may believe that it can subject its black citizens to horrors and indignities with impunity, Johnson indicates that there is a loophole to this policy: the nation's unjust and immoral domestic racial laws and customs have wide-ranging international consequences. Like Bowser and Jacobs, Johnson in his novel, autobiography, and New York speech illustrates not only how blacks have found loopholes of retreats into which to withdraw from and respond to racial intolerance but also how racial prejudice and violence on the part of United States whites works against their own best interests.

Similar to Jacobs, who, critics often remark, confines herself to circumvent the confinement of slavery, the figures examined in this collection turn apparent weakness into strength, defensiveness into offensiveness, and the machinery of oppression into the keys to liberation. In the opening essay, Jennifer Larson and Sarah Clere discuss how David Walker signifies on the Constitution of the United States, a document used as the legal justification for slavery, to make the case for abolition and racial tolerance. "David Walker's Vision: Constituting Black National Identity, Re-Constituting America in the *Appeal*" demonstrates how the vision of black identity, the tension between separatism and assimilation, the assertion of African American morality, and the endorsement of black nationalism in Walker's *Appeal* anticipates W.E.B. Du Bois's *The Souls of Black Folk*.

In their essays on *Incidents in the Life of a Slave Girl*, Isabel Soto establishes how the surveilled can engage in surveillance, and Shanna Benjamin examines how the folkloric figure of the spider converts confinement into dominance. Soto, in "'The Spaces Left': Ambivalent Discourses in Harriet Jacobs and Frederick Douglass," sees space as a major organizing principle in *Incidents* and the *Narrative of the Life of Frederick Douglass*. In contrast to Douglass, however, who follows a mostly linear trajectory through the various spaces that lead him from slavery to freedom, Jacobs must negotiate the limitations imposed on her by her "loophole of retreat." In "A Trickster in Transition: Nineteenth-Century Representations of Aunt Nancy," Benjamin argues that Joel Chandler Harris's Aunt Nancy and Harriet Jacobs's Linda Brent point to a folkloric African American female trickster tradition that complements and serves as an alternative to the black male trickster tradition.

Monique-Adelle Callahan, in "Translations of Transnational Black Icons in the Poetics of Frances Harper: Brazil's Zumbi and Cuba's Maceo," shows how Frances Harper the poet imaginatively journeys to sixteenth-century Brazil and 1890s Cuba to find inspiration for the black liberation struggle in the United States. Harper's Pan-African sensibility and transnational African American poetics, Callahan claims, arise from and call for an awareness of a multilingual, multicultural, trans-hemispheric conceptual framework. Meanwhile, DoVeanna Fulton looks at how Harper the temperance novelist depicts abstinence as the means to fulfillment in "Strong Drink, Strong Work: African Americans Working Race, Working Gender, Working Temperance." According to Fulton, race and gender serve as key subtexts in literary texts by Harper and other African American temperance advocates.

In a pair of essays devoted to Pauline Hopkins, Jessica Metzler argues that *Slaves' Escape; or the Underground Railroad* subverts the conventions of minstrelsy for the purpose of social critique, and Alisha Knight asserts that in her fiction and biographical writings Hopkins revises the individualistic white American rags-to-riches story for her *Colored American Magazine* readers. In "'Course I Knows Dem Feet!': Minstrelsy and Subversion in Pauline E. Hopkins's *Slaves' Escape; or the Underground Railroad*," Metzler sees the 1879 musical drama as a significant movement away from nineteenth-century blackface performance and toward politically progressive early twentieth-century black musical theater. Influenced by African American clubwomen such as Josephine St. Pierre Ruffin, Hopkins, according to Knight in "'All Things Work Together for Good': Pauline Hopkins's Race Woman and the Gospel of Success," adopts and adapts success literature to promote a community-based success paradigm unique to African American women.

Angelita Reyes, in her ambitious "Elusive Autobiographical Performativity: Vicey Skipwith's Home Place and Sarah Parker Remond's Italian Retreat," contends that two very different nineteenth-century African American women convert the filing or acquiring of public documents into private autobiographical acts. In the first half of the essay, Reyes examines the life of Vicey Skipwith, an illiterate former slave who became a property owner in her post-Reconstruction Virginia community of freedpeople and former slaveholders. Reyes then turns to the little-known later years of the Salem-born abolitionist Sarah Parker Remond, placing special emphasis upon the medical diploma she earned from the Santa Maria Nuova hospital school in Florence, Italy.

In "'Labyrinthine Memories': Charles Chesnutt and Zitkala-Ša's Navigation of the Old and the New in *Conjure Woman* and *American Indian Stories*," Mary Frances Jiménez investigates the use of elements from earlier conceptions of blacks and Native Americans to fashion a New Negro and a New Indian. The essay asserts that Chesnutt and Zitkala-Ša not only establish that the "already told" stories of plantation fiction and domestic sentimentalism were in fact untold but also present the stories of Old Negroes and Old Indians as crucial to charting a path for blacks and Native Americans at the turn of the twentieth century to reclaim and retell the past.

In the concluding essay of *Loopholes and Retreats*, "'Shrinking at No Lofty Theme': The Race Literature of Victoria Earle Matthews, Gertrude Mossell, and Katherine Tillman," Hanna Wallinger explains how African American women, one of the nation's most marginalized groups, promoted and produced a specific type of writing they termed race literature in order to effect political and social change. Mossell, Tillman, and others, as Wallinger makes clear, heeded Matthews's call in "The Value of Race Literature" for black women to aim for the highest ideals in both their lives and their writings.

[1] An expanded version of the reading of *Incidents* I offer in this and the two preceding paragraphs appeared in *Confluences* 107-14.

Works Cited

Burnham, Michelle. "Loopholes of Resistance: Harriet Jacobs' Slave Narrative and the Critique of Agency in Foucault." Harriet Jacobs. *Incidents in the Life of a Slave Girl.* Ed. Nellie Y. McKay and Frances Smith Foster. New York: Norton, 2001. 278-94.

"Dred Scott." *Wikipedia.* 21 April 2008. <http://en.wikipedia.org/Dred_Scott>.

Griggs, Sutton E. *Imperium in Imperio.* 1899. New York: Modern Library, 2003.

Grosvenor, Vertamae. "The Spy Who Served Me." NPR.org. 7 May 2008. http://www.npr.org/programs/morning/features/2002/apr/served.

Gruesser, John Cullen. *Confluences: Postcolonialism, African American Literary Studies, and the Black Atlantic.* Athens: U of Georgia P, 2005.

Jacobs, Harriet. *Incidents in the Life of a Slave Girl.* 1861. *The Classic Slave Narratives.* Ed. Henry Louis Gates, Jr. New York: Signet, 2002. 437-668.

Jacobs, John S. *A True Tale of Slavery.* Yellin 207-28.

Johnson, James Weldon. *Along This Way: The Autobiography of James Weldon Johnson.* New York: Viking, 1933.

—. *The Autobiography of an Ex-Coloured Man.* 1912. New York: Hill, 1960.

—. "Why Latin-America Dislikes the United States." *The Selected Writings of James Weldon Johnson: Vol. II: Social Political, and Literary Essays.* Ed. Sondra Kathryn Wilson. New York: Oxford UP, 1995. 195-97.

"Mary Bowser." *Wikipedia.* 7 May 2008. http://en.wikipedia.org/wiki/Mary_Bowser.

"Mary Elizabeth Bowser." AFRICANAMERICANS.com. 8 May 2008. http://www.africanamericans.com/MaryElizabethBowser.htm.

Warner, Anne Bradford. "Carnival Laughter: Resistance in *Incidents*." *Harriet Jacobs and Incidents in the Life of a Slave Girl.* Ed. Deborah M. Garfield and Rafia Zafar. New York: Cambridge UP, 1996. 216-232.

Williams, Jasmin K. "Mary Elizabeth Bowser – Tea and Secrets." *New York Post.* 27 March 2008: 34.

Wills, Garry. "The Negro President." *New York Review of Books.* 6 November 2003: 45-51.

Yellin, Jean Fagan. Introduction. Yellin xv-xli.

—, ed. *Incidents in the Life of a Slave Girl.* By Harriet Jacobs. Enlarged ed. Cambridge: Harvard UP, 2000.

David Walker's Vision: Constituting Black National Identity, Re-Constituting America in the *Appeal*

Jennifer Larson and Sarah Clere

As his title suggests, David Walker chose to model his *Appeal In Four Articles: Together with a Preamble, to the Coloured Citizens of the World, but in Particular, and Very Expressly to Those of The United States of America* (1829/1830) after the U.S. Constitution. The Constitution of the United States of America (1787) still serves as a major underpinning of American consciousness, outlining how American democratic principles can both thrive and endure. By creating the mechanics of the nation's government, the Constitution establishes and guarantees to all citizens the rights that have led the United States to call itself "the land of the free." Walker's designation of his audience as not only American blacks, but also "the Coloured Citizens of the World," indicates his strong association with other members of the African Diaspora, and a belief in blackness itself as an identifying marker. His use of the structure of the Constitution illustrates his view of himself as an American. Before the term African American became a commonplace, Walker attempts to provide a means for black residents of the United States to be American citizens without in any way renouncing and compromising their identity as blacks. In undertaking this project, Walker anticipates the idea of double-consciousness proposed nearly seventy years later by W.E.B. Du Bois.

Despite his indication that the audience for his pamphlet is "Coloured Citizens," the section of Walker's title page that reads "Appeal in Four Articles; Together with a Preamble" may have been designed to pique white patriotic interests. Walker appropriates the form of the Constitution to place his protest in a context and shape that would be immediately recognized by most Americans. By co-opting the narrative structure of this most foundational of American documents, and using it to illustrate a radical re-visioning of American racial policy, he shows his investment in principles of equality inherent in the Constitution. Through its re-fashioning of the Constitution, the *Appeal* aims to re-constitute America and redefine American identity by pointing out the hypocrisy and unfairness of the nation's racialized loopholes. In order to be compatible with Walker's vision of black identity, America must be re-constituted systematically and ideologically to outlaw slavery and afford citizens of African descent equal protection under the law. Walker's use of the Constitution is particularly radical given the incendiary nature of his *Appeal*. Shocking as his precepts were to nineteenth-century European American minds, Walker squarely situates himself as an American, asserting his claim to the rights of citizenship some twenty-seven years before the *Dred Scott* Case took the issue of black citizenship all the way to the Supreme Court.

To constitute black national identity, Walker rejects the idea of the Constitution as a static document, recognizing it as a dynamic and flexible entity capable of constituting – or defining and shaping – the people it governs; thus, each of Walker's articles speaks to an element of his vision for black national identity. Throughout the *Appeal*, Walker urges antebellum black Americans to claim their humanity and black identity as well as the American liberties they deserve but have been denied. At the same time, he rejects contemporary white constructions of American-ness and warns against embracing whiteness and its psychology of dominance and hypocrisy. In order to avoid emulating white Americans or being absorbed by their racialized ideologies, Walker implies that it is necessary to understand the dynamics of white America's tyranny. Such a project involves recognizing and naming specific modes of disenfranchisement and oppression. It also requires that black Americans actually look at themselves through a white gaze in order to understand the dehumanizing way they are viewed by their fellow Americans. This undertaking, troubling though it may be, is necessary in order to understand white attitudes toward black Americans rightly and combat oppression successfully. In the "Of Our Spiritual Strivings" chapter of *The Souls of Black Folk* (1903), W.E.B. Du Bois makes a similar distinction between black identity and American-ness.[1] Du Bois asserts that African American identity is born of an ability to look beyond the individual to see also the role of the self in a color-obsessed society:

> [...] the Negro is a sort of seventh son, born with a veil, and gifted with second-sight in this American world, – a world which yields him no true self-consciousness, but only lets him see himself through the revelation of the other world. It is a peculiar sensation, this double-consciousness, this sense of always looking at one's self though the eyes of others, of measuring one's soul by the tape of a world that looks on in amused contempt and pity. One ever feels his two-ness, – an American, a Negro; two souls, two thoughts, two unreconciled strivings; two warring ideals in one dark body, whose dogged strength alone keeps it from being torn asunder. (10-11)

Du Bois's agonizing sense of "looking at one's self through the eyes of others ... measuring one's soul by the tape of a world that looks on in amused contempt and pity" forms a disturbing corollary to the kind of knowledge that Walker, in the *Appeal*, believes black Americans must possess. In the same way that the Constitution in the *Appeal* is both a mutable palimpsest and a concrete document, double consciousness to Du Bois is an almost mythical gift, and a practical, if unfortunate, necessity.

By pointing to the need for both a consciousness of black identity and a consciousness of the racial complexities inherent in the label "American," Walker advocates an awareness not unlike the "second sight" Du Bois describes. Just as Articles I-III of the Constitution outline the separation of powers among the three branches of the United States government, so do Walker's articles outline the separation of black and American identities. Walker thus creates an intentional dichotomy that can be read as a nineteenth-century precursor of Du Bois's twentieth-century theory of double-consciousness. By charting the key similarities – as well as the obvious differences – between Walker's text and the U.S. Constitution as well as between Du Bois's and Walker's texts, we begin to see not only Walker's contributions to African American literary and cultural theory but also the historical, political, and philosophical changes that have shaped the evolution of double-consciousness in African American identity and literature. One of the central differences is that Walker seems to encourage double-consciousness: in Article II he admonishes blacks to compare their educational levels with those of whites. For Du Bois writing at the turn of the twentieth-century, such juxtapositions have become the inevitable result of an internalized white perspective.

When Walker was writing the *Appeal*, Constitutional questions about the role of African Americans in the republic were far from simple. Early in 1828, one year before Walker printed the first edition of his text, Congress was locked in a heated, sectional debate over federal compensation for the loss of slave property. Specifically, its members were reviewing an 1815 complaint filed by Marigny D'Autrieve, whose bondman Warwick was injured in the battle with the British at New Orleans (Fehrenbacher 7). Although debate focused on whether the Constitution defined enslaved men and women as people or as property, at the core of this issue – as of most others in antebellum Constitutional concerns – was the question of the framers' attitudes toward slavery (Fehrenbacher 12).

Most Southerners and some abolitionists believed the Constitution was a thoroughly pro-slavery document, while others were more optimistic. Frederick Douglass, for example, had come to believe by the time he wrote *My Bondage and My Freedom* (1855) that the Constitution "could not well have been designed [...] to maintain and perpetuate a system of rapine and murder like slavery; especially as not one word can be found in the constitution to authorize such a belief" (397). Rather, the document, Douglass writes, "is our warrant for the abolition of slavery in every state of the American Union" (398). Peter Hinks's interpretation of the *Appeal* suggests that Walker held a similarly positive view of the Constitution and American institutions: "According to Walker, the source of America's horrible problems with race and slavery was not in the nation's systems and institutions but in the hearts of Americans" ("Introduction" xxxiv). Thus, Walker draws our attention to a national quandary in the early nineteenth century: did the Constitution, as written, sanction slavery and white supremacy? Walker's personal views about the framers' motives aside, the text of the *Appeal* suggests that the Constitution proved to have limited provenance on racial matters because it was not specific enough to protect America's black citizens. Therefore, in order to protect themselves, African Americans needed to become keenly aware of their unique, separate, black identities – while still working both within and against dominant white attitudes toward American republicanism

Walker negotiates black Americans' precarious relationship with the nation by reaching out to a dual audience in the *Appeal*. As indicated by his title, Walker writes primarily to the "Coloured Citizens of the World, but in Particular, and Very Expressly, to those of The United States of America." However, as Herbert Aptheker points out, Walker knows that "the 'enemy' is reading" (57), and according to Ian Finseth, he "addresses his white readers fully, as often and as urgently as he does his black readers, notwithstanding his title" (359). The rhetorical trick of direct address to "Americans," then, plays a central role in the *Appeal*'s re-constitution efforts because it does not place the responsibility for reform solely on blacks or whites but instead calls both groups to action. Also, while Walker acknowledges that some whites would not even consider blacks human, he also notes that African Americans have many genuine white American friends. In his direct addresses and indirect references to white Americans, he employs multiple labels that draw clear distinctions between "Christians" and "My dear sirs," on the one hand, and "avaricious usurpers" and "avaricious oppressors," on the other. Thus, in Du Bois's words, the reader feels the *Appeal*'s "double aims" (11): On one side is Walker's vision for the ideal America possible by way of a re-invigorated dedication to the original principles of freedom and equality espoused by the Constitution; on the other is his fiery hatred for white oppression as well as his reverence for his people and their immeasurable contributions to the republic. Du Bois's *Souls* is similarly meant to reach both black and white American reading audiences, and functions as both an urgent appeal for racial equality and an exposition of the richness of African American culture. In the words of Arnold Rampersad, "*The Souls of Black Folk* sought to convert and seduce the American people, white and black, into sharing Du Bois's optimistic view of black culture in the United States" (68).

At the same time as it illustrates shortcomings in the white-authored U.S. Constitution, Walker's *Appeal* provides poignant messages aimed at constituting and strengthening black national identity. The Preamble to the U.S. Constitution concisely states the document's purpose: "[...] to form a more perfect Union, establish Justice, insure domestic Tranquility, provide for the common defence [sic], promote the general Welfare, and secure the Blessings of Liberty to ourselves and our Posterity." After setting up its claims and background, Walker's *Appeal* establishes a purpose of equal clarity: "to awaken in the breasts of my afflicted, degraded and slumbering brethren, a spirit of inquiry and investigation respecting our miseries and wretchedness in this *Republican Land of* Liberty*!!!!!!*" (5). Walker's Preamble, while confirming the possibility of a "*Republican Land of Liberty*," also includes a specific call-to-action not present in the framers' Preamble. Walker, like the framers, acknowledges his hope for the power of his words to shape history, policy, and sentiment, but he also indicts white American groups and institutions that have degraded his "brethren." At the same time Walker aspires "to awaken" African Americans from their "slumbering," so that they may find a productive and redemptive national identity.

Both Du Bois and Walker speak to the importance of "true self-consciousness" for African Americans by celebrating their own blackness and black history in America. Echoing Walker's goals as stated in the *Appeal*'s Preamble, Du Bois writes, "The history of the American Negro is the history of this strife, – this longing to attain self-conscious manhood, to merge his double self into a better and truer self. In this merging he wishes neither of the older selves to be lost. He would not Africanize America, for America has too much to teach the world and Africa. He would not bleach his Negro soul in a flood of white Americanism, for he knows that Negro blood has a message for the world" (11). The convergences between Walker's and Du Bois's visions of black identity reflect their shared ideologies: both seek to re-assert the claim for black humanity; both point to past, present, and future black contributions to the world; both advocate social and occupational elevation for African Americans; and both see this elevation as integral to the struggle for improved civil rights. These similarities to Du Bois establish Walker as an influential and canonical black American intellectual, rather than a literary anomaly.

Like the Preamble, the remaining four articles of Walker's *Appeal* signify on corresponding articles in the U.S. Constitution and anticipate Du Bois's theories. Article I of the Constitution establishes and describes legislative powers and representation, including the provision that a slave shall be counted as three-fifths of a person. Walker's "Article I: Our Wretchedness in Consequence of Slavery" focuses on this lack of African American representation and mentions repressive property laws. Walker asks to be shown not "a coloured President, a Governor, a Legislator, a Senator, a Mayor, or an Attorney at the Bar. – But [...] a man of colour, who holds the low office of Constable, or one who sits in a Juror Box, even on a case of one of his wretched brethren, throughout this great Republic!!" (10). By linking such protests to Article I of the Constitution, Walker seems to be questioning a country whose core governing document, regardless of original intent, legitimates enslavement through the legislative system it created and sanctioned. By denying African Americans the right to see themselves represented in even America's most basic representative positions, Walker shows how even the fundamental "Blessings of Liberty" promised by the Constitution have been undermined. Yet, Walker's terming the United States "this great Republic" indicates a belief in the potential for such blessings to be realized.

Walker's Article I takes the first steps toward constituting a black national identity by pointing to the need for blacks to reclaim the humanity stolen from them by the uniquely cruel system of American chattel slavery. In both Walker's and Du Bois's texts, the greatest obstacle to full citizenship for blacks is simply the ubiquitous, oppressive, and hypocritical ideologies of black inferiority perpetrated by white society since before the American Revolution. In

Article I of the *Appeal*, Walker argues "that we, (coloured people of these United States of America) are the *most wretched, degraded* and *abject* set of beings that *ever lived* since the world began, and that the white Americans having reduced us to the wretched state of *slavery,* treat us in that condition *more cruel* (they being an enlightened and Christian people,) than any heathen nation did any people whom it had reduced to our condition" (9). This hypocritical subjugation is not only physically oppressive to African Americans but also has profound psychological effects on both blacks and whites. In *Narrative of the Life of Frederick Douglass* (1845), Douglass's illustration of the way the institution of slavery corrupts white slaveholders still resonates as a potent condemnation of slavery as a cancer that poisons society as a whole

Like Walker, Du Bois addresses a republican hypocrisy in the first chapter of *The Souls of Black Folk*: the black American "simply wishes to make it possible for a man to be both a Negro and an American, without being cursed and spit upon by his fellows, without having the doors of Opportunity closed roughly in his face" (11). Du Bois also believes that black Americans' quest "to satisfy two unreconciled ideas, has wrought sad havoc with the courage and faith and deeds of ten thousand thousand people, – has sent them wooing false gods and invoking false means of salvation, and at times has even seemed about to make them ashamed of themselves" (12). Walker and Du Bois seem to agree that a people cannot realize true potential or find true identity under an identity paradigm that oppresses and degrades them. The white American nation of the nineteenth-century allowed no room for a black American nation to co-exist within its geographical or ideological boundaries. Since there was never any provision made for an autonomous black state within the United States, it became necessary for black Americans to be given full political enfranchisement within the country to which they had already contributed so much economically and culturally.

Walker continues his indictments against white America in Article II, and this article offers what are perhaps the most poignant parallels between Walker's *Appeal* and the Constitution, thereby clarifying his vision for a black national identity and his call for a re-constituted America. In the Constitution, Article II speaks to the roles and powers of the President and other members of the Executive branch, and Walker, in "Article II: Our Wretchedness in Consequence of Ignorance," attacks former president Thomas Jefferson and his *Notes on the State of Virginia* (1787). Walker challenges Jefferson's assertions about the physical and mental inferiority of African Americans with his own evidence of black moral superiority, claiming that African Americans will have to "contradict" Jefferson "by [their] own actions" (30). Walker thereby challenges intellectual and institutional racism and establishes the demolition of these stereotypes as a project that must be undertaken by black Americans.

Located at the physical center of the Appeal, Article II is the cornerstone for Walker's constitution of black national identity. Beyond debunking Jefferson's "'natural observations'" about the servile and simple nature of African

Americans, Article II focuses on casting off ignorance and creating a powerful African-American brotherhood. Walker asserts that blacks must "let the aim of [their] labours among [their] brethren, and particularly the youths, be the dissemination of education and religion" (32). He urges them to move toward a more collective mentality "for the salvation of our whole body" (32). Hinks notes the uniqueness of Walker's call for worldwide black cooperation: "No one had asserted it previously with such vehemence. Walker recognized that the security of African Americans was in jeopardy so long as blacks anywhere in the world were enslaved and treated like subhuman brutes" (*To Awaken* 179).

One of the white oppressor's most powerful tools for keeping African Americans degraded and enslaved, according to Walker – and later Du Bois – is imposed ignorance. Walker especially targets the type of ignorance (which he sees exhibited most obviously in blind submission to white Americans) that leads to intra-racial strife. For Walker the betrayal of blacks by other blacks is one of the most painful legacies of white oppression. Walker claims that such betrayals are "not the natural element of blacks as Americans try to make us believe" (23), indicating that he seeks to separate black identity from stereotypes imposed by dominant white culture. Walker connects formal education directly to black political empowerment and resistance to white oppression: "I would crawl on my hands and knees through mud and mire, to the feet of a learned man, where I would sit and humbly supplicate to instil [sic] into me, that which neither devils or tyrants could remove, only with my life – for coloured people to acquire learning in this country, makes tyrants quake and tremble on their sandy foundation" (34). Self-awareness, education, and unity, then, are essential elements in Walker's constitution of black national identity.

Although Du Bois does not mention Jefferson specifically in "Of Our Spiritual Strivings," he nevertheless reaffirms Walker's claims from Article II by challenging stereotypes about African American character and reasserting the value of education. "By the poverty and ignorance of his people, the Negro minister or doctor was tempted toward quackery and demagogy" (11), writes Du Bois, and he describes how, even after emancipation, an African American "felt the weight of his ignorance, – not simply of letters, but of life, of business, of the humanities; the accumulated sloth and shirking and awkwardness of decades and centuries shackled his hands and feet" (14). And, like Walker, he calls for expanded access to education: "The training of the schools we need today more than ever, – the training of deft hands, quick eyes and ears, and above all the broader, deeper, higher culture of gifted minds and pure hearts" (15). Both Walker and Du Bois believe that black Americans must strive for genuinely intellectual education and not be content with merely baseline literacy and vocational training. Thus, both Walker's and Du Bois's writings point to ignorance as one of the greatest obstacles to a more complete understanding of racial and national identity on the part of African Americans.

Articles III and IV of the *Appeal* speak of other obstacles to a fully realized personal and racial identity among African Americans. While not as rich as the previous two Articles, Articles III and IV are nevertheless compelling because of their topical significance. Whereas the Constitution's Article III outlines judicial power, Walker's Article III speaks to "Wretchedness in Consequence of the Pretended Preachers of Jesus Christ" and focuses on biblical, rather than secular, judgment. According to Walker, God's judgment on slavery will de-constitute the Americans by destroying the republic through civil strife and division (41, 45). Du Bois similarly asserts in 1903 that "the Nation has not yet found peace from its sins" (12). The Constitution's Article IV focuses on the formation and rights of states, and Walker's "Article IV: Our Wretchedness in Consequence of the Colonization Plan" condemns the colonization project which would send black Americans to colonies, such as Liberia, outside America, rather than granting them equal rights within the United States. Walker shrewdly notes that a major aim of the colonization plan is the removal of free blacks from America so that those black people who are still enslaved may be kept in a situation of oppression and ignorance: "For if the free are allowed to stay among the slaves, they will have intercourse together, and, of course, the free will learn the slaves *bad habits*, by teaching them that they are MEN as well as other people, and certainly *ought* and *must* be FREE" (49). As Wilson J. Moses explains, black intellectuals of the early nineteenth-century almost uniformly opposed colonization; however, once the Fugitive Slave Law was enacted in 1850, many black Americans became more amenable to colonization, since an integrated bi-racial society seemed to be ever more impossible (27). Walker, writing before the passage of the Compromise of 1850, possesses more hope for a re-constituted America than did many of his mid-century intellectual successors. Du Bois does not speak directly to colonization in "Of Our Spiritual Strivings," but he does point out that, even after the Civil War that Walker predicted, "the freedman has not yet found freedom in his *promised land*" (12, emphasis added).

Just as each article of the Constitution defines a particular branch of government or guarantees another right – thereby adding another limb to the political body – each article of Walker's Appeal constructs the black national self that he seeks to constitute. Walker urges African Americans to recognize and embrace their dormant selfhood and repressed humanity; at the same time he provides a blueprint for a new identity and nationhood. Each article is another exhortation of the slumbering black nation – Article III calls for religious devotion; Article IV implies a right to land and free labor, establishing both as national black causes. And each article bolsters the argument for black humanity and unity.

A prerequisite for national harmony, however, available only to a reconstituted America, is freedom. To underscore this, Walker includes an excerpt of from The Declaration of Independence (1776) within the text of Article IV of the *Appeal*. Similarly, in "Of Our Spiritual Strivings," Du Bois asserts, "there are to-day no truer exponents of the pure human spirit of the Declaration of Independence than the American Negroes" (16). By including the Declaration in the *Appeal*, Walker reminds his readers, black and white, that despite the ideals espoused in *The Declaration of Independence,* the Revolutionary War led to freedom only for white men. America's re-constitution, then, must be neo-revolutionary and must include freedom for black Americans as well. Walker thus re-claims Jefferson's *Declaration* by incorporating it into a militant black nationalist call to arms, as a component of his re-envisioned Constitution. He thereby shows that black Americans must declare and fight for the freedom to claim, and to constitute, a national identity understood as separate from, yet wholly compatible with, America – as long as America re-constitutes itself (in accordance with the Constitution's implicit ideals) to allow for difference but not for racism.

The parallels between Walker's *Appeal* and the U.S. Constitution as well as those between Walker's and Du Bois's visions for black identity are not exact. And in fact, the divergences between the *Appeal* and the Constitution and between Walker and Du Bois are as significant as the convergences. Some elements of the *Appeal* have no direct Constitutional parallel, because neither Walker's newly constituted black America nor the racially healed, re-constituted United States he envisions is fully compatible with the status quo. Walker's *Appeal* thereby correctly anticipates that only what the framers considered a drastic action, amending the Constitution, might lead to the type of change necessary to abolish slavery, protect African Americans, legitimize racial identity, and ensure black participation in and access to "the Blessings of Liberty" – manifested most obviously in the right to vote.

The ultimate difficulty for Walker, as for the framers of the U.S. Constitution, was balance. Just as the framers struggled with the separation of powers and the autonomy of the states compared to the central government's authority, so too does Walker seem to struggle with the balance of power and identity between his re-constituted white America and his newly constituted black America. At times, Walker sounds like an ardent separatist, while just a few pages later he seems committed to a bi-racial *United* States. This apparent paradox in Walker's text points to the two audiences the Appeal addresses: black and white Americans. The hope of Walker's constitution and re-constitution is that, in spite of this paradox, we may all come to see each other and ourselves as members of "the WHOLE human family" (7).

The tension between separatism and assimilationalism is evident in both Walker's and Du Bois's texts. Both men at times claim a specific African American cultural and moral identity and even superiority, yet neither is willing to negate white America entirely. Walker, in the *Appeal*, articulates principles connected to early black nationalism, and Du Bois in *The Souls of Black Folk* was himself involved in the black nationalist movement. Moses points out that although *Souls* "is often viewed as an assimilationist manifesto," the book stresses the particularity of black culture, taking the almost mystic view of African Americans frequently associated with black nationalism at the turn of the century. According to Moses, the very "ambivalence" of *Souls* "makes it impossible to neatly pigeonhole Du Bois into either the black nationalist or the radical assimilationist tradition" (136). Walker's nationalism in the *Appeal* is strikingly more insurgent and religious than is Du Bois's in *Souls*. The militancy of this nationalism is the focus of the most enduring critical debates on Walker's text. Like Du Bois, Walker speaks of "human brotherhood," but focuses on God's impending judgment against whites as well (16). His inclusion of phrases such as "kill or be killed" shows that he is willing to imagine some form of physical, even violent, deliverance for African Americans alongside the vision of intellectual and artistic deliverance that he shares with Du Bois (28). Walker, in addition to alluding to African contributions to America and the world community, asserts the moral superiority of the African race. According to Leonard Sweet, Walker believed "blacks had a legitimate right to question whether whites were physically and morally equal to blacks at all" (113). Walker juxtaposes the true faith of black Americans with the religious hypocrisy of white America.

The *Appeal* clearly strives to be a Christian text, and its rhetorical techniques link it to the Protestant sermon as well as the colonial pamphlet. Walker wrote in an atmosphere of mounting sectionalism and was inspired by insurrections, successful and failed. Colonial America's resistance to tyranny in the not-so-distant American Revolution itself also inspired Walker to bellicosity, enabling him to envision the potential for God's justice to become manifest in militant black nationalism and armed revolution, even if only as a last resort. Walker writing in 1830 truly envisioned a war which overthrew slavery as "the coming of the Lord." But years after Walker's death, the failure of the Civil War and Reconstruction to refine America into a racially perfected ideal was profoundly disillusioning.

Walker's evangelical and prophetic tone, which differs dramatically from the Constitution's legalism, strongly suggests that the *Appeal* advocates a more active role for religion in American government. The *Appeal* itself functions as a kind of jeremiad, warning both white and black America that they are in error. Walker felt that God would deliver black America from oppression and that a racially healed America must truly be united "under God." He believed unwaveringly that God would rise up against the white oppressor and deliver to African Americans the equality and the American liberties they deserved. Hinks clearly outlines Walker's grounding in religious thought and discusses Walker's Millennial brand of Christian citizenship, which led him to envision "a sense of national identity and collective mission among blacks founded on their special relationship to God" (*To Awaken* 242-243). Black America must be truly religious, focused on serving the Lord. Walker's *Appeal* therefore advocates unseating the "pretended preachers" of the Southern slaveocracy through a kind of republican revival.

Du Bois, in partial contrast to Walker, believes changes in the condition of black Americans will occur primarily through cultural and intellectual means rather than biblical deliverance, remarking in connection with voting rights and "freedom":

> Work, culture, liberty, – all these we need, not singly but together, not successively but together, each growing and aiding each, and all striving toward that vaster ideal that swims before the Negro people, the ideal of human brotherhood, gained through the unifying ideal of Race; the ideal of fostering and developing the traits and talents of the Negro, not in opposition to or contempt for other races, but rather in large conformity to the greater ideals of the American Republic, in order that some day on American soil two world-races may give each to each those characteristics both so sadly lack. (15-16)

Du Bois's reliance on secular mechanisms (conformity to the ideals of the Republic rather than the Bible) for racial progress reflects an increasingly progressive, programmatic America, as well as his own training as a sociologist. After the Millennial fervor of the nineteenth-century, mainstream American religion itself became increasingly focused on the "Social Gospel," and the responsibilities that Christians bore toward their fellow human beings as well as their God. When viewed in a turn-of-the-century context, Du Bois's faith in secular systems of reform is not particularly remarkable. In *Up from Slavery* (1901) Booker T. Washington himself lauds his own initiative and American philanthropic benevolence far more than he invokes the Deity. While Du Bois in *The Souls of Black Folk* denigrates the type of narrowly conceived religion that privileges denominational squabbling over racial uplift, the common view of him as somehow irreligious is false. In his 2007 book, *W.E.B. Du Bois: American Prophet*, Edward J. Blum reevaluates Du Bois's religiosity and questions why historians who debate every other aspect of his life are content to accept an uncomplicated view of Du Bois's religious belief. Blum shows Du Bois as having "multiple religious selves" and claims that one of these "selves" "was a stirring prophet who felt that a higher power had called him to challenge white supremacy and economic exploitation" (12). In that role he bears a striking similarity to David Walker.

Indeed, Walker's ultimate plan for racial reconciliation and healing, another component conspicuously absent from the U.S. Constitution, relies heavily on God's redemption. Walker's Article IV is significant not only because it questions the motives of those in support of colonization, but also because it seems to suggest the possibility of a state – a government and a way of life – founded on racial reconciliation through Christian morality. He envisions the United States as a racially healed space, a space with room for black national identity, created with God's help. Walker writes, "Treat us then like men, and we will be your friends. And there is not a doubt in my mind but that the whole of the past will be sunk into oblivion, and we yet, under God, will become a united and happy people" (73). In spite of all his anger, Walker stresses forgiveness and Christian cooperation, not the oppressive and bloody past.

Du Bois, writing about "Spiritual Strivings," ends his chapter with a similar vision of human cooperation and divine oversight:

> Will America be poorer if she replace her brutal dyspeptic blundering with light-hearted but determined Negro humility? or her coarse and cruel wit with loving jovial good-humor? or her vulgar music with the soul of the Sorrow Songs?
>
> Merely a concrete test of the underlying principles of the great republic is the Negro Problem, and the spiritual striving of the freedmen's sons is the travail of souls whose burden is almost beyond the measure of their strength, but who bear it in the name of an historic race, in the name of this the land of their fathers' fathers, and in the name of human opportunity. (16)

Here Du Bois's faith lies with African Americans' strength and American justice – yet, unlike Walker he does not wish the past to "be sunk into oblivion" but rather sees African Americans as a "historic race" deriving their strength in part from what they have endured. While still holding on to a belief in a purer version of American republicanism, Du Bois suggests that the best chance for black advancement lies in pursuing peace with America, even as it stands, all the while hoping that black America will become stronger in the process, and that the whole of America will become more like "the great republic" the founders imagined. Du Bois asks America to reform itself, not only for fear of judgment, but primarily because the United States will be a stronger, happier nation for the change.

In Walker's vision of racial and national identity, however, it would only be possible to be black and American when white Americans reformed their attitudes and actions to show that they were no longer the "natural enemies" of African Americans. It is evident early in his text that Walker does not aspire to whiteness of any kind nor to any kind of American-ness that privileges whiteness. White Americans, he explains, "think because they hold us in their infernal chains of slavery, that we wish to be white, or of their color – but they are dreadfully deceived – we wish to be just as it pleased our Creator to have made us [...]" (14). He offers a striking indictment of whiteness, contending that "the whites have always been an unjust, jealous, unmerciful, avaricious and bloodthirsty set of beings, always seeking after power and authority" (19). Here the staunch black separatist, Walker can imagine co-existence only with a radically reformed, bi-racial, Christian America.

Walker, writing his *Appeal* over thirty years before the emancipation in which he places so much faith, could not foresee that the end of slavery would not mean the end of segregation and that slavery would be so easily replaced by other codified forms of white supremacy. Seven decades after the *Appeal*, Du Bois saw that the majority of white America remained committed to racial oppression, and his theories reflect frustration with an unreconstructed America that even an amended Constitution could not fully reform.

Du Bois himself saw Walker as a foundational, yet enigmatic, figure. In *Efforts for Social Betterment Among Negro Americans* (1909), he calls Walker's *Appeal* "the first full-voiced, almost hysterical, protest against slavery and the color line" (109). But Du Bois does not fully give Walker his due: Walker's *Appeal* is much more than the *hysterical* and exclamation-point laden sections of promised retribution and insurrection that are so often excerpted in anthologies. The text, as its parallels with the Constitution and "Our Spiritual Strivings" demonstrate, offers a complex and theoretical analysis of American republicanism and African American identity. Such a view of Walker encourages us not only to reconsider his legacy, but also to reread and reconsider other nineteenth-century figures, such as Maria Stewart and Walker's friend Henry Highland Garnet, who have been similarly dismissed and neglected. Even if Walker's prophecies were not fully realized, reading him as a cultural critic capable of simultaneously signifying on the U.S. Constitution and anticipating a theory as ground-breaking as Du Boisian double-consciousness rescues him from critical judgments that hold that his significance lies only in the conspiracy theories surrounding his untimely death or in his emotional brand of early black nationalism. Seen in the context of his own time and in relation to the trajectory of black political thought, David Walker becomes one of the most important and groundbreaking writers in African American literary history. In Article IV of the *Appeal* he anticipates intellectuals like Du Bois, eagerly looking forward to a time "when the Lord shall raise up coloured historians in succeeding generations, to present the crimes of this nation, to the then gazing world" (61).

[1]Like a number of the chapters from *The Souls of Black Folk*, "Of Our Spiritual Strivings" appeared in an earlier version in 1897 as "Strivings of the Negro People" in *The Atlantic*.

Works Cited

Aptheker, Herbert. *"One Continual Cry": David Walker's Appeal to the Colored Citizens of the World (1829-1830), Its Setting & Its Meaning*. New York: Humanities, 1965.

Blum, Edward J. *W.E.B. Du Bois: American Prophet*. Philadelphia: U of Pennsylvania P, 2007.

Douglass, Frederick. *My Bondage and My Freedom*. 1855. New York: Dover, 1969.

Du Bois, W.E.B. *The Souls of Black Folk*. 1903. New York: Norton, 1999.

—."Strivings of the Negro People." *The Atlantic Monthly* Aug. 1897: 194-98.

—. Ed. *Efforts for Social Betterment Among Negro Americans*. Atlanta: Atlanta UP, 1909.

Fehrenbacher, Don E. *The Slaveholding Republic: An Account of the United States Government's Relations to Slavery*. New York: Oxford UP, 2001.

Finseth, Ian. "David Walker, Nature's Nation, and Early African-American Separatism." *Mississippi Quarterly* 54.3 (2001): 337-62.

Hinks, Peter P. Introduction. Walker xi-li.

—. *To Awaken My Afflicted Brethren: David Walker and the Problem of Antebellum Slave Resistance*. University Park: Penn State University Press UP, 1997.

Moses, Wilson Jeremiah. *The Golden Age of Black Nationalism, 1850-1925*. Hamden: Archon, 1978.

Rampersad. Arnold. *The Art and Imagination of W.E.B. Du Bois*. Cambridge: Harvard UP, 1976.

Sweet, Leonard I. *Black Images of America 1784-1870*. New York: Norton, 1976.

Walker, David. *David Walker's Appeal to the Coloured Citizens of the World*. 1830. Ed. Peter P. Hinks. University Park: Penn State UP, 2000.

"The Spaces Left": Ambivalent Discourses in Harriet Jacobs and Frederick Douglass

Isabel Soto

This essay addresses the *topos* of space in *Incidents in the Life of a Slave Girl* (1861) and *Narrative of the Life of Frederick Douglass* (1845). In what follows, I propose that space functions as a major organizing principle in these two works; more particularly, I consider the extent to which the spatialization of experience, a strategy common to the two texts, endorses agency and freedom as viable goals, or, alternatively, demystifies them. Certain questions invite themselves: who or what defines and controls space? Who or what determines entry to it and, indeed, exit from it? My analysis exposes gender-identified responses and strategies. The narrators of *Incidents* and the *Narrative* engage space, and hence agency and freedom, in contrasting ways; they stand in eloquent counterpoint to one another, with the narrator of the former text performing an ironic revision of the latter. While Frederick Douglass negotiates a linear trajectory through the spaces that will lead him from slavery to freedom in an almost teleological realization of the narrator's purpose, the narrator's strategies of empowerment in *Incidents* are qualified repeatedly throughout the text. Together, the narrators frame the terms of the debate concerning how agency and freedom should be represented and raise questions as to whether it is possible to represent them at all within the context of a slaveholding economy. As Saidiya V. Hartman declares with reference to historical narratives constructed by victims of slavery and post-emancipation oppression, the "tactics of resistance, modes of self-fashioning, and figurations of freedom" in these narratives "[are] enmeshed with the relations of power and dominance that [they] strive [...] to write against" (11).

Hartman's statement invites a closer scrutiny of the role of the narrator in *Incidents* and the *Narrative* with regard to issues of control and authority. This task acquires special urgency in the case of the former text in which, though conforming to the specific type of life writing which is the slave narrative, one must distinguish not only between narrator and character, but further between narrator/character, on the one hand, and, on the other, author. Despite presenting real facts and events, *Incidents* famously provides an instance of a differentiated narrative persona, that of Linda Brent (the putative narrator/character) and Harriet A. Jacobs (the "real" narrator/character *and* author). Perhaps driven by Jean Fagan Yellin's investigative scholarship which established the text to be a stunning example of what Robert Stepto has described as "personal history in – and as – a literary form" (20), critics do not always differentiate between character (Linda Brent) and author (Harriet Jacobs). For the purposes of this essay, "Linda Brent" will be used to refer to the main character in *Incidents* and "Harriet Jacobs" to the author. The term "narrator" is used in reference to the discursive device or agent who actually tells the story, bearing in mind that that agent is itself far from being a straightforward construct.[1] Ultimately, in both *Incidents* and Douglass's *Narrative*, the narrator speaks with a double voice, engaging both the overarching first-person storyteller and the character about whom the story is being told.

Reading *Incidents* against the *Narrative* undoubtedly illuminates the specificity of each. The comparatively unambiguous relationship of Douglass's narrator to freedom, as opposed to Jacobs's more equivocal stance towards the potential exercise of freedom untainted by "relations of power and dominance," has predictably generated a wide and contrasting range of reader responses. With regard to *Incidents*, readers tend to fall into several camps, reflecting perhaps the rich ambiguities the narrative itself presents. On the one hand, there are those such as Hazel Carby who celebrate the author's resourcefulness in the face of, and resistance to, a legally enforced system of brutal curtailment of agency: "[A] spirit of defiance characterized Jacobs's representations of all Linda Brent's encounters with her master. Conventional feminine qualities of submission and passivity were replaced by an active resistance" (*Reconstructing* 56).[2] Other readers have argued that the heroine's relationship to such agency is equivocal and paradoxical. Consistent with this reading, Yellin, in her pathbreaking 1987 edition of *Incidents*, notes Jacobs's doubling strategies, "transforming herself into a literary subject in and through the creation of her narrator, Linda Brent," the text's "contrasting literary styles" and "contradictory thrusts of the story," and the "deep conflict" of the narrator's voice (Introduction xiv). Mary Helen Washington likewise highlights the challenge Jacobs faced in revealing the desperate facts of her life while endeavouring not to offend the prevailing sensibilities of her targeted audience: white, female, northern readers (*Invented Lives* 5). Other classic readings such as Valerie Smith's "'Loopholes of Retreat': Architecture and Ideology in Harriet Jacobs's *Incidents in the Life of a Slave Girl*" (1990) and Michelle Burnham's "Loopholes of Resistance: Harriet Jacobs's Slave Narrative and the Critique of Agency in Foucault" (1993) argue that the ambivalence is mediated through a certain material reality, namely, the famous garret or loophole of retreat where Linda Brent spends seven years in her bid for freedom. That her freedom can only be acquired at the expense of physical mobility and, ultimately, as the result of a bill of sale for her person, exposes the harsh reality that the heroine's agency is – and has always been – profoundly compromised.[3] More recently, readers juxtapose Jacobs's equivocal text to Frederick Douglass's *Narrative* which portrays a seemingly unproblematic transformation from slave to free man: "I was now my own master [...]. It was to me the starting point of a new existence" (150). Samira Kawash observes that Jacobs "insists on the gap between the rhetoric of freedom and its material reality" (74),[4] while Douglass suppresses the complications, qualifications and points of resistance that Jacobs makes manifest in her narrative: "Douglass attempts to neutralize the ambivalence of the freedom available to him as self-possessed subject by availing himself of the power of Enlightenment rhetoric" (74).[5] In the same vein, Stepto believes the *Narrative*'s closing lines, in which the narrator recounts his first experience in public speaking (bringing, incidentally, the text full circle to William Lloyd Garrison's Preface, in which Garrison recalls this very incident), demonstrates how "In one brilliant stroke, the quest for freedom and literacy, implied from the start, even in the narrative's title, is resolutely consummated" (26).

Space theories such as Paul Gilroy's *Black Atlantic* give voice to an organization of reality that, since the beginning of the twentieth century (one could start with Bakhtin's chronotope), has gained increasing purchase. Today everything, it seems, including, and possibly most of all, the body, is vulnerable to spatialization. Nearly half a century ago, Foucault was already declaring in "Of Other Spaces": "The present epoch will perhaps be above all the epoch of space," adding that "our experience of the world is less that of a long life developing through time than that of a network that connects points and intersects with its own skein" (par. 1). Time, it seems, has become de-emphasized in favour of space in the ways in which we theorize and experience the world.

It is perhaps no accident that a privileged understanding of how space works and mediates individual experience lies at the heart of African American writing. Katherine Clay Bassard, implicitly endorsing Foucault's temporal de-emphasis and privileging of space, notes in her article "Crossing Over: Free Space, Sacred Place and Intertextual Geographies in Peter Randolph's *Sketches of Slave Life*" that the slave's subjectivity was by definition spatially organized since "a sense of self was determined by the master's mandate that [the slave] account for his movements in space at every hand" (122). Slavery, further, "order[ed] experience according to free space and captive space" (Bassard 116), i.e. plantation and town, master and slave quarters, free and slave states, north and south, black and white. Ultimately, we are talking about the spatialization of power (or the power of spatialization) – how, where and by whom. The contrasting responses can be read, as stated earlier, as expressive of the specificity of the narrating voice. Accordingly, Douglass's experience "is unique and representative [...] [and] also male," (Carby *Reconstructing* 46) while Jacobs "locates freedom in feminized spaces [...] as a slave and in particular as a female slave she *is* the domestic" (Sánchez-Eppler 87).

More than half of the Douglass narrative is characterized by a "spatially-organized narrative strategy" (Bassard 7) or, following Foucault, the absence of temporal markers: "I have no accurate knowledge of my age [...]. By far the larger part of the slaves know as little of their ages as horses know of theirs [...]. I do not remember to have ever met a slave who could tell of his birthday"; and so forth (47). Temporality takes over from space with the announcement "I have now reached a period of my life when I can give dates [...]" (95).

The emergence of temporality gives rise to the triumph over Covey, illiteracy and, eventually, bondage. Subjectivity is realized, it would seem, not only through spatial negotiation but also "the acquisition of temporal markers" enabling "an entry into the cultural symbolic equated with the acquisition of literacy," as Bassard declares (123).

The space-time-literacy triad is not mere geometry; rather it is a relationship of interdependence and mediation. The mature, literate and *narrating* subject provides a telling example of this through what Robert Stepto has called Douglass's syncretic phrasing. Citing the well-known example, "My feet have been so cracked with the frost, that the pen with which I am writing might be laid in the gashes" (72), Stepto applauds "Douglass's ability to conjoin past and present and to do so with images that [...] speak of his evolution from slavery to freedom" (20). The spatial metaphor of the gash and the metonymic use of the pen, that "symbol [...] [of] the quest for literacy fulfilled" (20), are mediated through temporal process. To white society's imposition of what W.E.B. Du Bois a half century later would term double-consciousness, the author responds with a strategy of syncretism. Douglass may well have suffered gashes on his feet the width of a pen, but until the two images – gash and pen – are temporally retrieved through memory and the act of writing, their equivalence will have escaped us.

Throughout the *Narrative* (and African American writing in general) we are reminded of the materiality of experience, and the slave's experience in particular, mediated and determined through spatial sequencing. The physicality of the pen/gash image[6] eventually yields to the memorable sequences of the narrator's acquisition of literacy. Having experienced a truncated schooling in letters, Douglass finds alternative classrooms and teachers, revealing not only the narrator's resourcefulness and singleness of purpose, but also the blunt materiality in which his apprenticeship unfolds. Yet while the acquisition of literacy as a marker of freedom is a *topos* of the slave narrative, it is rarely read against the *topos* of space. In Douglass's *Narrative*, the process of acquiring literacy is manifested through a spatial sequence, indeed, a sequence of free spaces, syncretically figuring process and outcome, the mastery of letters and freedom. The spaces are: the streets of Baltimore, the shipyard and, finally, the "spaces left" in his young master's discarded copy book in which Douglass writes his own letters and words. The latter spaces are not just blanks on a page, but the crucial site mediated through time and memory in which he forges a fully realized subjectivity. Note also how Douglass's text uses thresholds as narrative enablers: the narrator crosses a series of thresholds – literal and figurative – in the course of his story. Perhaps the one that springs most readily to mind is the "blood-stained gate, the entrance to the hell of slavery" (51), figuring the narrator's cognition of the full, material implications of bondage. Thresholds of course establish the limits, entrance and exit to spaces. Together with thresholds, space becomes, according to Bassard, the "chief organizing principle for the narrativization of events" (116) such as we find in the works of slave authors, but also of neo-slave authors and other African American authors.[7] Much African American narrative is thus articulated through the paratactical arrangement of spatial configurations: that is how the story gets told.

I want to consider a little more closely the individual's relation to space insofar as that relation is inscribed within a larger structure and dynamic of power relations. Again, Foucault is instructive here. His recognition of the spatial as central to contemporary experience is indebted to previous spatial models, such as the Panopticon, an architectural structure designed to guarantee maximum visible surveillance of the inmates of prisons, lunatic asylums, schools, and so forth. Foucault notes in *Discipline and Punishment: The Birth of the Prison* that the disciplinary coerciveness of the Panopticon ultimately depends on it being internalized by the individual who will eventually act as if under constant surveillance even if s/he is not. The individual's radical disempowerment is effected through the visual control of his/her access to, exit from, and performance within space. An inescapable and defining part of Douglass's experience as a slave, such disempowerment is effected through the visual control of his access to, exit from, and performance within slave-plantation space. He tells us that there was no deceiving the overseer Covey, and "work went on in his absence almost as well as in his presence," because "he had the faculty of making us feel that he was ever present with us. This he did by surprising us [...]. His comings were like a thief in the night. He appeared to us as being ever at hand. He was under every tree, behind every stump, in every bush, and at every window, on the plantation" (103).

That spatial arrangements lead to certain configurations of power relations is merely acknowledged by Douglass. Fellow slave-narrator Jacobs goes somewhat further in her attempts to re-draw the lines of power by removing her body from the spatial coerciveness of the slave economy and inserting it into an alternative and resistant space. Much has been written about Linda's "loophole of retreat," the cramped garret in which she hides, as a preliminary space/phase to her reaching freedom in the northern United States. As Valerie Smith argues, the nominal designation of her hiding place invites scrutiny, drawing attention to its "closeness" and "the passivity that even voluntary confinement imposes," adding that the phrase, "loophole of retreat," possesses an ambiguity of meaning that extends to the literal loophole as well: "if a loophole signifies for Jacobs a place of withdrawal, it signifies in common parlance an avenue of escape" (212). Smith also notes that the garret is preceded by a series of similar (and, I would argue, prefigurative) structures of confinement, with the narrative unfolding in a series of receding spaces that culminate in the tiny attic space. Linda can go no further. She has literally backed herself into a corner, a confined space which paradoxically removes her from the economy of slavery. Her declaration that "There was no place, where slavery existed, that could have afforded me so good a place of concealment" (117) manifests an understanding of the ambiguities of her situation, ambiguities located in the very syntax of the sentence itself (Kawash 76). At the least, Linda seems to be saying, she is concealed in a space/place where slavery does not exist. It is from this "no place" that in spite, or precisely because, of the material implications of her confinement, Linda wrests the practice of surveillance from slavery itself. Whereas the slave's experience of reality is of unbroken surveillance in which distinctions between the private and the public, the seen and the unseen, are irrelevant, Linda contrives to occupy a space which is unobserved because invisible, undetected and beyond the law.

For Smith, Linda responds to the sexual persecution by her employer, Dr. Flint, by "repeatedly [...] choosing her own space of confinement" (213), though I propose that the verb "choose" is clearly problematic in the context. Her strategies of resistance are indeed repeated – repeated as often as Flint's attempts to coerce her into becoming his concubine – her taking a white lover, thus becoming the agent of her own de-flowering, being one of the most celebrated. Dr. Flint's ambition is to gain full control of Linda's person, that is, her body, though the means he uses are less physical than verbal, reminding us that the slave narrative conjoins language and body at the same site – as, indeed, it does in Douglass's syncretic conjoining of pen and gash. It is through language, whether spoken "foul words" (27) or other semiotic means – "What he could not find opportunity to say in words he manifested in signs. He invented more than were ever thought of in a deaf and dumb asylum" (31) – that Dr. Flint persecutes Linda. Linda, for her part, retreats to, takes refuge in (the spatial metaphors are unavoidable) strategic silences, feigned ignorance, and a series of literal spaces, from a space under the floor boards and an attic in a friend's house to, finally, her "loophole of retreat."

The extent of Linda's inventiveness and subversiveness can be seen in her appropriation of the "overseer's gaze" Foucault identifies as the Panopticon's core instrument of power (*Power/Knowledge* 147). *Incidents* provides striking corroboration of the panoptic effect characteristic of the slave plantation noted by Douglass, a model which Linda vexes by frequently placing herself in the space which the agent of surveillance would normally occupy and from which she or he invigilates, controls, and polices the movements of those within the visual and physical purview of the Panopticon.[8] From within her garret, she is able to follow movements in the street below, including and especially Dr. Flint's. At the same time, Linda's retreat into ever-receding spaces in order to escape Dr. Flint's unwelcome advances is a *forced* retreat and illustrates the cramped garret's equivocal status *both* as the endpoint of her defensive flight *and* a site of resistance, the place from which to plan and launch her children's and her own final bid for freedom.[9]

Ultimately, the model of empowerment represented by the Panopticon is never wholly realized. This would require the full relational possibilities to be transferred: a Panopticon works because there is an understanding *on both parts*, a dynamic that implicates the individual in control of surveillance and the individual at its mercy, the latter knowingly acquiescing in the controlling power of the former's gaze. The Panopticon model in *Incidents*, then, is flawed, since, for the surveillance to be effective within the terms of the narrative, indeed to be possible at all, the "surveilled" (read: Dr. Flint) cannot be aware of the "surveiller" (read: Linda). The panoptic contract, therefore, is not fulfilled. Yet the measure of Linda's achievement is undeniable: her attempt to subvert the power relations encoded in the panoptic model through a bodily and architectural substitution places her to a remarkable extent in possession and control of the "overseer's gaze."

As has been advanced throughout this essay, a salient feature of the slave narrative is the spatialization of experience reflective of the slave's severely curtailed agency; the Panopticon model, which engages simultaneously an external and internal spatialization, provides perhaps the most dramatic example of the slave's spatialized existence. Examples of slaves occupying confined, even smaller hiding spaces than Linda's are prevalent, as they are in much later writings, and support Hazel Carby's view that African American writing locates a common ancestor in the historical experience of slavery. Though all such examples demonstrate the commonality of spatialized existence, not all the protagonists are able to exploit the advantages of such spaces. The instances are too numerous to cite but Henry Box Brown's story makes common cause with Linda's experience, even while it also highlights the singularity of her response. Brown's escape to freedom "enclosed in a box 3 feet long and 2 feet wide," uses space to the slave's advantage: he willingly encloses himself in a coffin-like box and is thus transported from bondage to freedom. While the ruse is successful, the fact that he has to resort to it at all and the means he adopts raise questions about his achievement. Brown's story confirms Hartman's wry observation that such "tactics of resistance" are inevitably determined by "the relations of power and dominance that [slave narratives] strive [...] to write against" (11). Moreover, his sensory agency is severely curtailed – he can only hear with difficulty and is deprived of sight, an essential faculty for the Panopticon to work.[10]

Examples such as Henry Box Brown's coffin-like hiding place and means of transport bear some resemblance to Linda's loophole of retreat, yet draw our attention to the specificity of her strategy as well as its parodoxical potentialities. On the one hand, Linda is fully cognizant of the potential advantage her position – her emplacement – affords, duly noting on arriving at her grandmother's cramped garret and her hiding place for the next seven years that "I was eager to look on [my children's] faces; but there was no hole, no crack, through which I could peep" (114). Her visual agency, in ironic counterpoint to her physical containment (passivity, according to Smith), is recovered when she finds a gimlet with which to bore small holes in the wall and gain the ability to see without being seen. On the other, her sense of triumph and the restored ability to follow movements in the street below, including and especially Dr. Flint's, remain in (literally) painful tension with the harsh material implications of her situation. Her confession that her body suffers from the effects of her prolonged imprisonment reveals the permanently marked status of the slave's body, even as it bespeaks her free status: it is, in short, the price she has had to pay. Similarly, she exercises agency through a sort of virtual mobility which transports her to other spaces through the manipulative device of her letters to Dr. Flint. Kawash notes that the letters' false address "project [...] her body into a virtual space, where in fact she is not" (78-9). However, adds Kawash, "The circumstance of Jacobs's body in the loophole reinforces the significance of property in the determination of the subject" (79). What the narrator of *Incidents* thus stunningly exposes is that a site of contestation such as the slave's body may well remain just that: contested, and the agency over that site inevitably qualified. Ultimately, as Carla Kaplan observes, "Although Brent does eventually get out of her miserable attic hideaway, Jacobs does not escape the impasse this narrative so brilliantly renders. And that is the narrative's point" (qtd. in Kawash 79).

That critics are concerned with the extent and efficacy of Jacobs's strategy is reflective of the text's own ambivalent discourse. For Smith, Jacobs "inscribes a subversive plot of empowerment" (213), while others consider it expressive of the ways in which women's agency has historically been obliged to enter into dialogue with the discourse of oppression. At the end of her narrative, Linda herself maintains a qualified attitude toward her status, resigned to a problematic freedom acquired as a result of her "reinsert[tion] into the economy of property" (Kawash 79) through Mrs. Bruce's purchasing of her person, that is, her body. The narrative concludes with a reflection expressive of Linda's unresolved ambivalence: "It has been painful to me… to recall the dreary years I passed in bondage. I would gladly forget them if I could. Yet the retrospection is not altogether without solace; for with those gloomy recollections come tender memories of my good old grandmother, like light, fleecy clouds floating over a dark and troubled sea" (201). The phrases "dreary years," "gloomy recollection," "dark and troubled sea," contrast with words such as "solace," "tender memories" and "light, fleecy clouds." The irreducible doubleness of the discourse comes on the heels of Linda's more widely quoted ambivalence regarding freedom a few lines earlier, which not coincidentally rewrites the formulaic ending of sentimental fiction: "Reader, my story ends with freedom, not in the usual way, with marriage. I and my children are now free!" (201). The passage immediately following provides further reflection on the ambiguities attached to the condition of freedom, ambiguities which Brent astonishingly extends here to include white northerners, the *narratees* otherwise courted throughout her narrative: "We are as free from the power of slaveholders as are the white people of the north; and though that, according to my idea, is not saying a great deal, it is a vast improvement in *my* condition" (201, emphasis in original). John Cullen Gruesser argues that what truly sets off this passage from previous self-interrogations about Brent's own freedom is that it expresses the same ambivalence towards the freedom of whites living in the North: "[Brent] not only questions the legitimacy of her own freedom but also the freedom of the white people in the North [...]. Here she no longer writes *to* northern white women, [...] but instead writes *about* them, using her own experiences [...] to expose the limitations of *their* freedom" (114, emphases in original). Compare these passages from *Incidents* with Douglass's coda: "I was now my own master. It was a happy moment, the rapture of which can be understood only by those who have been slaves [...]. It was to me the starting point of a new existence" (150). Douglass's unironic and totalizing celebration of his new status is in sharp contrast to Jacobs's strategy of ambivalence. By insisting throughout her narrative, up to and including the ending, on the uniqueness of the black woman slave's experience, Jacobs simultaneously subverts the teleological structure of the male-authored slave narrative and proposes an alternative and more critical exploration of what agency and freedom might entail in a slave-holding economy.

Throughout the narrative, each time Linda responds to her condition – by managing her own sexuality, by refusing to comply with Dr. Flint's orders, by opting not to flee but remain hidden in a place where she can remain close to her children and retain visual access to events outside – her response is simultaneously driven and mediated by the limitations imposed by the very nature of her condition. Inevitably, her range of "choice" is qualified. Jacobs's sober presentation of such realities is in stark contrast to Frederick Douglass's *Narrative*, in which the protagonist processes and resolves dialectically the competing realities denotative of double-consciousness – as in, for example, his title's self-designating "An American Slave." Through an active syncretism, the narrator creates fresh sites undetected and unforeseen by white society into which he could move and continue "writing in the spaces left." Douglass's liberatory/celebratory narrative of seizure and occupation of such spaces is severely interrogated by Jacobs's more nuanced narrative of "the loophole of retreat."

[1] Foucault cautions us not seek an author in a first-person narrator, since "neither the first person pronoun, the present indicative tense, nor, for that matter, its signs of localization refer directly to the writer, either to the time when he wrote, or to the specific act of writing; rather, they stand for a 'second self' whose similarity to the author is never fixed and undergoes considerable alteration within the course of a single book" ("What" 1631). Albert Murray reinforces the notion of the narrator as a construct in its own right, as distinct from the author and with specific attributes: "[In] autobiography as in fiction, nothing has more to do with what the story is really about than the voice of the narrator. So the main thing [is] to get his voice on the page [...]. It is always the storyteller's story [...]. It is still his voice that provides the emotional as well as the physical context in terms of which everything else is told" (31).

[2] Other examples include Jon Hauss's argument that *Incidents* is "remarkable [...] in its [...] strategically revelatory storytelling, of underground passageways of solidarity and

resistance" (145); he concludes that *Incidents* "recovers [...] an alternative body of cultural beliefs and practices sustained within slave-woman centred networks of resistance to slavery" (163). See also Claudia Tate who asserts: "[*Incidents*] switches the gender network in the seduction story so that Jacobs can momentarily become the free agent [...]; we can see Jacobs playing the role of the seductress instead of the seduced victim. This is indeed radical, revolutionary autonomy for a woman [...]" (109).

[3] In the interests of fairness, Carby does acknowledge a certain tension in the narrative, such as the "struggle of Linda Brent to retain some control over her sexuality," and observes how Jacobs's narrative "negotiated the tension between satisfying moral expectations [of her readers] and challenging an ideology that would condemn her as immoral" (*Reconstructing* 58).

[4] Smith calls attention to "three narrative spaces" in *Incidents,* spaces analogous to the garret, and which the critic identifies as examples of the author's control over the form – sentimental fiction – she has appropriated to tell her story ("Loopholes" 223).

[5] Hartman's more recent reading of Jacobs's and Douglass's writings suggests that Douglass himself was ambivalently positioned vis-à-vis his own seemingly absolutist and totalizing narrative of emancipation. In the introduction to her work *Scenes of Subjection: Terror, Slavery and Self-Making in Nineteenth-Century America* (1997), she declares that "the entanglements of slavery and freedom" (9) exposed in Jacobs's narrative are a common theme in pre- and post-emancipation texts. Hartman candidly admits that her own archival enquiry "is enmeshed with the relations of power and dominance that it strives to write against" (11). Hartman locates Douglass's critique of freedom in his "decrial of slave holidays [...] [whose] pleasures thwart the emergence of an oppositional consciousness" (47), on the one hand, and his emphasis, on the other, on the "singularity of sorrow [songs], thus hoping to establish an absolute division between diversion and the glimmerings of protest" (48). Hartman's examples are taken from *Life and Times of Frederick Douglass.*

[6] This is echoed in the later testimony: "Mr. Covey gave me a very severe whipping [...] raising ridges on my flesh as large as my little finger" (101).

[7] Carby locates the collective ancestry of African American writing in the experience of slavery: "Slavery haunts the literary imagination [in African American writing] because its material conditions and social relations are frequently reproduced in fiction as historically dynamic [...]. The economic and social system of slavery is thus a prehistory (as well as a pre-text to all Afro-American texts), a past social condition that can explain contemporary phenomena" ("Ideologies" 125-26). While not necessarily endorsing a myth of origins, critics consistently point to the slave narrative as the urtext of the African American literary tradition. Robert Stepto (*From Behind the Veil: A Study of the Afro-American Tradition*) and Henry Louis Gates, Jr. (*The Signifying Monkey*) have compellingly argued in favor of a rhetorical line of descent from the slave narrative to the present day.

[8] *Incidents* abounds with instances of ubiquitous surveillance consistent with the Panopticon. Rescuing her sleeping daughter from underneath her master's house, Linda speaks her fears out loud and is startled to find Dr. Flint standing next to her and privy to her spoken thoughts (87); overhearing a comment by Mrs. Flint in reference to her (Brent's) children, Linda declares "My heart was on watch all the time" (93); from a prior "loophole of retreat," Linda observes that from the window to the small space where she is temporarily hiding, "I could lie perfectly concealed, and command a view

of the street through which Dr. Flint passed to his office. Anxious as I was, I felt a gleam of satisfaction when I saw him" (100). There are many more similar examples before Linda's final retreat to her "loophole."

[9] Cf. "[E]ach moment of [Jacobs's] apparent enclosure actually empowers her to redirect her own and her children's destiny" (Smith Introduction: xxxiv).

[10] In an example from a twentieth century neo-slave narrative, *Beloved* (1987), the loft from which Halle witnesses, hidden and unobserved, Sethe's violation at the hands (and mouths) of Schoolteacher's nephews, tragically enables all of Halle's senses; the brutally unmediated scene to which he is a helpless witness however reverses the empowering Panopticon model and results in his psychological collapse.

Works Cited

Bassard, Katherine Clay. "Crossing Over: Free Space, Sacred Space and Intertextual Geographies in Peter Randolph's *Sketches of Slave Life*." *Religion and Literature* 35.2-3 (Summer-Autumn 2003): 113-41.

Brown, Henry Box. *Narrative of Henry Box Brown, Who Escaped from Slavery Enclosed in a Box 3 Feet Long and 2 Wide. Written from a Statement of Facts Made by Himself, With Remarks Upon the Remedy for Slavery. By Charles Stearns*. 1849. 30 January 2008. <http://docsouth.unc.edu/neh/boxbrown.html>

Burnham, Michelle. "Loopholes of Resistance: Harriet Jacobs's Slave Narrative and the Critique of Agency in Foucault." *Arizona Quarterly* 49.2 (Summer 1993): 53-73.

Carby, Hazel V. *Reconstructing Womanhood: The Emergence of the Afro-American Woman Novelist*. New York: Oxford UP, 1988.

—. "Ideologies of Black Folk: The Historical Novel of Slavery." *Slavery and the Literary Imagination*. Ed. Deborah E. McDowell and Arnold Rampersad. Baltimore: Johns Hopkins UP, 1989. 125-43.

Douglass, Frederick. *Narrative of the Life of Frederick Douglass, an American Slave. Written by Himself*. 1845. Harmondsworth: Penguin, 1982.

Foucault, Michel. *Discipline and Punish*: The Birth of the Prison. New York: Pantheon, 1977.

—. "Of Other Spaces, Heterotopias." 1967. Trans. Jay Miskoview. 22Dec. 2007. <http://foucault.info/documents/heteroTopia/foucault.heteroTopia.en.html>

—. *Power/Knowledge: Selected Interviews and Other Writings (1972-1977)*. Ed. C. Gordon. Brighton: Harvester, 1980.

—."What is an Author?" 1969. Leitch 1622-1636.

Gates, Jr., Henry Louis, ed. *Reading Black, Reading Feminist: A Critical Anthology*. New York: Penguin, 1990.

—. *The Signifying Monkey*. Oxford: Oxford UP, 1988.

Gilroy, Paul. *The Black Atlantic: Modernity and Double Consciousness*. Cambridge: Harvard UP, 1993.

Gruesser, John Cullen. *Confluences: Postcolonialism, African American Literary Studies, and the Black Atlantic*. Athens: U of Georgia P, 2007.

Hartman, Saidiya V. *Scenes of Subjection: Terror, Slavery, and Self-Making in Nineteenth Century America*. Oxford: Oxford UP, 1997.

Hauss, Jon. "Perilous Passages in Harriet Jacobs's *Incidents in the Life of a Slave Girl*. Plasa and Ring 44-165.

Jacobs, Harriet. *Incidents in the Life of a Slave Girl, Written by Herself.* 1861. Ed. Jean Fagan Yellin. Cambridge: Harvard UP, 1987.

Kawash, Samira. *Dislocating the Color Line: Identity, Hybridity, and Singularity in African American Literature*. Stanford: Stanford UP, 1997.

Leitch, Vincent B., ed. *The Norton Anthology of Theory and Criticism*. New York: Norton, 2001.

Murray, Albert. *The Blue Devils of Nada*. New York: Vintage, 1997.

Morrison, Toni. *Beloved*. 1987. New York: Vintage, 1997.

Plasa, Carl, and Betty J. Ring, ed. *The Discourse of Slavery*. London: Routledge, 1994.

Sánchez-Eppler, Karen. *Touching Liberty: Abolition, Feminism, and the Politics of the Body*. Berkely: U of California P, 1993.

Smith, Valerie. "'Loopholes of Retreat': Architecture and Ideology in Harriet Jacobs's *Incidents in the Life of a Slave Girl*." Gates 212-226.

—. "Introduction." Harriet Jacobs. *Incidents in the Life of a Slave Girl*. New York: Oxford UP, 1988. xxvii-xl.

Stepto, Robert. *From Behind the Veil: A Study of Afro-American Narrative*. Urbana: U of Illinois P, 1991.

Tate, Claudia. "Allegories of Black Female Desire; or Re-Reading Nineteenth Century Sentimental Narratives of Black Female Authority." Wall 98-126.

Wall, Cheryl A., ed. *Changing Our Own Words: Essays on Criticism, Theory, and Writing by Black Women*. London: Routledge, 1989.

Washington, Mary Helen. *Invented Lives: Narratives of Black Women 1860-1960*. London: Virago Press, 1989.

Yellin, Jean Fagan. "Introduction." Jacobs. xiii-xxxiv.

A Trickster in Transition: Nineteenth-Century Representations of Aunt Nancy

Shanna Greene Benjamin

In short, the trickster hero of West Africa has been transplanted to America.
Zora Neale Hurston, "Characteristics of Negro Expression"

All of the standard tricksters are male.
Lewis Hyde, "Where Are the Women Tricksters?"

Male figures dominate the African American trickster tradition and define critical analyses of the African trickster's influence on black literature and culture. During the nineteenth century, Joel Chandler Harris helped to preserve the African American trickster tradition by collecting folktales of the American South in his Uncle Remus stories. Rearticulations of West African animal tales, his most popular stories feature the exploits of Brer Rabbit: a small, unlikely hero who uses verbal dexterity to outwit his more powerful animal enemies. For slaves, the stories about rabbit, fox and turtle that were told for entertainment in Africa became New World allegorical tales of resistance. In the twentieth century, literary critic Henry Louis Gates, Jr., codified a vocabulary to define the influence of African myth upon black literary and cultural traditions. His seminal text, *The Signifying Monkey: A Theory of Afro-American Literary Criticism*, traces the folkloric roots of the black vernacular tradition to the Yoruba trickster and god of crossroads, Esu-Elegbara, thereby naming the mythic source of the double-voiced discourse within African American oral and narrative traditions. Gates's study, while groundbreaking in its analysis of the relationship between West African myth and black American trickster tropes,[1] nonetheless uses a male archetype – whose symbol is coincidentally a phallus – to define the trickster's place within the entire black literary tradition.

Yet there is another figure within black folklore that offers an alternative approach to reading the black trickster tradition: Aunt Nancy, the American version of the Ghanaian trickster spider Kwaku Ananse.[2] The American descendent of a delightful rogue known both for his greediness and altruism, Ananse experienced a sea change during the Middle Passage that altered his name and function in diasporic society.[3] In Ghana, Ananse was a "creative culture hero" while in Jamaica and other parts of the Caribbean he became a "trickster par-excellence" (Tanna 77). In the United States, he became she:

Aunt Nancy the witch and trickster who morphed, among other things, into a mediator between slavery and freedom in nineteenth-century texts.[4]

Since studies of the African American trickster typically privilege Joel Chandler Harris's Brer Rabbit, Henry Louis Gates's Esu-Elegbara[5] or the signifying monkey, "A Trickster in Transition" asks, what happens to our understanding of the black trickster tradition if we rewrite this genealogy of influence to include Aunt Nancy? How does the work of this female trickster complement the work of her male counterparts? What criteria can we use to identify a trickster whose presence has remained mostly hidden in plain view? "A Trickster in Transition" reads Aunt Nancy's explicit presence in Joel Chandler Harris's "Brother Rabbit Doesn't Go to See Aunt Nancy" and figurative emergence in Harriet Jacobs's *Incidents in the Life of a Slave Girl* to reveal the origins a black female trickster tradition within African American literature and culture. Specifically, this essay explains the three ways Aunt Nancy's emergence is marked in nineteenth-century folklore and literature: by occupying an "absent presence"[6] within the dominant culture, lurking, like spiders, in areas up above and on the margins to surreptitiously execute her ruse; by employing the "text as textile"[7] technique where she weaves a narrative web that ensnares readers and rivals alike to her advantage; and by enacting "integrative liminality" where, like spiders that spin their webs between opposing spaces, Aunt Nancy bridges the gap between disparate ideologies to complement the deconstructive qualities of traditional, male tricksters.[8]

In the *Seven Tales of Uncle Remus*,[9] a series of "hitherto uncollected" stories by Joel Chandler Harris (5), Aunt Nancy appears in "Brother Rabbit Doesn't Go to See Aunt Nancy," a narrative where Remus recounts the time of year when Aunt Nancy summons the animals of the forest to visit her home and "make der peace" with her (27). When the animals feel a particular "creepy feelin'" in the air, a chill in their bones, they know it is time to make their ascent to Aunt Nancy's hideaway (27). One year, Brother Rabbit decides that he wants no part of this yearly ritual and announces to the other animals of the forest that he is not going, adding that if they knew what he knew, they would avoid her as well. The animals fear Aunt Nancy more than they are persuaded by Rabbit's admonition so, sans Rabbit, they collectively trek to Aunt Nancy's house.

Once all are seated, Aunt Nancy takes account of each animal and, after noticing that Rabbit is missing, inquires about his whereabouts. Brer Bear remarks that Rabbit instructed the animals to tell her "howdy" in lieu of attending and suggested that they shake hands with her to understand his reasons for bypassing the meeting. At this, Aunt Nancy "roll her red eye" and declares, "Well you des tell 'im, dat ef he'll come ter dis place I'll shake han's wid 'im, an' ef he don't come ez hard ez his legs'll fetch 'im, I'll go an' shake han's wid' 'im whar he lives at" (Harris 27). In response, Brer Bear exclaims, well, we're here – why don't you shake hands with us? As Aunt Nancy stands to address Brer Bear, her cloak slips away, revealing a body that is half woman and half spider. Mortified after noticing that "She had sev'm arms an' no han's" (28), the creatures run back into the forest only to realize that Aunt Nancy's foggy lair is, in fact, a spider's web. When they tell Brer Rabbit what transpired, he simply sits "chawin' his cud" like nothing happened (28).

Like most of Harris's Uncle Remus stories, this Aunt Nancy tale exists as the internal narrative within a larger frame tale that situates Uncle Remus as storyteller and a young white boy as his attentive audience. Couched in a period reminiscent of simple plantation life "befo' de wah," Harris's frame narrative regulates the allegorical and often violent internal narrative where the black slave (Brer Rabbit) regularly triumphs over his white master or overseer (Brer Fox/Brer Bear). Written in the plantation tradition style – where happy darkies enthusiastically sing songs, cheerfully tell stories, and endlessly demonstrate their loyalty to master and plantation – the frame narrative maintains the social stratification that the Civil War and emancipation of slaves threatened.[10]

The thread motif in the frame of "Brother Rabbit Doesn't Go to See Aunt Nancy" foreshadows the spider imagery dominating the internal tale and establishes the underlying thematic line's text as textile technique. "Brother Rabbit" opens with Uncle Remus "doing his best to patch an old waistcoat" trying "once and again [. . .] to thread the large needle with which he was doing the work" (Harris 26). Read against the internal narrative, hereafter referred to as the folktale, the image of Uncle Remus mending his clothes serves a dual purpose: it anticipates the "yarn" Remus is about to spin and gestures toward trickster Aunt Nancy's presence as the binding force behind both the folktale and its narrative frame.

In the frame story, we see the intersection of text and textile – the linking of narrative line and fiber motif – that connects "Brother Rabbit" to a traditional Ananse tale where Ghanaians situate the spider man as the source of all stories. Reminiscent of the spider trickster who weaves his way to the heavens for the stories that will later become his legacy, Uncle Remus spins a tale that ensnares the young boy in a captivating narrative about a domineering spider witch. In this familiar West African story, "Trickster Gets Sky-god's Stories," Kwaku Ananse weaves his way to the heavens to broker a deal with Sky-god and acquire his trunk of stories.[11] In exchange for Onini the python, Osebo the leopard, Mmoatia the fairy, and Mmoboro the hornet, Sky-god agrees to relinquish his stories to Ananse so that the people on earth may enjoy them. With cunning precision, Ananse captures these elusive figures and brings them to Sky-god who renames the tales "Spider Stories" in honor of the one who rescued them for the world's enjoyment. This early Ananse story establishes an African folkloric tradition where storyteller and weaver are one. Similarly, as Remus mends in the narrative frame, he physically and figuratively manipulates the thread – both as the seam of his coat and the narrative line – using folklore to teach the young boy about the seasonal movement of animals and creating a text with textile qualities that enmeshes the young boy and readers alike in an enticing story line.

Symbolically, Harris's folktale – the internal narrative about Aunt Nancy and her lair – offers a textually vivid representation of Nancy's role as a nineteenth-century trickster who not only functions as a mediator and master of liminality like Ananse before her, but also embodies integrative liminality in her physical form. Instead of moving *between* heaven and earth like Ananse,[12] Aunt Nancy exists in both worlds simultaneously, fusing physical and spatial mediation at the same time: physically, she embodies duality with a body that is at once animal and human; spatially, she unites the distance between the celestial and the animal worlds by spinning her web between heaven and earth. Unlike traditional black male tricksters that function as a fragmenting force, Aunt Nancy exemplifies the integrative impulse by assimilating opposing epistemologies and spaces to create a realm where "both/and" exist as a philosophical norm.[13]

Mirroring Aunt Nancy's liminal lair where the heavens and earth meet, the spider and female forms inscribed upon Aunt Nancy's body unite the otherwise distinctive animal and human tricksters, enabling Aunt Nancy to embody the mediation that tricksters like Esu Legba merely perform. The unique duality that is part and parcel of the black female trickster tradition involves a careful negotiation between pragmatism and idealism exemplified in Aunt Nancy's physical assimilation of otherwise mutually exclusive African American trickster traditions. In *Black Culture and Black Consciousness*, Lawrence Levine defines the difference between black animal- and human-based trickster stories. Here, he explains how the transplanted animal stories that migrated with Africans during the Middle Passage existed within a slave culture that limited the psychological dreams of transplanted Africans as much as it restricted the physical freedom of these slaves. As a result, African American animal and human tricksters expressed success in vastly different ways.

On the one hand, the victories of animal tricksters were limitless – they existed in an imaginary setting where animals lived as humans but were free from the realism of chattel slavery, psychological degradation and the physical abuse of the Peculiar Institution. On the other hand, restricted and bound by a "more conscious and more realistic world," Levine asserts, "The exploits of the human trickster functioned as a carefully constructed rationale for the actions slaves found themselves resorting to" (132). Therefore, while the ploys of the human trickster were primarily limited to "making his master look foolish and thus exposing the myth of white omniscience and omnipotence," the animal trickster violated social boundaries and cultural taboos, delighting in the "death of the oppressor, the love of the oppressor's woman, or the inheritance of the oppressor's material empire" as a result of his trickery (132). Since, as spider and woman, Aunt Nancy embodies both sides of Levine's trickster equation, she is uniquely positioned to enact transcendent trickery, to perform a hoax that goes beyond the one-time scamming of Brer Rabbit and instead, employ a "long con": an extended trick that is both pragmatic and visionary given the racialized restrictions of nineteenth-century America. Her trick is integrative liminality, where Aunt Nancy complements the work of Esu by linking disparate ideologies, reconciling binaries, or uniting that which he traditionally breaks apart.

Aunt Nancy's integrative liminality is made possible through the absent presence of her suspended lair: a spider's web masquerading as a cloud of fog. Hovering between heaven and earth, Aunt Nancy's web home positions her between the "roun' worl'" and the celestial space above (Harris 27). While her position does not grant her the ability to observe action on earth (if it did, she would have known that Brer Rabbit remained behind even before calling the roll) her absent presence allows her to have a direct effect on the creatures of that world. Aunt Nancy can communicate viscerally with the animals of the forest with a simple inhalation and make her presence felt while she remains invisible. In so doing, Aunt Nancy denotes the absent presence and integrative liminality of black female tricksters.

Inspired by the way Aunt Nancy "hangs out" in her lair, absent presence defines the unique position black female tricksters assume before employing their trick; modeled after the way spiders bridge the gap between opposing spaces with their webs, integrative liminality names black women's linking of disparate ideologies, traditions, and conventions and their reconciliation of binaries in a discursive space between dominant discourses. Seeing all without being seen and spinning their webs between two distinct spaces at once, black female tricksters occupy absent presence in relation to the world around them and employ integrative liminality to join otherwise disconnected spaces. Aunt Nancy's position on the margins, both literal and figurative, provides the space for black female tricksters to execute their trickery; and like spiders that dwell on the margins of rooms, black women during slavery exist without autonomy or agency on the periphery of a sexist and racist society that privileges maleness and whiteness. Where the "totem pole" trope obscures black women beneath a hierarchy of white men, white women and eventually, black men, absent presence affords black women perspective despite their alienation from agency. From the outskirts of access, black women are able to see and evaluate virtually everything and everyone, often unnoticed because of their presumed inferiority.

As Harris's Aunt Nancy lurks above, observing without being observed, her emergence in Harriet Jacobs's *Incidents* prompts us to look to the margins of dominant society for insight into black women's hidden power and the relationship between that power and the black female trickster tradition.[14] In *Madcaps, Screwballs, and Con Women: The Female Trickster in American Culture*, Lori Landay asserts that domestic sites of women's power, traditionally marginalized by mainstream culture, are an ideal space to locate female tricksters: "In order to identify female tricksters [...] we must turn from the margins of dominant society to the centers of women's space – the parlors, kitchens, and bedrooms of domesticity" (3). Consider, for example, Linda Brent's aunt Nancy and her vital yet invisible service to the Flint household in *Incidents*. Even as she nurses and attends to others, sharing a physical space with the Flint family, her physical presence and value as a servant is all that matters; her humanity is inconsequential. As the household "factotum" who serves as the "housekeeper and waiting-maid in Dr. Flint's family," every night, aunt Nancy sleeps on the floor by the door to Mrs. Flint's chamber (Jacobs 113). Supporting the Flint's domestic needs as a body of labor, instead of as a human being, aunt Nancy nurses Mrs. Flint's children even as her regular miscarriages leave her childless. As a black slave, aunt Nancy literally and figuratively lives her life on the margins. And even though, to our knowledge, aunt Nancy engages in no specific trickery within the Flint household, she does support Linda's subterfuge by sharing insider information about the Flints and encouraging Linda's efforts to escape even while her friends tried to "discourage [her] from running away" (113). Both aunt Nancy and Linda Brent utilize their absent presence, their position on the margins, in different ways. Because of aunt Nancy's peripheral position within the Flint home, she is able to observe the private lives of Dr. and Mrs. Flint and share privileged information with Linda; Brent's stint in the garret allows her to occupy an absent presence and demonstrate the marginal position of power that black female tricksters must assume before enacting the text as textile and integrative liminality of their trick.

The trickster energies in *Incidents* enter the narrative in "The Loophole of Retreat": a chapter positioned at the structural crossroads of Jacobs's text where Brent begins a nearly seven-year stay in her grandmother's garret. Situated at exactly the center of the narrative, "Loophole" transitions parts one and two of *Incidents* and serves as "the hinge which balances twenty chapters on either side" (Burnham 278). In "Loopholes of Resistance: Harriet Jacobs' Slave Narrative and the Critique of Agency in Foucault," Michelle Burnham observes "This chapter's central location, whether the result of accident or design, would seem to suggest its structural significance in Jacobs' narrative. Yet its central location is by no means obvious, for 'The Loophole of Retreat' goes just as easily unnoticed in the middle of forty-one unnumbered chapters" (278). What is important to Burnham structurally, is important to us folklorically as this organizational crossroads is the point at which Esu Legba enters into the narrative to symbolically undo the bind of slavery that has held Brent hostage and create a space for the integrative energies of Aunt Nancy to enter and facilitate Brent's transition from slavery to freedom.[15] The "sole messenger of the gods," Esu is the "guardian of the crossroads" known for disrupting and undoing our suppositions (Gates 6). As Edward Pavlic explains in "'Papa Legba, Ouvrier Barriere Por Moi Passer': Esu in *Their Eyes* and Zora Neale Hurston's Diasporic Modernism," crossroads imagery "might make readers attuned to West African cultural traditions edgy, even suspicious" – for the "Little Lord of the Crossroads" is none other than Esu, the transitional force that creates space "anew" (61).[16] As a space of ambiguity and interpretation, Brent's "Loophole" is the ideal space for Linda to begin her transition to freedom. Since she is not-quite free and not-quite enslaved, her work toward freedom requires a liminal space to enact her trick – an area of absent presence where she will have the time and opportunity to weave her web and spring her trap.[17]

While in the garret, Linda Brent assumes an absent presence and develops the critical and narrative skills that prepare her to perform the text as textile trick of Aunt Nancy. Observing life through her "peep-hole" (96), Brent's physical position in the garret "afford[s] her both concealment and a point of observation" in relation to both the street below and the discourse surrounding her disappearance (Warner 224). This space, Brent explains, "was only nine feet long and seven feet wide. The highest part was three feet high, and sloped down abruptly to the loose board floor. There was no admission for either light or air" (Jacobs 91-92). Within the stifling confines of the garret, Brent hides out for seven years, enduring tortuous heat and agonizing cold, awaiting the day when Dr. Flint's hunt for her abates and it becomes safe to leave.[18] What Brent has not personally been able to see (or hear) through the chink in her "little den" she is able to glean from her aunt Nancy, who regularly brings her niece "all the news she could hear at Dr. Flint's" (93). Above the activity of everyday life yet below the sky above, Brent exists liminally between heaven and earth. She does not actively participate in the events in or around town, nor has she left the place where she was enslaved. Instead, unable to talk above a whisper with family or friends, she lingers in a physical and discursive purgatory, wanting to move beyond a crawl,[19] but being unable; having something to say but often without anyone with whom she can speak. Moreover, she lives in a world somewhere between slavery and freedom: freed from her responsibilities as a slave and the unwanted advances of Dr. Flint yet bound by the confines of the garret in the land of her oppressors.

In this liminal space, where Brent occupies an absent presence in relation to the slave world below, she prepares herself to weave the text as textile narrative that will trap Dr. Flint and upend his relentless search for her. With limited movement, constrained by the tightness of the garret, Linda "contrive[s] to read and sew" and begins to develop the literacy, both cultural and narrative, that will enable her to fool Dr. Flint and perform her ultimate trick: escape (Jacobs 93). The work of reading and sewing – Linda's engagement with both text and textile – may not have been a conscious effort by Jacobs to invoke Aunt Nancy, but it nonetheless positions Brent to enact the integrative liminality of this trickster as she uses letters to close the space between Linda's imposed enslavement and her desired freedom.

By reading in the garret, Brent becomes attuned to the nature of texts and nuances of narrative and resists the efforts of both Dr. Flint and Mrs. Emily Flint – later Mrs. Dodge – to return her to slavery. In the chapter "Competition in Cunning," Brent enacts a ruse that demonstrates her ability to weave an intricate narrative line that brings her closer to freedom. Here, she describes Dr. Flint's incessant pursuit and feeble attempts to fool others into revealing her whereabouts: "Every now and then he would say to my grandmother that I would come back, and voluntarily surrender myself and that when I did, I could be purchased by my relatives, or any one who wished to buy me. I knew his cunning nature too well not to perceive that this was a trap laid for me" (Jacobs 101). Unimpressed by his tactics, Brent resolves "to match my cunning against his cunning. In order to make him believe that I was in New York, I resolved to write him a letter dated from that place" (101). Brent's mastery of discourse, developed while occupying an absent presence within the confines of the garret, allows her to successfully fabricate, quite literally to weave, a narrative that performs the integrative liminality of trickster Aunt Nancy, bringing Brent ever closer to freedom.[20]

The success of Brent's trick and, by extension, her facility as a trickster, depends on her ability to weave her text as textile with the interlocking threads of both textual literacy (her ability to interpret written texts and write narratives of her own) and cultural literacy (her understanding of the slave system and ability to negotiate its terms) to reverse the master/slave dynamic and seize Dr. Flint's power. Brent's deceptive letters to Dr. Flint and her grandmother offer the ideal locus to see text as textile in action, but it is impossible for readers to experience her letters firsthand since we do not know exactly what Brent wrote. She excludes the correspondences themselves, leaving to the reader's imagination the presumably provocative content that provoked Dr. Flint to replace her letter with one of his own. Even though there is no letter, no primary text, to analyze, Brent offers circumstantial information that hints at her trickery – her skills in verbal expression and narrative construction – which function as an absent presence in Dr. Flint's replacement letter. Brent summarizes her letter to her grandmother as follows: "I expressed a wish to have my children sent to me at the north, where I could teach them to respect themselves, and set them a virtuous example; which a slave mother was not allowed to do at the south" (Jacobs 101-102). Dr. Flint paints a very different picture: "Dear Grandmother: I have long wanted to write you; but the disgraceful manner in which I left you and my children made me ashamed to do it. If you knew how much I have suffered since I ran away, you would pity and forgive me. I have purchased freedom at a dear rate" (102-103). The principles of virtue, respect and a mother's love for her children stand at the core of Brent's letter; in contrast, notions of disgrace, shame, suffering and desperation characterize Dr. Flint's rewrite.

This stark difference in tone and content suggest that Brent's trickery – her exploitation of Dr. Flint's underestimation of her power – is the product of a letter that ignites his rage for the way that it exceeds his expectations. Immediately after reading the false letter aloud to her grandmother, Dr. Flint smugly asserts, "It is very much as I expected it would be" (103). The irony, of course, is that Brent's original letter is nothing like he expected. If it had met his expectations – if it were anxious, fearful, apologetic and rambling – he would not have had to rewrite it. Given Dr. Flint's retort, one may gather that Brent's letter was not only good, but it was also biting, assertive, and even eloquent.

Complementing her cultural literacy, Brent's textual literacy, employed specifically through her letter writing, invokes the qualities of a trickster when she, because of her marginalized position as black/slave/woman, manipulates language to subversively embark on a freedom quest, even when she is unable to do so directly. In the garret Brent develops the writing and reading skills that transform her into Aunt Nancy: a trickster whose absent presence permits her to ensnare her prey in a narrative web that baits with stereotype – Dr. Flint's bias that because of her position as a slave, Brent's capacity for deception could never outweigh his – and binds with substance – the reality that with language as her tool, Brent is more than capable of fashioning an effective ruse against her oppressor.

In addition to furthering her pursuit of freedom, Brent's trickery is also an attempt to assert her wit in the face of whites who question her intellect. After Linda has successfully escaped north and found work with a prominent New York family, Miss Emily Flint, "now Mrs. Dodge," attempts to seduce Linda into returning south by intimating in a painfully transparent letter that Brent will be able to purchase her freedom if she comes back to Edenton (Jacobs 144). Annoyed, Brent rejoins: "Of course I did not write to return thanks for this cordial invitation. I felt insulted to be thought stupid enough to be caught by such professions. 'Come up into my parlor,' said the spider to the fly; ''Tis the prettiest little parlor that you ever did spy'" (145). By quoting this section of Mary Howitt's poem "The Spider and the Fly," Brent reverses the power dynamic Mrs. Dodge attempts to assert in her letter. Where Mrs. Dodge fancies herself the spider and Linda the fly, Brent's ingenuity and ability to see through Mrs. Dodge's obvious ruse thrusts her in the position, quite literally, of spider. At this point in the narrative, in chapter thirty-eight, just three chapters from the text's conclusion, Brent has, in fact, become a sly spider. Writing from a liminal, abolitionist space, Brent weaves the story of her life safely from the north, linking the slave and free worlds with a text that re-members her slave past by piecing together the most impressionable incidents in her life into a patchwork narrative of freedom.

From Joel Chandler Harris's Aunt Nancy to Harriet Jacobs's Linda Brent, the folkloric and symbolic emergence of the black female trickster points to an alternative trickster tradition where women complement the work of their male counterparts by stitching together that which they undo, and unifying that which they fragment. Like other female tricksters, Aunt Nancy transforms gendered spaces of alienation into powerful spaces of exile. Her presence infuses the African American literary tradition with a trickster whose subversive power is matched only by her ability to transform the social and psychological fragmentation of the black slave experience into opportunities for personal integration, wholeness and strength.

[1] In *The Signifying Monkey,* Gates invokes the Yoruba trickster Esu-Elegbara as the mythic forefather of the Signifying Monkey defined as "the great trope of Afro-American discourse" (21). Together, Gates identifies the significance of these figures: "First, they and the myths in which they are characters function as focal points for black theories about formal language use," "[s]econd, in the myths of Esu and the Monkey the tradition defines the role of the figurative," and "[t]he third conclusion that we can draw from the myths of Esu and the Monkey concerns the indeterminacy of interpretation" (21-22).

[2] See Newall.

[3] *Drums and Shadows: Survival Studies Among the Georgia Coastal Negroes* is one of several texts that provides evidence of Aunt Nancy's presence on American shores even into the twentieth century. In response to questions about Aunt Nancy, spiders, or spider stories, one interviewee responds that the spider is "bote good and ebil an is useful tuh man" because medicine can be made from the webs (56). Another cautions, "I dohn fool wid no spiduh. Dey is bad luck. All duh time dey drop down right out ub a tree" (157).

[4] The case of Kwaku Ananse's gender switch from Ghana to the United States is particularly interesting because, even after the Middle Passage, he remained a male figure in the Caribbean (Anancy the Spider *Man*). There are several reasons which are, at this stage of research, speculative at best, that may account for the gender switch. The first, and most obvious, centers on a question of linguistic corruption or the Anglicization of the Ghananian Ananse into an Americanized version: Aunt Nancy. The second takes into account the trauma of the Middle Passage and the shift in social structure where slave women played a more prominent role in family life. This may also have been reflected in the re-naming of Ananse as Aunt Nancy. The third possibility is that the name change is the product of a masking device that allowed slaves to invoke the power of a mythical force by calling the name of someone who sounded like a friend or relative. Like Santeria, which hides African deities under the guise of Catholicism, it is entirely possible that Sea Island slaves enacted the same with Ananse (to Aunt Nancy). Fourth, given the Sea Island connection with Native American cultures, the possibility also exists that the Native view of the Americas as a feminine land may have also encouraged the gender switch. While all of the reasons behind this gender switch are not one hundred percent clear, textual evidence indicates that Ananse survived the Middle Passage and lived on as a real presence within the African American folkloric tradition.

[5] Esu-Elegbara, Esu and Esu Legba will be used interchangeably throughout this essay.

[6] My use of absent presence signifies upon Jacques Derrida's presence/absence explored in his essay "Différance." It is necessary to make a distinction between his presence/absence and my absent presence because each works from a different set of cultural assumptions. In his essay, Derrida explores how language is built out of words that refer endlessly in a chain of deferral to other words and never to the signified (concept) or the real thing (referent). This principle of deferral of meaning links up with presence/absence because meaning (the signified and the referent) is absent from the signifier (the word/language). The word, or the signifier, is its own "presence." Although there are certainly similarities between Derrida's theories and my own, our differences point to one crucial epistemological distinction: where Derrida's presence/absence points to the fissure between text and referent, my theory of absent presence highlights the connection between texts and their historical and material realities.

The historical and material base of my theory is the one produced by slavery in the New World.

[7] The etymology of both text and textile is the Latin *textere*, which means "to weave" or, according to the Proto-Indo-European *teks,* "to fabricate." As trickster, Aunt Nancy links the fabrication of literary texts with the weaving of narrative webs. See Friedman, Gubar, Marcus, J.H. Miller, N.K. Miller and Showalter for woman-centered analyses of writing and weaving as modes of critical inquiry and metaphors for the narrative process.

[8] These principles are part of a larger work-in-progress by the author entitled *The Ananse Aesthetic*. The literature and fiber art of black women who create within the Ananse aesthetic bear the imprint of many, if not all, of the following principles: *text as textile* (presence of a patchwork motif in literature or the weaving of a narrative web); a *verbal/visual nexus* (the unity between visual and oral or written texts); *absent presence* (an indeterminate and marginal presence that enhances critical perspective); *interiority* (the creation of a separate psychological space held sacred from the outside world and owned solely by *black* women); a *conversant warp and weft* (literary and artistic work that dialogues with the warp of history and culture through an individualized, creative weft that inserts black women into otherwise restricted discourses); *dynamism* (a purposeful, innovative, and improvisational revision of tradition to ensure its evolution and permanence); *boldness and attack* (womanish subversion, sassy display, and diva resistance in the articulation of a creative voice); and *integrative liminality* (the linking of disparate ideologies or reconciliation of binaries in a discursive space between dominant hegemonies). *The Ananse Aesthetic* explores these in relation to African American folklore and black women's nineteenth- and twentieth-century texts and textiles; this essay explores three of these principles in relation to nineteenth-century folklore and literature specifically.

[9] Since first fictionalizing and publishing the folktales, songs and sayings of African Americans, Harris and the stories penned by this "accidental folklorist" (Baer 185) have been met with a bevy of critical responses. Some praise the tales for their preservation of (black) folk heritage (Bone 131), while others denounce Harris for his use of the stereotypical Uncle Remus to frame otherwise subversive tales, thereby "almost emasculat[ing] [the genuine folk] into the cute folksy" (Wolfe 75). However, what characterizes Joel Chandler Harris/Uncle Remus criticism most is the drive by scholars to create a discourse for understanding or reconciling these tensions.

[10] See Hedin.

[11] See Courlander, Feldman, and Rattray.

[12] The survival of Harris's folktales provides a point of departure for pinpointing the entry of Ananse stories into the American trickster tradition. Scholars have long recognized that the space between Brer Rabbit and Ananse is not as vast as some believe. In "Uncle Remus Again," an anonymous review of Joel Chandler Harris's *Told by Uncle Remus: New Stories of the Old Plantation* published in 1905, the writer suggests a connection between Uncle Remus's stories and tales told in "the West Indies and Africa," and identifies "Annancy" as a "West Indian Brer Rabbit" (44). To the author, "[t]he cunning spider called Annancy seems to be Brer Rabbit, and to hear his adventures told in any language one understands is to be convulsed with the same droll mirth that has endeared Uncle Remus" (44). Likewise, in "Anansi and Brer Rabbit," Wenzel Brown acknowledges the influence of Anansi stories on the content of the Brer Rabbit

tales. In the spirit of Brown, Julius Lester, who has published several retellings of Uncle Remus stories, maintains that "The Brer Rabbit tales transplanted from Africa are merely variants of the tales about Anansi the Spider, still current in West Africa" (viii).

[13] Scholars capture Ananse's multiple functions in African diasporic culture from his mocking unscrupulousness to his wicked irony. Joyce Jonas describes Ananse as a master of commerce and exchange who faces both ways in "perpetual ambiguity, inviting – even provoking – intercourse between inside and outside" (30). In "Ananse the Akan Trickster," Christopher Vecsey notes Ananse's cathartic function in Ghana as the trickster who provides the Akan with an outlet for social dissent: "he gives the individual the opportunity to mock society's authority. He is able to do what the ordinary Akan cannot: act unscrupulously with relative impunity" (118). The underlying premise of Ananse's cathartic function among the Akan people is what Robert Pelton, in "West African Tricksters: Web of Purpose, Dance of Delight," calls Ananse's "rejection of order" (125). In essence, Ananse transcends his "rogue" moniker, and works as a rousing transitional and mediating force by establishing a worldview that resists comfortable binaries and instead delights in the contradictory (129). Through tricksters, Pelton elaborates, "in whom the anomalous and the ordered, the sacred and the profane, the absurd and the meaningful are joined, we have an image of irony and the working of the ironic imagination itself" (133).

[14] See Smith and Jurich.

[15] In "Keep the White Folks from Meddling: Africanisms in Slave Narratives," Kimberly Rae Connor presents another West African-inspired way of reading Jacobs's narrative and, more importantly, pinpoints specific examples of African survivals in Jacobs's narrative. Among the Africanisms included in Jacobs's narrative, Connor designates the "Methodist camp meeting, [...] Jacobs's report on the Johnkannaus, or John Kooner dancers, [... her] use of charms and fetishes, [... and] Jacobs's narrative surround[ing] death and funerals" as the major sites of African influence (51, 52). Connor is not specific about the tribal or geographic origins of most of these Africanisms; however, she does mention Yoruba culture as a touchstone for Jacobs's use of "metal as a curative [that] may be related to Ogun, a powerful god of the Yoruba people whose spirit lives in iron and brass" (52). For, as Jacobs related the stories of slave life, O'Connor claims, she implicitly documented African American rituals and rites with African origins. O'Connor's African-inspired reading of Jacobs's autobiography prompts us to take a closer look at *Incidents* to uncover the various West African cultural influences that may otherwise go overlooked.

[16] See Benjamin.

[17] Anne Bradford Warner explores Brent's function as a "trickster narrator" in "Carnival Laughter: Resistance in *Incidents.*" Generally, Warner posits the Johnkannau in Chapter Twenty-Two of *Incidents* as "a central trope for the multiple concerns of [Jacobs's] slave narrative" (216); specifically, she names one of those concerns as the way in which Brent serves as a "female appropriation of an African American trickster figure" (217), the "orchestrating female trickster" (224), and an "inspired trickster" (229) in the narrative.

[18] In her absent presence and slow and deliberate approach to trickery, Aunt Nancy the trickster connects *Incidents* to scholarship that examines the relationship between Jacobs's autobiography and the trickster tradition, "Africanisms," negotiations of space, and subversive acts of resistance. In "Escaped Tricksters: Runaway Narratives

as Trickster Tales," Alexis Brooks DeVita compares and contrasts the function of the trickster in African societies with his purpose in diasporic literature. Using Oyekan Owomoyela's work on Yoruba tricksters as a touchstone, DeVita focuses on the transportation of "Yorubean ethics" (1) through non-folklore-related African trickster tales and identifies the ways in which various writers employ the trope of the trickster as a mode of resistance. DeVita paints the trickster's influence on Jacobs's *Incidents* with broad strokes, focusing primarily on how "Jacobs' writings exhibit the traditional oral qualities of signification to sway the readership to one's viewpoint to highlight the virtues of one's supporters and the contrasting lack of virtue among one's adversaries" (2, 3). DeVita's article is useful for its positioning of *Incidents* within a tradition of African American literature that demonstrates trickster sensibilities.

[19] Once in the garret – which Linda describes as her "little den" (Jacobs 93), "little cell" (98), "dungeon" (101) and even "living grave" (116) – Brent, unable to stand, "crawls about [...] for exercise" (92) and complains often about her "cramped limbs" (96) which were often "benumbed by inaction" (97).

[20] See Braxton and Zuber's "Silences in Harriet 'Linda Brent' Jacobs's *Incidents in the Life of a Slave Girl*" for a discussion of the ways in which Jacobs moves between speech and silence to comment on issues like sex, literacy, and agency.

Works Cited

Baer, Florence. "Joel Chandler Harris: An 'Accidental' Folklorist." *Critical Essays on Joel Chandler Harris.* Ed. R. Bruce Bickley, Jr. Boston: Hall, 1981. 185-195.

Bone, Robert. "The Oral Tradition." *Critical Essays on Joel Chandler Harris.* Ed. R. Bruce Bickley, Jr. Boston: Hall, 1981. 130-145.

Benjamin, Shanna Greene. "Weaving the Web of Reintegration: Locating Aunt Nancy in *Praisesong for the Widow.*" *MELUS* 30.1 (2005): 49-67.

Braxton, Joanne M., and Sharon Zuber. "Silences in Harriet 'Linda Brent' Jacob's *Incidents in the Life of a Slave Girl.*" *Listening to Silences: New Essays in Feminist Criticism.* Ed. Elaine Hedges and Shelley Fisher Fishkin. New York: Oxford UP, 1994. 146-55.

Brown, Wenzell. "Anansi and Brer Rabbit." *The American Mercury* Oct. 1949: 438-443.

Burnham, Michelle. "Loopholes of Resistance: Harriet Jacobs' Slave Narrative and the Critique of Agency in Foucault." *Incidents in the Life of a Slave Girl.* Ed. Nellie Y. McKay and Frances Smith Foster. New York: Norton, 2001. 278-294.

Connor, Kimberly Rae. "'Keep the White Folks from Meddling': Africanisms in Slave Narratives." *MultiCultural Review* 5.2 (1996): 44-53.

Courlander, Harold. "Anansi Owns All Tales That Are Told." *A Treasury of African Folklore.* New York: Crown, 1975. 137-139.

Derrida, Jacques. "Différance." *Speech and Phenomena.* Trans. David Allison. Evanston: Northwestern UP, 1973.

DeVita, Alexis Brooks. "Escaped Tricksters: Runaway Narratives as Trickster Tales." *Griot: Official Journal of the Southern Conference on Afro American Studies* 17.2 (1998): 1-10.

Feldman, Susan, ed. *African Myths and Tales.* New York: Dell, 1963.

Friedman, Susan Stanford. *Penelope's Web: Gender, Modernity, H.D.'s Fiction.* Cambridge: Cambridge UP, 1990.

Gates, Henry Louis, Jr. *The Signifying Monkey: A Theory of Afro-American Literary Criticism.* New York: Oxford UP, 1988.

Gubar, Susan. "'The Blank Page' and the Issue of Female Creativity." *Critical Inquiry* 8.2 (1981): 243-263.

Harris, Joel Chandler. *Seven Tales of Uncle Remus.* Atlanta: Higgins-McArthur, 1948.

Hedin, Raymond. "Uncle Remus: Puttin' On Ole Massa's Son." *Southern Literary Journal* 15.1 (1982): 83-90.

"How Spider Obtained God's Sories." Feldman 129-32.

Hurston, Zora Neale. "The Characteristics of Negro Expression." *Norton Anthology of African American Literature.* Ed. Nellie Y. McKay and Henry Louis Gates, Jr. New York: Norton, 1997. 1019-1032.

Hyde, Lewis. "Where Are the Woman Tricksters?" *Trickster Lives: Culture and Myth in American Fiction.* Ed. Jeanne Campbell Reesman. Athens: U of Georgia P, 2001. 185-193.

Jacobs, Harriet. *Incidents in the Life of a Slave Girl.* 1861. New York: Norton, 2001.

Jonas, Joyce E. "Wilson Harris and the Concept of Threshold Art." *Journal of West Indian Literature* 1.2 (1987): 29-34.

Jurich, Marilyn. *Scheherazade's Sisters: Trickster Heroines and Their Stories in World Literature.* Westport: Greenwood, 1998.

Landay, Lori. *Madcaps, Screwballs, and Con Women: The Female Trickster in American Culture.* Philadelphia: U of Pennsylvania P, 1998.

Lester, Julius. *More Tales of Uncle Remus: Further Adventures of Brer Rabbit, His Friends, Enemies, and Others.* New York: Dial, 1988.

Levine, Lawrence. *Black Culture and Black Consciousness: Afro-American Folk Thought From Slavery to Freedom.* New York: Oxford UP, 1978.

Marcus, Jane. "Still Practice, A/Wrested Alphabet: Towards a Feminist Aesthetic." *Tulsa Studies in Women's Literature* 3.1/2 (1984): 79-97.

Miller, J. Hillis. "Ariadne's Thread: Repetition and the Narrative Line." *Critical Inquiry* 3 (1976): 57-77.

Miller, Nancy K. "Arachnologies: The Woman, the Text, and the Critic." *The Poetics of Gender.* Ed. Nancy K. Miller. New York: Columbia UP, 1986. 270-295.

Newall, Venetia. "The Hero as Trickster: The West Indian Anansi." *The Hero in Tradition and Folklore.* Ed. Hilda Davidson. London: Folklore Soc., 1984. 46-89.

Pavlic, Edward. "'Papa Legba, Ouvrier Barriere Por Moi Passer': Esu in *Their Eyes* and Zora Neale Hurston's Diasporic Modernism." *African American Review* 38.1 (2004): 61-85.

Pelton, Robert D. "West African Tricksters: Web of Purpose, Dance of Delight." *Mythical Trickster Figures.* Ed. William J. Hynes and William G. Doty. Tuscaloosa: U of Alabama P, 1993. 122-40.

Rattray, R.S. "How it Came About That the Sky-god's Stories Came to be Known as 'Spider-stories.'" *Akan-Ashanti Folk Tales.* Oxford: Clarendon, 1930. 54-59.

Showalter, Elaine. "Piecing and Writing." *The Poetics of Gender.* Ed. Nancy K. Miller. New York: Columbia University Press, 1986. 222-247.

Smith, Jeanne Rosier. *Writing Tricksters: Mythic Gambols in American Ethnic Literature.* Berkeley: U of California P, 1997.

Tanna, Laura. *Jamaican Folk Tales and Oral Histories.* Kingston: Institute of Jamaica, 1984.

"Uncle Remus Again." *Critical Essays on Joel Chandler Harris.* Ed. R. Bruce Bickley, Jr. Boston: Hall, 1981. 43-44.

Vecsey, Christopher. "The Exception Who Proves the Rules: Ananse the Akan Trickster." *Mythical Trickster Figures: Contours, Contexts, and Criticisms.* Ed. William J. Hynes and William G. Doty. Tuscaloosa: U of Alabama P, 1993. 106-121.

Warner, Anne Bradford. "Carnival Laughter: Resistance in *Incidents*." *Harriet Jacobs and Incidents in the Life of a Slave Girl.*" Ed. Deborah Garfield and Rafia Zafar. New York: Cambridge, UP, 1996. 216-232.

Wolfe, Bernard. "Uncle Remus and the Malevolent Rabbit: 'Takes a Limber-Toe Gemmun ferter Jump Jim Crow.'" *Critical Essays on Joel Chandler Harris.* Ed. R. Bruce Bickley, Jr. Boston: Hall, 1981. 70-97.

Writer's Project/Work Projects Administration. *Drums and Shadows: Survival Studies Among The Georgia Coastal Negroes.* Athens, Georgia: U of Georgia P, 1940.

Translations of Transnational Black Icons in the Poetics of Frances Harper: Brazil's Zumbi and Cuba's Maceo

Monique-Adelle Callahan

In the introduction to *American Literary History*'s special issue on "Hemispheric American Literary History," Caroline F. Levander and Robert S. Levine pose key questions about the purview of American literature:

> What happens to US and American literary and cultural studies if we recognize asymmetry and interdependency of nation-state development throughout the hemisphere? What happens if we let this recognition of the nation as historically evolving and contingent – rather than already formed – revise our conceptions of literary and cultural genealogies? Finally, what happens if the "fixed" borders of a nation are recognized not only as historically produced political constructs that can be ignored, imaginatively reconfigured, and variously contested but also as component parts of a deeper, more multilayered series of national and indigenous histories? (401)

While the idea of a nation imposes imaginary boundaries, Levander and Levine challenge the idea of "fixed borders," suggesting that our cultures and literatures are formed through border crossings. Studies of gender and race help to deconstruct the boundaries imposed by a nation-based concept of literary studies. They do so by undoing the perceived fixedness of national histories. The forced migration of Africans into the "New World" is one example. As the descendants of enslaved Africans began to articulate themselves and project a space for themselves in emerging "New World" nations, they challenged national and hemispheric boundaries.

For African American writers in particular, the scope of "America" extended beyond the national boundaries of North America proper. In *The Book of American Negro Poetry* (1922), for example, one of the first attempts to document a cohesive African American poetic canon, James Weldon Johnson included references to nineteenth century writers in Cuba, Brazil, Haiti and Mexico such as Cuban poets Gabriel de la Concepción Valdés or "Placido" and Francisco Manzano, and Brazilian poet Machado de Assis.[1] While anthologies like Johnson's demonstrate the fact that *afrodescendente*[2] peoples have written prolifically throughout the western hemisphere, Frances Ellen Watkins Harper's poetics suggest the possibility of a transnational and hemispheric discourse in the early poetry of African Americans writing in the United States. Frances Harper's artistic and intellectual contributions are already well documented (Foster; Boyd; Hill; Still). Her popularity made her one of the first black women to earn a living as a poet. She toured the United States giving lectures and reading her poetry to blacks (free and enslaved) and whites alike and was a strong advocate of both racial and gender equality. What has yet to be sufficiently explored, however, is the degree to which we might consider her work in the context of a larger, transnational discourse on race and nation in the nineteenth century.

There are, in fact, two outstanding instances in which it is clear that Harper is *explicitly* transnational and hemispheric in her poetics. Harper's treatment of Zumbi, in "Death of Zombi, the Chief of a Negro Kingdom in Latin America" (1857) precedes more recent appropriations of Zumbi by a century. Brazilian black nationalists, writers, artists, and scholars during the twentieth century in particular have appropriated Zumbi – leader of a society of escaped slaves in colonial Brazil – to represent Afro-Brazilian resistance to oppression. Harper suggests that Zumbi's significance extends beyond the Brazilian national sphere. Zumbi's struggle in "Death of Zombi," mirrors the struggle of African Americans in North America during the nineteenth century who had to daily negotiate the choice between a life of slavery and death. Like Zumbi, the Afro-Cuban general Antonio Maceo has emerged as an iconic figure. His role in the Cuban struggle for independence at the end of the nineteenth century made him one of the most well known Afro-Cuban leaders in world history. Harper's poem "Maceo" (1900), draws attention to the complex intersection of North American nationhood and Latin American struggles for national sovereignty. Harper depicts Maceo as a martyr for the cause of Cuban independence and uses his death to question the reality of freedom in the United States. In doing so, Harper bridges hemispheric struggles for freedom in the Americas.

In a second phase of its "Manifest Destiny," the United States sought to extend its national sovereignty to new territories beyond the boundaries of the continent. The post-Reconstruction era saw African blacks systematically stripped of the legal rights gained after the Civil War and subject to unchecked racial violence. Moreover, the United States victory in the war with Spain – a war fought primarily in Cuba with a predominantly Afro-Cuban Cuban Liberation Army – which made the nation an imperial power, caused African Americans to question their status vis-à-vis the colonized people newly under American control. Through her representation of Maceo – a man who emphasized the ideological connection between Cuban national freedom and that of black slaves in and outside of Cuba – Harper suggests that the freedom of nations was inextricably linked to the freedom of oppressed peoples. Harper conjoins the struggle for freedom in the United States not yet realized by African Americans with that of nations that, like Cuba, were struggling for national freedom. In doing so, Harper characterizes African American identity in the nineteenth century as a negotiation between a North American politics of race and a transnational politics of race manifested largely in debates about racial slavery and national sovereignty.

"Death of Zombi" was published in the wake of the Fugitive Slave Act and "Maceo" during the nadir and in the aftermath of the United States victory in the war with Spain. In these poems, Harper links the organized resistance of Africans in Brazil to Portuguese rule and the Cuban struggle for political "freedom" from Spanish rule, to the plight of African Americans during the national crisis that would evolve into civil war and the racist aftermath of a failed Reconstruction. She bridges the gap between Cuban, Brazilian, and United States legacies of slavery and struggle for an ideal of national freedom. At two critical periods in its national history when the United States was internally conflicted about the terms of its own nationhood, Harper uses poetry to challenge African Americans to conceptualize identity beyond national borders. Harper posits African American identity as what Paul Gilroy calls "a process of movement and mediation" (19) characterized by transnational movement not only of people, but also of ideas, tropes, and symbols.

In her analysis of Phillis Wheatley – whom she defines as the "invent[or] of transatlantic literature," Colleen Glennes Boggs highlights the multiple connotations of translation (2). Using Noah Webster's 1828 definition of the term *translation*, Boggs explains how translation depicts both the "literal sense of conveyance" or "movement across space" in the natural realm as well as the transition into a transcendent state in the spiritual sense (25). Just as a single word might be taken from one lexical context and translated into another for the purpose of attaining meaning, so can a symbolic figure be translated into an "other" lexicon, a lexicon defined by a different geographical, temporal, cultural space. The act of translation bridges a perceived gap by showing that, ultimately there is no gap, that meaning in an "other" – be it linguistic or nonlinguistic – context can be achieved through a bidirectional and persistent negotiation of one with an "other." Harper's treatment of Antonio Maceo and of Zumbi constitutes a form of translation. Not only does Harper effectively translate these figures through the act of memorializing them poetically – that is to say facilitating their transition from the physical world to a transcendent world of collective memory – but Harper also moves these figures across an imaginary hemispheric space, ultimately making them relevant to North American slavery and struggles for freedom.

> *From the beginning, however, it should be carefully emphasized that the slave trade was accompanied stride for stride by slave revolts and rebellions. In the sixteenth century there were revolts by black slaves in America, and the organized rebellions by slaves called Maroons had already begun in Cuba, Jamaica, Haiti, Mexico, and Brazil. Du Bois points out, as the trade increased, so too did the rebellions. Throughout the seventeenth century actual wars went on against slavery. There were nine major revolts in Jamaica, Barbados, Haiti, and the forming of an independent state, Palmares, in Brazil. This state was founded by Afro-Brazilians fighting against the Portuguese slavers – they were called Zombis! The name has been used as a negative and metaphysical term to characterize these warriors as rising from the dead and being unkillable, because of the ferocity with which these Afro-Brazilians fought against slavery.*[3]
>
> Amiri Barka

The Death of Zombi: Harper's Mythology of Black Resistance

Leading figure of the Black Arts Movement Amiri Baraka identifies maroonage as a primary manifestation of black resistance to slavery. For Baraka, the enslavement of African peoples went hand in hand with an unrelenting determination on the part of the enslaved to pursue freedom through active resistance. He uses the term "Zombi" to characterize Afro-Brazilian fugitive slaves and their efforts to secure their freedom, thereby suggesting a transnational context in which to locate the themes of freedom and resistance in the history of African American peoples. In the Brazilian context, "Zombi," more commonly written "Zumbi," was the name of the last chief of the Republic of Palmares, a *quilombo* (society of escaped slaves) now legendary in Brazil. [4] Baraka's appropriation suggests that African Americans and African descendants as a larger "imagined" community of *afrodescendentes,* might understand their own history by seeing "Zombi" as an immortal legacy of human agency against slavery and its dehumanization of black peoples.

But Baraka was far from the first to venture such a claim. Perhaps we might expect that, as an aesthetic sister to and historical contemporary of the Black Power Movement, the Black Arts Movement and its political engagement might result in such a Pan-African sensibility. Less predictable, however, is Frances Ellen Watkins Harper's allusion to Zumbi over a century before Baraka's in the poem "Death of Zombi, the Chief of a Negro Kingdom in South America." Harper constructs a narrative of this leader of a fugitive slave community, presenting Zombi as a heroic figure who chooses physical death rather than accepting the "death" (i.e. demise) of a realized ideal of freedom and citizenship in a community. Harper thereby translates Zombi from a tragic figure, contained in the historical time period and geographical space of seventeenth-century northern Brazil, to a nineteenth century icon for resistance to the oppressive forces of racial slavery in North America. Ultimately, Harper translates Zombi from a symbol of African resistance in Brazil, to a figure for the transnational phenomenon of black resistance in the Americas as a whole.

Published in a collection entitled *Poems* (1857), Harper's "Death of Zombi" narrates the invasion and eventual destruction of Palmares and culminates in the heroic suicide of its leader, Zumbi (1655-1695). One of the most legendary and longest-lasting societies of fugitive slaves in the Americas, the Republic of Palmares flourished for almost a century in the northern region of Brazil in the Barriga Mountains between Alagoãs and Pernambuco. Pernambuco was one of the major centers of Portuguese colonial activity in Brazil. By the end of the sixteenth century there were sixty-six *engenhos* (sugar mills) in Pernambuco and approximately ten thousand African slaves. Both numbers continued to grow over the next century as the Portuguese imperial economy became more and more dependent on the sugar industry (Gomes 43). Alongside the panoply of plantations and slaveholders, Palmares maintained a thriving society of fugitive slaves.

Primarily of Angolan descent, the citizens of Palmares, or *palmaristas*, had been brought from Africa to Brazil. For the duration of its existence, Palmares was under the constant threat of attack, first by the Dutch and then the Portuguese. Eventually, after one final invasion at the end of the seventeenth century, Palmares was destroyed by the Portuguese. Harper's dramatic monologue "Death of Zombi" begins at the moment of Portuguese invasion:

> Cruel in vengeance, reckless in wrath,
> The hunters of men bore down on our path;
> Inhuman and fierce, the offer they gave
> Was freedom in death or the life of a slave. (1-4)

As Harper's speaker, a member of this community attacked by a cadre of "inhuman" hunters, retells the story, the reader participates as listener and is urged to recognize the speaker as a human survivor of an *in*humane attack. The musicality and rhythmic structure of the lyrical ballad evokes the rhythm of speech, further emphasizing this speaker-listener interaction. The reflection of the "inhuman and fierce" attackers on the faces of the people of Palmares further highlights the humanity of the *palmaristas* in their encounter with the inhumane and oppressive forces of the colonial invaders. The primary opposition here, however, is that of death and freedom. By choosing death over enslavement, Zombi gains freedom and becomes a mythological symbol of resistance to slavery. The resolution of this opposition through self-sacrifice complicates the relationship between life and death in that it suggests that freedom in life can be achieved through physical death.

In the very same year that "Death of Zombi" was published, the United States Supreme Court declared Dred Scott an illegal fugitive, ineligible for citizenship because of his race. Scott was re-enslaved after living "free" in Illinois for close to ten years. The *Dred Scott* ruling highlighted the fact that the presence of slavery in North America was no longer bound to regional demarcations of "free" and "slave" states. Just seven years earlier, Harper herself was forced to flee her home state of Maryland after the passing of the Fugitive Slave Law as a part of the Compromise of 1850 marked the legal denial of self-ownership to African Americans and threatened the nominal freedom of the small population of free blacks in the United States. Harper suggests that even "free" blacks – a major contingent of her audience – had to walk the line between freedom and slavery as they negotiated a life of second-class citizenship and the constant threat of slavery posed by the Fugitive Slave Law.

While Harper's involvement with the Underground Railroad placed her in close contact with a large number of fugitive slaves in North America, *they* are not the subjects of her only poem depicting such a community. Harper does not write about the many fugitive slave communities in Virginia or South Carolina. Nor does she write about any of the other approximately twenty thousand fugitive slaves and descendants of fugitive slaves living in maroon societies in the United States between the seventeenth and nineteenth centuries (Price 152). Instead, Harper transports her readers to seventeenth century Brazil via a narrative poem about the demise of a free "Negro Kingdom" there. As fugitive slaves in North America faced death in the pursuit of freedom (or at the very least virtual death through re-enslavement), Harper suggests a larger historical and mythological scope within which to place their experience, one that takes into account the presence of enslaved *afrodescendentes* throughout the Americas and conjectures an "imagined" transhemispheric space.

Zumbi was born in Palmares and fought in the fateful war against the Portuguese. While it is documented that Zumbi was in fact captured by the Portuguese and publicly beheaded, a version of the story survives through folklore that Zumbi chose to commit suicide rather than be captured. By using this version of the story, Harper emphasizes the significance of Zombi's self-sacrifice as a resolution to the threat of re-enslavement. Turning to poetry to actively construct memory rather than to simply regurgitate historical fact, Harper treats Zombi as both a historical and mythological figure.

Harper continues to contrast the humanity of the *palmaristas* and the inhumanity of their attackers:

> The cheek of the mother grew pallid with dread,
> As the tidings of evil around us were spread,
> And closer and closer she strained to her heart
> The children she feared they would sever apart.
> The brows of our maidens grew gloomy and sad;
> Hot tears burst from eyes once sparkling and glad.
> Our young men stood ready to join in the fray,
> That hung as a pall 'round our people that day.
> Our leaders gazed angry and stern on the strife,
> For freedom to them was dearer than life.
> There was mourning at home and death in the street,
> For carnage and famine together did meet.
> The pale lips of hunger were asking for bread,
> While husbands and fathers lay bleeding and dead. (5-18)

Harper highlights the intensity of the desire for freedom among the *palmaristas* as her narrator claims that "freedom to them was dearer than life." The desire for freedom is coupled with a natural hunger for "bread." The speaker emphasizes the loss of "husbands and fathers, thereby humanizing the *palmaristas*." In contrast to the *palmaristas* who are depicted as members of a family, the colonists are portrayed as "hunters of men," lacking domestic titles. As "tempests of wrath," the colonists acquire an elemental quality (natural in their force but not human) that stands in opposition to the familial humanity of the *palmaristas*. Harper concludes the first section of the poem by emphasizing the death of the kingdom as it yields to the force of history itself.

> For days we withstood the tempests of wrath,
> That scattered destruction and death in our path,
> Till, broken and peeled, we yielded at last,
> And the glory and strength of our kingdom were past. (19-22)

When death and destruction overwhelm the *palmaristas* to the point of complete acquiescence, Zombi enters as a heroic figure. Harper presents the figure of "Zombi" as a resolution to the contending forces of life and death, freedom and slavery, humanity and inhumanity. His introduction into the narrative interrupts the pattern of oppositions.

> *But Zombi*, our leader, and warlike old chief,
> Gazed down on our woe with anger and grief,
> The tyrant for him forged fetters in vain,
> His freedom-girt limbs had worn their last chain.
> Defiance and daring still flashed from his eye;
> *A freeman he'd* lived *and free he would die.*
> So he climbed to the verge of a dangerous steep,
> Resolved from its margin to take a last leap;
> For a fearful death and a bloody grave
> Were dearer to him than the life of a slave.
> Nor went he alone to the mystic land –
> There were other warriors in his band,
> Who rushed with him to Death's dark gate,
> All wrapped in the shroud of a mournful fate. (*My Italics*) (23-36)

Here the poem shifts from the invasion story to focus on the story of Zombi and his heroic rejection of slavery through suicide. His resistance to physical enslavement demonstrated in his rejection of "fetters" and chains on his "freedom-girt limbs," culminates in a rejection of physical life. For him "a fearful death and bloody grave / Were dearer to him than the life of a slave." (31-32)

Zombi emerges in the poem, then, as a symbol of resistance to the colonial rapacity. Harper contrasts the freedom of Zombi's limbs with the "chains" and "fetters" of the colonial "tyrant," using parallelism to reinforce his defiance – "A freeman he'd lived and free he would die." Here life and death are *linked* by freedom, rather than in tenuous conflict with one another. The image of Zombi gazing down on the scene hearkens back to the moment of the invasion when the leaders "gaze" at the Portuguese attack. As a God-like presence, Zombi observes the scene and transcends the binary oppositions. He lives free and dies free, becoming a symbol of resistance to colonial imperialism and slavery. He leads his followers into a "mystic land," a place where the freedom they fought to maintain in life can be sustained in death.

Harper's narrator, who has witnessed the event in the past, now relays it in the present, taking us from the "reckless wrath" of the ensuing attackers to the fated death of Zombi and his followers. As a performance of *telling*, "Death of Zombi" becomes meaningful in its performance of this re-membering of a collective history of escaped slaves. This type of re-membering suggests that the pursuit of freedom on the part of African descendants – rather than a passive acceptance of enslavement – constitutes a tradition of struggle for freedom in the Americas. The poem also serves as a testament to the existence of African descendants outside of the United States whose lives are also inscribed by the tension between a desire for freedom and the reality of slavery in the Americas. Additionally, Zombi functions as a link between the past and the present. This linkage is again mirrored in the structure of the poem. After the speaker and the other *palmaristas* have been "broken and peeled" and succumb to the colonial invaders, "Zombi" enters as a redemptive force.

In "Death of Zombi," Zumbi becomes a figure for "Negro" freedom, while demonstrating through his demise the double bind confronting enslaved peoples for whom the terms of "freedom" require physical death. By commemorating Zombi's "freedom in death" the poem confers immortality on its protagonist. By alluding to this double bind in which death in fact becomes synonymous with freedom and life under slavery becomes a type of death, Harper highlights the dialectic between freedom and death imposed by the system of racial slavery. Zombi emerges as a type of resolution, synthesizing freedom and death in a single act of heroic self-sacrifice.

As Zombi transitions into the "mystic land" of death, "fearful death" and the "bloody grave" become "dearer" than a life of slavery. Zombi's act of resistance reconfigures the relationship between freedom, slavery, life and death. Unable to realize freedom in life, the fugitive redefines the very terms of freedom itself. As the slave system creates a cosmos in which life becomes synonymous with death, the fugitive who faces death heroically sustains the spirit of resistance. It is this process that Harper portrays in "Death of Zombi," thereby arriving at the more familiar notion of the *zombie* as a person in a liminal space between life and death.

The *Dred Scott* decision affirmed slavery's hold on the South and confirmed the fact that freedom for blacks in North America – like that of the *palmaristas* – was under constant threat of attack. Through her depiction of Zumbi as the quintessential fugitive hero who defies slavery in life and achieves freedom in death, Harper highlights the transnational context of slavery and black experience in North America. Harper effectively "translates" the history of fugitive Brazilian slaves into the language of African Americans in the United States whose autonomy was also threatened by slaveholders. Harper's celebration of one man's choice of death over slavery in seventeenth-century Brazil, challenged her readers in the United States – black and white alike – to recognize not only the pervasive nature of slavery in the Americas but also the legacy of heroic black resistance to it.

> *En nuestra desgraciada patria ha sonado nuevamente el grito de !Libertad! Ha llegado el momento oportuno de que hagamos conocer al mundo entero que el cubano sabe morir por la redención de su patria ...*[5]
>
> Antonio Maceo
> Kingston, Jamaica, September 5,1879

The "Bronze Muse" and the "Bronze Titan"

Harper thematizes black resistance to not only racial slavery but also colonial oppression. One of history's most apparent instances of black resistance to colonial oppression is that of the largely Afro-Cuban *Independentista* army against the Spanish Crown during the late nineteenth century. One the most well known leaders of this army was Antonio Maceo y Grajales (1845-1896) who famously demonstrated his willingness to die for the "redemption" of Cuba. His leadership in the Cuban wars of independence won him the sobriquet "The Bronze Titan." Just four years after his death, Harper's "Maceo" appeared in her 1900 collection *Poems* published in Philadelphia.

Beginning as an elegy lamenting and commemorating Maceo's death, Harper's poem also incorporates elements of the dramatic monologue and eventually evolves into a prayer. Maceo's death prompts the anonymous speaker to interrogate the role of death and bloodshed in struggles for freedom:

> Maceo dead! a thrill of sorrow
> Through our hearts in sadness ran
> When we felt in one sad hour
> That the world had lost a man. (1-4)

In very first stanza of "Maceo," the oxymoronic notion of a "thrill of sorrow" alludes to what will not only emerge as a commentary on Maceo, but also on the implications of his life and ideology for the United States, a nation riddled with its own contradictions. The rise of Jim Crow in the southern states reflected the belief of many white Americans – namely that white supremacy was indeed the solution to "the problem of black freedom" (Clark 193). Racial violence increased drastically in the South as blacks were systematically excluded from politics (Clark 194-198).

Ironically, war in Cuba provided a premise for U.S. national unity, a unity reinforced by a belief in white supremacy. According to Kathleen Ann Clark, the Spanish-American War and the rise of North American imperialism "further fueled both national reconciliation and racial antagonism. As northern and southern whites joined together to defeat a common – and darker – foe, they celebrated the decline of 'sectional feeling' and bolstered the power of white supremacy at home and abroad" (194). Politicians and journalists began to represent the Spanish-American war as continuation of the Civil War, promising to "re-unite North and South in a united fight and heal the wounds and divisiveness of internecine war" (Kaplan 122). In fact, convinced that black Cubans were also unfit to rule themselves, the United States government used the racial composition of the Cuban Liberation Army to justify its intervention in Cuba. The blurring of racial lines in the military – on both the Cuban and United States side – threatened the integrity of domestic racial divisions (Kaplan 124-128). This thinking ultimately led the United States government to implement Jim Crow in Cuba during its four-year-long occupation. Rumors spread throughout the United States, Cuba, and Spain about the predominantly black presence in the Cuban Liberation Army as it fought vehemently for Cuban independence. Antonio Maceo and other leaders of the army denied such claims but at the same time advocated a Cuba free of any outside intervention, even that of the United States. A number of black newspapers sided with black Cubans and argued against the exportation of American racism through American imperial presence in Cuba (Kaplan 135).

"Death of Zombi" explores the relationship between human life and freedom in the shadow of the transatlantic slave trade; "Maceo" likewise engages the theme of freedom, but does so in national rather than individual or even regional terms. Harper uses the death of Maceo – a black leader internationally known for his struggle against racial and national oppression – to prescribe her a solution for a racially divided United States, a nation whose avid pursuit of nationhood too often coincided with racial violence and the disenfranchisement of African Americans. She calls for heroic men who, like Maceo, can lead the nation towards a utopian vision of nationhood rooted in biblically based morality. The poem's celebration of Maceo's manhood – expressed in his willingness to fight and die for an ideal of freedom and his vision of national independence and racial equality – highlights the failure of the United States to realize its own ideals.

As Amy Kaplan notes, the black male body posed a problem for American national identity. "Black and white male bodies," she asserts, "had different symbolic resonance, a different signifying function in the political landscape. The foundation for the construction of the white male body as figure for American nationhood lies in the subjugation of black male bodies at home and abroad" (142). It is significant, then, that Harper begins "Maceo" with a reference to Maceo's manhood and uses it as an entry point for her vision of an integrated American nation that embraces the goal of global peace.

Harper expounds on the vision of a *free* Cuba as the literal and figurative link between Maceo's life (i.e. his "latest breath") and his death:

He had clasped unto his bosom
The sad fortunes of his land –
Held the cause for which he perished
With a firm, unfaltering hand.

On his lips the name of freedom
Fainted with his latest breath.
Cuba Libre was his watchword
Passing through the gates of death. (5-12)

Harper evokes the image of Maceo holding "the sad fortunes of his land" to his chest and "the cause" of freedom in his hand. In his death he "names" or identifies freedom as "Cuba Libre," his "watchword."

An iconic symbol for the struggle for Cuban independence, Maceo pursued a delicate and strategic balance of Cuban nationalism and a species of "New World" black transnationalism. While he fought for a collective and racially integrated *Cuba Libre*, Maceo also believed that the history of slavery in the Western Hemisphere had inextricably linked the history of Cuba and those of other countries with a similar legacy of racial slavery.

In an effort to garner support for the cause of Cuban independence, Maceo traveled to Jamaica, Haiti, and the United States to talk with black leaders there. As secretary of the Cuban Anti-Slavery Committee, black abolitionist and separatist Henry Highland Garnet (1815-1882) addressed a mixed crowd of Cubans and North American blacks at a meeting in New York in 1872. Garnet assured the Cuban "defenders of freedom" (16) that African Americans who had "passed through the terrible ordeal of the struggle for freedom and equal rights" would recognize the similar plight of their "enslaved fellow-men" in Cuba (15). In 1878, the same year that Antonio Maceo visited the United States, *La Verdad* – a newspaper in New York – published a letter to Maceo from Cuban Anti-Slavery committee chairman S. R. Scrotton. "The friends of liberty in America as in Europe," Scrotton wrote, "have their eyes anxiously fixed on you, hoping that perhaps you will save that noble Cuban army which successfully sustains the flag of liberty" (qtd in P. Foner *History*: 270).

Regarding himself as an "emissary for a slave 'people,'" Maceo believed Cuba and Haiti had a connection based on a common history of racial slavery. He wrote in a letter to the Haitian General José Lamothe

> … la historia de Cuba es igual a la de Haití; es la historia de todas las colonias … allí, la mayor parte de la población compuesta de hombres de nuestra raza, se ve privada de todos los derechos políticos y civiles y sujeta a las más estúpidas preocupaciones y allí, en fin, 350 mil hombres yacen aún en la más dura servidumbre y nacen y mueren bajo el férreo yugo de la esclavitud ... Me bastaría decirle que hay en Cuba cerca de medio millón de hombres que son de la propiedad exclusiva de unos cuantos que tienen sobre ellos derechos de vida y muerte, que pueden comprarlos y venderlos, que les hacen trabajar día y noche sin ninguna retrobución, que los mandan azotar por la más libera falta y que assimilándolos completamente a las bestias, les niegas hasta el derecho de tener una familia. (Maceo "Carta" 48)

> [The history of Cuba is the same as that of Haiti; it is the history of all the colonies ... there, the majority of the population is comprised of men of our race; they are deprived of all political and civil rights and subject to the most frivolous concerns and there, lastly, 350 thousand men remain still in the most harsh servitude and are

> born and die beneath the iron yoke of slavery ... I can tell you myself that in Cuba there are almost half a million men who are the sole property of a few who have the rights over their life and death, who can buy and sell them, who can make them work day and night without retribution, who can order them to be whipped for the slightest fault, and considering them to be completely equivalent to beasts, deny them even the right to have a family. (*My Translation)*]

Maceo believed that it was the obligation of "hombres de color que hemos tenido la fortuna de no nacer en la esclavitud" (men of color who had the fortune of not being born into slavery) to liberate the enslaved who were "cansados del látigo y de las cadenas" (tired from the whip and the chains) and "demasiado débiles para romperlas por sí solos" (too weak to break them by themselves) (Maceo, "Carta" 49). His contention that the African slave trade and its legacy in the Americas were intricately linked to the pursuit of cross-racial freedom, significantly informed his conception of the Cuban national project. Maceo the Cuban nationalist, then, did not separate the legacy of black oppression in Cuba from the cause of liberty in Cuba. In his speech "A Los Cubanos de Color" ("To Cubans of Color"), Maceo identified the Cuban government, in its loyalty to the Spanish Crown, as "enemigos de la humanidad negra" (enemies of black humanity), while in the same breath he called black Cubans to arms *united* with "los blancos, hijos del país que os defienden vuestros derechos" (the whites, sons of the country, who defend your rights) (50).

By identifying himself as the emissary of an enslaved "people" fighting for independence, Maceo linked the pursuit of freedom for and by *afrodescendente* slaves and the national freedom of Cuba from the "yoke" of European colonialism. He drew parallels between the enslavement of "el hombre negro" (the black man) in Cuba and that of the Cuban nation, "yoked" under the colonial grip of Spain. For Maceo, the rise of the "bandera de Cuba" (Cuban flag) – that is to say the new, independent, egalitarian Cuba that was an expressed ideal of the Cuban independence struggle – would effectuate the freedom of the slaves and of the Cuban nation (Maceo, "Proclama" 46).

Maceo's Pan-African sensibility, however integrated with the struggle for Cuban independence, made him the object of much criticism. News of the Cuban wars for independence with a largely Afro-Cuban army began to fuel white fear in Cuba, Spain, and the United States of another slave revolt like the Haitian Revolution in 1791 (Helg 49-51, 80, 89). Maceo was accused of favoring his black troops and of trying to build a "Negro Republic." He denied these accusations vehemently and repeatedly expressed his commitment to an integrated struggle for Cuban independence. Identifying himself as a member of "the colored race," he believed in an integrated and egalitarian nation that would "recognize no hierarchy" of races and stated that he "entered the revolution for no other reason than to shed his blood to see the slaves and his country free" (P. Foner *Antonio*, 62-63).

Frances Harper's poetic rendering of Maceo's death emerges out of this larger historical and political context. By the time Harper published the poem,

Maceo was already an established figure closely aligned with racial and national struggles for freedom. Harper not only celebrates his life, but also links him to the continued struggle of African Americans for social and political freedom in the United States as well as to the American nation's failure to realize its ideals. By aligning Maceo with Christ, Harper challenges an American nation founded on Christian ideology to note the contradiction between Christian values and racial or colonial oppression.

After identifying Maceo with Cuban national freedom in the first three stanzas, Harper's speaker calls upon other Christians to consider Maceo's death in light of Christic typology:

> With the light of God around us,
> Why this agony and strife?
> With the cross of Christ before us,
> Why this fearful waste of life?
>
> Must the pathway to freedom
> Ever mark a crimson line,
> And the eyes of wayward mortals
> Always close to light divine. (13-20)

Like Christ, Maceo is martyred because of the ignorance of "wayward mortals" with "eyes…close[d]" to the divine who make the "pathway to freedom" one of bloodshed and death.

Harper's typological linking of Christ and Maceo places her within a tradition of American writers who, from the seventeenth century on, as Werner Sollors notes, "develop Christic parallels" in their work, relating a secular American history to biblical types (51). Harper draws a parallel between Christ's death on the cross for "wayward mortals" and that of Maceo. Both Maceo and Christ walk the "pathway of freedom." They shed "crimson" blood on behalf of the freedom or redemption of mankind. Both Christ and Maceo gain immortality through death. As Maceo becomes *im*mortal through the eulogizing process of the narrative, Harper opposes him to the "mortals" who do not see the spiritual divinity in his human form. As Christ's death brings about a plan for spiritual redemption, Maceo's death redeems Cuban nationhood by making him the quintessential citizen of a new Cuba – one who, in his own words, "sabe morir por la redención de su patria" (knows how to die for the redemption of his country) (Maceo, "Proclama" 46). Maceo's heroic self-sacrifice for the "redemption of his country" aligns him with the crucified Christ, who shed his blood for the purpose of *earthly* redemption. Furthermore, Maceo's disappearance in the poem is as meaningful as his initial appearance. While the poem bears his name, Maceo is not explicitly mentioned after the third stanza. However, I suggest that this "disappearance" is actually a textually implied metamorphosis. After "[p]assing through the gates of death" Maceo disappears, effectively *becoming* Christ as we are prompted to perceive him in the "light of God."

Harper does not reject North American Christianity; she reinterprets it. Harper's appropriation of Christic typology places her within a tradition of biblical reinterpretation in African American poetry. Allen Dwight Callahan cites the Negro Spirituals as prime examples of such a phenomenon. Callahan maintains that the Negro Spirituals in fact created a context in which the Old and New Testaments were *correlated* rather than dichotomized:[6]

> But in the Negro spirituals, the New does not supersede the Old. The two Testaments, Old and New are correlated to each other. Moses is not a "type" of Jesus. Both bear witness – eternally, equally valid witness – to what God has done and is doing in the world. They are placed side by side with others in the Bible, that "great cloud of witnesses," as the writer of the Epistle to the Hebrews puts it, who *corroborate* each other's testimony. (Callahan 189)

Joshua did not "foreshadow Jesus" but is identical to Jesus, his New Testament antitype (Callahan 193). On the one hand, Maceo's suffering and death in "Maceo" ties him to the New Testament Christ, a correlation that is performed in the very structure of the poem. On the other hand, his heroic and militaristic death identifies him with the often vengeful God of the Old Testament as well as the vision of the Christ predicted in the Book of Revelation.

This connection between Maceo and Christ not only places "Maceo" in a tradition of African American literary meditations on Christ, but it also suggests that the poem has implications that go beyond religious symbolism. The speaker suggests that Maceo's death repeats Christ's sacrifice and questions whether or not the eyes of the global community are truly open to the "divine light." In doing so, Harper evokes the contradictions that plagued nineteenth-century North American national consciousness. For instance, Harper's critique of American nationalism aligns her with her contemporary Frederick Douglass, who also drew a line between the "Christianity of Christ" and the Christianity of the American nation. He called the Christianity of the "master class" – as distinct from the "faith of the slave" – "corrupt, slave-holding, women-whipping, cradle-plundering, partial and hypocritical" (qtd in Callahan 212). And yet American nationalist rhetoric thrived on the idea that the United States was a Christian nation. In his observation of a burgeoning American nation, French political scientist Alexis de Tocqueville asserted that "America [was] nevertheless still the place in the world where the Christian religion [had] retained the greatest true power over souls" (132). America fulfilled its desire for a distinctly American character, a national character, by positing itself as a nation chosen by God, a "Promised Land" (Friedman 164; Grosby 221-224). Harper's meditation on Maceo's death in "Maceo," suggests that this "promised land" of freedom had yet to be fully realized in the Americas. Maceo's death and the ongoing wars for independence in Cuba signaled this fact. The correlation between the fight for freedom and death, death being the "pathway to freedom" that "mark[s] a crimson line," recalls "Death of Zombi" in which freedom becomes associated with bloodshed. Christianity being a central component of nineteenth-century American nationalism, Harper tropes on this dialectic between freedom and death through an allusion to Christ in the context of Maceo's death, considering his death in a larger discourse about freedom and Christianity.

This correlation also resonates with the Civil War in North America for which the relationship between freedom and national unification was central. Harper's speaker questions a world that kills its "heroes" and she calls for human and *humane* intervention:

Must the hearts of fearless valor
Fail 'mid crime and cruel wrong,
When the world has read of heroes
Brave and honest, true and strong?

Men to stay the flood of sorrow
Sweeping round each war-crusted heart;
Men to say to strife and carnage –
From our world henceforth depart. (21-28)

After questioning a failing humanity, Harper's speaker addresses God directly in a plea for the "reign" of Christ as "redeemer":

God of peace and God of nations,
Haste! oh, haste the glorious day
When the reign of our Redeemer
O'er the world shall have its sway.

When the swords now blood encrusted,
Spears that reap the battle field,
Shall be changed to higher service,
Helping earth rich harvests yield. (29-36)

This redemption is not transcendental or escapist. Instead, the "higher service" is the act of causing the earth to be fruitful. The God here is one of nations *on earth.* Harper's "Redeemer" does not "reign" over a heavenly kingdom but an earthly one. Harper grounds the "heavenly" in the earthly world of the poor, the widowed, the orphaned child:

Where the widow weeps in anguish,
And the orphan bows his head,
Grant that peace and joy and gladness
May like holy angels tread.

Pity, oh, our God the sorrow
Of the world from thee astray,
Lead us from the paths of madness
Unto Christ the living way. (37-44)

Beyond its moralistic or didactic function, the assertion of movement *towards* Christ from the "paths of madness," suggests a subtle but specific interpretation and appropriation of Christ. Harper identifies Maceo with a Christ who himself became a victim, "the 'lamb that was slain'...whose perennial wound signifies his suffering" (Callahan 238). This suffering Christ, however, brings peace and change to the downcast and the marginalized:

> Year by year the world grows weary
> 'Neath its weight of sin and strife,
> Though the hands once pierced and bleeding
> Offer more abundant life. (45-48)

From this point forward the poem becomes an intercession. It extends beyond the specific Cuban national context and acquires a transnational, even global scope. After lamenting the condition of a world that "grows weary '[n]eath its weight of sin and strife," the speaker asks that the "old and sweet refrain" be sung until there is peace:

> May the choral song of angels
> Heard upon Judea's plain
> Sound throughout the earth the tidings
> Of that old and sweet refrain.
>
> Till our world, so sad and weary,
> Finds the balmy rest of peace –
> Peace to silence all her discords –
> Peace till war and crime shall cease.
>
> Peace to fall like gentle showers,
> Or on parched flowers dew,
> Till our hearts proclaim with gladness:
> Lo, He maketh all things new. (49-60)

Addressing a higher power that might grant this request for peace, the speaker intercedes on behalf of a world plagued with "war and crime." This peace is not simply a transcendental peace of death in which death functions as a metaphor for a mystic translation into heaven. In fact, heaven does not appear here at all. Maceo's new "Cuba Libre" remerges at the end of the poem in the form of a new earth. Like Zumbi, the iconic figure of Maceo effects a peculiar relationship between life, death, and freedom, such that freedom is achieved only in and by death. Maceo's death in the first line of the poem culminates in "all things new" in the last. In both cases, freedom requires death, the shedding of blood.

In connection with the overall structure of "Maceo," Harper's sensibility for oral performance becomes particularly important. The poem functions as a quasi-sermonic performance, beginning with an event, commenting on that event using biblical allusions, and finally ending in a prayer. The implied audience in "Maceo" is divided between "the people" (i.e. in the United States) and God himself, as it culminates in a collective prayer. In this sense the poem progresses from the regionally specific and isolated death of Antonio Maceo, towards a collective prayer on behalf of "nations" and "worlds." Maceo transforms from individual to icon signifiying a symbolic redemption. Harper adopts the figure of Christ – with its biblical notions of freedom through self-sacrifice – and aligns it with the cause of earthly (political, economic, racial, social) redemption through the death of Maceo. Maceo becomes a black Christ – the synthesis of sacrifice and struggle. In her translation of Maceo, Harper configures him as a *sign* for the African American struggle for freedom during the post-Reconstruction era in the United States.[7] Harper urges blacks facing government sanctioned violence and persecution to see their fight against oppression in a larger, transnational context of the struggle of African descendants. Harper suggests that this struggle calls into question the very tenets of North American national identity. For Harper, the progress and spiritual health of an evolving United States at the turn of the century, depends on recognizing the death of men like Maceo as both tragic *and* redemptive.

Conclusion

Harper's emphasis on the common humanity of blacks and whites falls in line with many other abolitionists at the time that made a deliberate effort to counteract the belief that blacks were less than human. In a speech delivered to the New York Anti-Slavery Society in 1857, Harper asks

> Could we trace the record of every human heart, the aspirations of every immortal soul, perhaps we would find no man so imbruted and degraded that we could not trace the word liberty either written in living characters upon the soul or hidden away in some nook or corner of the heart. The law of liberty is the law of God, and is antecedent to all human legislation. It existed in the mind of the Deity when He hung the first world upon its orbit and gave it liberty to gather light from the central sun. (Harper "Could We Trace")

Not only does Harper allude to a common, transcendent humanity, but she also argues that liberty is fundamental to any conception of the human. The "law of liberty" precedes any legislation or epistemological theory that might place limitations on humanity and the human desire for and entitlement to freedom. In "How We Mistook the Map for the Territory," Sylvia Wynter explains how a secularized, "biocentric" definition of "Man" evolved in the second half of the nineteenth century, a European conception of man that became synonymous with the definition of *hu*man and precipitated in the *othering* (i.e. the dehumanization) of Native Americans and especially of Africans (119). It also produced a "color line" that then translated into the idea of race. This process was intimately related to conceptions of "races" of people and to a racial hierarchy in which white was ultimately superior and black (and to some degree non-white peoples in general) bore the weight of "*désêtre*," or "wrongness of being" (118). Both "Death of Zombi" and "Maceo" challenge such definitions of humanity influenced by Darwinian and Positivist thought.

Harper *explicitly* transnationalizes the question of freedom and humanity for African Americans in the nineteenth century. In a country torn between a national rhetoric of freedom and a social and economic dependency on slavery, she offered a vision of a free black republic, evoking the history of what would become a celebrated symbol of struggle against colonial imperialism – the Republic of Palmares. Four decades later, in the aftermath of a failed Reconstruction leading to racial violence and the exclusion of blacks from United States citizenship, Harper wrote about a black Cuban leader who fought to quell racial conflict in his country for the sake of national unity and independence. By using black figures outside of the United States, she suggests that the scope of African American experience extends beyond regional and national boundaries.

The idea that a "Negro Kingdom" could exist in Brazil and be relevant to the history of African Americans suggests the peculiar relationship of *afrodescendente* peoples to their national identities – identities that evolve from a condition of exile – and shows that neither African American racial identity nor North American national identity respected national borders. This "New World" black consciousness is born out of a fundamental *condition* of diaspora. It is neither simply a desire for a return to Africa nor an essentialist concept of blackness or of African ancestry. It is rather a product of an interweaving of historical process contingent upon the multidirectional movement not only of people but of narratives, symbols, typologies, and other such literary elements. Likewise, Harper appropriates Maceo's death in an effort to resolve a perceived inconsistency between human behavior and a transcendent morality that might restore black (and white) humanity and create "free" nations. As "Cuba Libre" (i.e. a new, free Cuba) here becomes synonymous with freedom, Maceo's death acquires a larger meaning with implications beyond the Cuban context. By inserting this text into this larger discourse, Harper also places American nationalism in a transnational context.

Well before the Harlem Renaissance and Negritude movements popularized internationalism in poetry, Harper began using poetry to challenge African Americans to conceptualize identity beyond national borders. Harper's appropriations of Zumbi and Maceo are signs not only of Harper's Pan-African sensibility but also of her early transnational African American poetics, a poetics demanding a certain kind of critical analysis – one that recognizes the permeability of national boundaries. Because her work demonstrates a keen trans-hemispheric sensibility, future scholarship on Harper should take into account the transnational currents instigated by the transatlantic slave trade and their influence on Harper's poetry. In fact, as part of a collection of transnational poetic allusions in African American literature, Harper's "Death of Zombi" and "Maceo" suggest that transnational readings of African American poetry need to go beyond the scope of such explicitly Pan-African movements as Negritude and the "third world consciousness" of Black Arts Movement poetics and consider all African American writing within a persistent transnational context that has influenced black literary aesthetics from the earliest moments of black literary production in the "New World." To do so, African American literary studies requires a trans-hemispheric – and therefore multilingual, multicultural, and pan-American – conceptual framework.

[1] In his discussion of Paul Laurence Dunbar, Johnson also refers to other "outstanding" figures among "the Aframericans of the whole Western world." Johnson continues: "There are Plácido and Manzano in Cuba; Vieux and Durand in Haiti; Machado de Assis in Brazil, and others that might be mentioned, who stand on a plane with or even above Dunbar. Plácido and Machado de Assis rank as great in the literatures of their respective countries without any qualifications whatever. They are world figures in the literature of the Latin languages. Machado de Assis is somewhat handicapped in this respect by having as his tongue and medium the lesser known Portuguese, but Plácido, writing in the language of Spain, Mexico, Cuba and almost the whole of South America, is universally known. His works have been republished in the original in Spain, Mexico and in most of the Latin-American countries; several editions have been published in the United States; translations of his works have been made into French and German" (7). In addition to being one of the earliest known Afro-Cuban poets, Juan Francisco Manzano (1797-1854) wrote the only known slave narrative in the Spanish-speaking world. Machado de Assis (1839-1908) was a Brazilian novelist, poet, short-story writer and one of the most well known and highly acclaimed writers of his time. While Johnson does mention Frances Harper, he does so only briefly and in the context of Dunbar's use of dialect. Analysis of Frances Harper in the larger context of Johnson's Aframerican "world," allows us to consider the role of African American women poets in this hemispheric vision.

[2] I use the term *afrodescendente* here to refer broadly to an imagined (not to be confused with imaginary) literary community of writers of African descent. While the hyphenated "*afro-descendente*" refers to peoples of African descent *in* Brazil, *afrodescendente* refers more broadly to peoples of African descent in the North and South America and in the space in between. The Portuguese term allows for a single term to refer to what I posit as a singular "imagined space." This designation is not arbitrary. I focus here on the United States, Cuba, and Brazil, not to the exclusion of other countries where colonialism and the slave trade dispersed African communities. I suggest instead that this literature constantly, on one level or another, engaged with the symbolic presence of an imagined, transnational community. Ultimately, by *afrodescendente*, then, I mean those whose identity by virtue of historical process has relied on the negotiation of an African ancestry, a particular relationship to the "memory" of transatlantic slavery and to the cultural, sociological, psychological and political implications of its occurrence. The term *afrodescendente* literally contains within one semantic unit this concept of ancestry and "Africa" – itself an "imagined" space that should not be confused with an extremely diverse and multicultural continent – accounting for the implications of this ancestry on the terms by which Africans entered colonial societies, but does so in a way that synthesizes the two, performing textually the symbiotic nature of these two components. The term *afrodescendente* also incorporates the political and cultural-historical aspects of race while not disavowing the specific ways in which such race concepts have evolved in the United States, Cuba, and Brazil respectively over the course of the twentieth century. At times I use the term "black" interchangeably, maintaining always a commitment to the terms used by the poets/poems themselves to refer to themselves or their readership.

[3] This historical figure is most commonly referred to as "Zumbi" both in Brazil and in the United States. Some historical documents transcribe the name "Zombi." For the purposes of this paper, I use "Zumbi" to refer broadly to the historical figure and "Zombi" to refer to Harper's character in "Death of Zombi."

[4] Baraka 228.

[5] In our wretched country the cry of Freedom has sounded once again! The opportune moment has arrived that we will make the whole world know that the Cuban knows how to die for the redemption of his country… (*My Translation*)

[6] In *The Talking Book: African Americans and the Bible*, Allen Dwight Callahan argues that in fact African American literature does not "properly begin with writing" but rather that "it begins with religion" and, more specifically, Christianity. He argues that African American interpretation of the bible and symbolic use of the Christ figure has permeated African American culture and, at a fundamental level, informed African American artistic production. He further maintains that "African Americans read their own collective experience into the agony and exaltation of Jesus. The story of the Christ child, blessed by God yet born in the shadow of poverty and violence, was their story. Jesus' humble birth in antiquity signified the humble origins of African peoples in modernity. In his impoverished entry into the world, Jesus turned the tables on earthly valuations" (236).

[7] My use of the term "sign" here and discussion of Maceo as a figure "signifying" a symbolic redemption draws on Ferdinand de Saussure's theory of "the sign" as described in his *Course in General Linguistics* (1916). Saussure maintained that language is comprised of a series of linkages between sound and thought which ultimately constructs a system of language made up of pairings between signifier (form) and signified (concept). The *signifier* and the *signified* combine to produce the *sign*. We can understand this poem's process in the same way. Harper employs the figure of Maceo as a signifier, signifying the concept of freedom and nationhood. The poem is structured around this process of signification; Maceo as a historical figure is semiologically linked to the African American racial and United States national contexts. Ultimately, Maceo becomes a *sign* for the African American struggle for freedom during the post-Reconstruction era in United States.

Works Cited

Baraka, Amiri. "Notes on History of African/Afro-American Culture." *Daggers and Javelins: Essays, 1974-1979*. New York: Morrow, 1984.

Boggs, Colleen Glenney. *Transnationalism and American Literature: Literary Translation 1773-1892*. New York: Routledge, 2007.

Boyd, Melba Joyce. *Discarded Legacy: Politics and Poetics in the Life of Frances E. W. Harper 1825-1911*. Detroit: Wayne State UP, 1994.

Callahan, Allen. *The Talking Book: African Americans and the Bible*. New Haven: Yale UP, 2006.

Clark, Kathleen Ann. *Defining Moments: African American Commemoration and Political Culture in the South, 1863-1913*. Chapel Hill: U of North Carolina P, 2005.

Fitz, Earl. "In Quest of Nuestras Américas." AmeriQuests [Online] Vol. 1, No. 1.1 (8 November 2004). 28 Aug. 2007 <http://ejournals.library.vanderbilt.edu/ameriquests/viewarticle.php?id=14>

Foner, Eric. *Forever Free: The Story of Emancipation and Reconstruction*. New York: Knopf, 2005.

Foner, Philip Sheldon. *Antonio Maceo: The "Bronze Titan" of Cuba's Struggle for Independence*. New York: Monthly Review, 1977.

—. *A History of Cuba and Its Relations with the United States, Vol. II, 1845-1895*. New York: International Publishers, 1963.

Foster, Frances Smith, ed. *A Brighter Coming Day: A Frances Ellen Watkins Harper Reader*. New York: Feminist, 1990.

Friedman, Lawrence J. *Inventors of the Promised Land*. New York: Knopf, 1975.

Garnet, Henry Highland. "Excerpt of the Speech of Rev. Henry Highland Garnet." *Slavery in Cuba: A Report of the Proceedings of the Meeting Held at Cooper Institute, New York City, December 13, 1872*. New York: Office of the Cuban Anti-Slavery Committee, 1872.

Gilroy, Paul. *The Black Atlantic: Modernity and Double Consciousness*. Cambridge: Harvard UP, 1993.

Gomes, Flávio. *Palmares: escravidão e liberdade no Atlântico sul*. São Paulo: Contexto, 2005.

Grosby, Steven Elliott. *Biblical Ideas of Nationality: Ancient and Modern*. Winona Lake: Eisenbrauns, 2002.

Harper, Frances Ellen Watkins. "Could We Trace the Record of Every Human Heart." *National Anti-Slavery Standard*, May 23, 1857: 3.

—. "Death of Zombi, the Chief of a Negro a Negro Kingdom in South America." Foster 172-173.

—. "Maceo." Foster 374-376.

Helg, Aline. *Our Rightful Share: The Afro-Cuban Struggle for Equality, 1886-1912*. U of North Carolina P, 1995.

Hill, Patricia L. "'Let Me Make the Songs for the People': A Study of Frances Watkins Harper's Poetry." *Black American Literature Forum* 15.2 (1981): 60-65.

Humphrey, Edward Frank. *Nationalism and Religion in America, 1774-1789*. Boston: Chipman, 1924.

Johnson, James Weldon. *The Book of American Negro Poetry*. 1922. New York: Harcourt, 1958.

Kaplan, Amy. *The Anarchy of Empire in the Making of U.S. Culture*. Cambridge: Harvard UP, 2002.

Levander, Caroline F., and Robert S. Levine. "Introduction: Hemispheric American Literary History." *American Literary History* 18.3 (2006): 397-405.

Maceo, Antonio. "A Los Cubanos de Color." *Pensamiento cubano: siglo XIX*. Ed. Isabel Monal and Olivia Miranda. La Habana: Editorial, 2002: 50.

—. "Carta al General José Lamothe." *Pensamiento cubano: siglo XIX*. Ed. Isabel Monal and Olivia Miranda. La Habana: Editorial, 2002: 48-49.

—. "Proclama !Viva Cuba Independiente! [1879]." *Pensamiento cubano: siglo XIX*. Ed. Isabel Monal and Olivia Miranda. La Habana: Editorial, 2002: 46-47.

Price, Richard, ed. *Maroon Societies: Rebel Slave Communities in the Americas*. 3rd ed. Baltimore: Johns Hopkins UP, 1996.

Sollors, Werner. *Beyond Ethnicity: Consent and Descent in American Literature*. New York: Oxford UP, 1986.

Still, William. *The Underground Rail Road*. Philadelphia: Porters, 1872.

Tocqueville, Alexis de. *Democracy in America*. Trans. Stephen D. Grant. Indianapolis: Hackett, 2000.

Wynter, Sylvia. "On How We Mistook the Map for the Territory, and Re-Imprisoned Ourselves in our Unbearable Wrongness of Being, of Désêtre: Black Studies toward the Human Project." *Not Only the Master's Tools: African-American Studies in Theory and Practice*. Ed. Lewis Gordon and Jane Anna Gordon. Boulder: Paradigm, 2006: 107-120.

Strong Drink, Strong Work: African Americans Working Race, Working Gender, Working Temperance

DoVeanna S. Fulton Minor

From its earliest inception, temperance reform garnered African American support. In 1788 the Free African Society of Philadelphia banned alcoholic drinking among its members.[1] While the initial object of the temperance movement was to counsel moderate consumption of alcoholic beverages, eventually temperance societies and advocates demanded total abstinence from drinking intoxicating liquids. Although the earliest temperance organizations were founded in the first decade of the nineteenth century, the movement did not experience substantial growth until the 1830s and 1840s, when the abolitionist and women's rights movements also began gaining strength and recognition. Temperance activists identified the "demon drink" as the root cause of social crises like spousal abuse, indolence and domestic impoverishment. For many white abolitionists and temperance advocates – although these groups were not mutually inclusive – slaveholding and drunkenness occasioned similar disapprobations; both constituted transgressions of Christian principles. Not above exploiting images of slavery and discourses of freedom, temperance artwork, including scenes like the one in *Going into Captivity*, struck terror into white hearts with depictions of scores of white workers, businessmen, women and children chained together and driven in a slave coffle by whip-wielding saloon keepers (Fig. 1).[2] Andrew Sinclair points out the appeal to freedom and women's rights in "dry" literature, which reasoned, "How could drinkers claim that their personal liberty was being attacked when their wives were slaves? Did not freedom to drink for men mean mere freedom for women to drudge, to scrape, and to starve? Could any woman be called free who did not have a decent home and husband? Did not women have the right to ensure the health of their children? Was not the real slave the drink slave?" (59)

This reasoning equating intemperance and women's repression with slavery was often employed without its authors recognizing the reductive and disingenuous comparison to the lives of antebellum African Americans whose empirical realities of slavery in the South and nominal freedom in the North belied such equations. Both before and after emancipation, many mainstream temperance organizations exploited this discursive incongruence and simultaneously ignored and dismissed the intersections of race and temperance as "*Going into Captivity*" (Fig. 1) demonstrates. Although the work depicts a commonly portrayed slave scene, ironically, all the captives are white – thus, ignoring the reality of slavery in America. This situation was not the case in the temperance activism of Martin R. Delany, Frederick Douglass, William Wells Brown and Frances E. W. Harper. Their work illustrates that when African Americans engaged and interacted with the mainstream temperance movement, the complexities of race, equality, and temperance were at the forefront of their work. By locating the intersection of race and gender politics at the center of their work, these activists demonstrated that they recognized the significant impact of categories of difference on temperance reform. The troubled relationship between the mainstream temperance movement and African Americans occasioned multiple approaches to race(ing) temperance by African American writers, innovative approaches in which race, whether as a subtext or foregrounded, operates as an always already present social factor. Social activism and literary texts by African American advocates of temperance reveal the diverse routes they took in the anti-drink movement while struggling for social and political equality. Douglass's "The Heroic Slave" and Harper's *Sowing and Reaping*, moreover, combine the discourses of gender and temperance to interrogate and challenge racial pejoratives and assumptions.

Although William Lloyd Garrison, publisher of *The Liberator*, the leading abolitionist newspaper, proclaimed "The Temperance and abolition enterprises are the hope of our country, identical in principle, based on the same broad foundation of human brotherhood, and animated by the same spirit of Christian benevolence and charity," many white temperance activists failed to sufficiently connect the two "enterprises."[3] In fact, Frederick Douglass was strongly criticized by white American Temperance delegates at the 1846 World's Temperance Convention in London for speaking out against slavery. After accusing Douglass of inappropriately introducing antislavery concerns into temperance discussions in a letter to the *New York Evangelist*, Reverend Samuel Hanson Cox declared, "the cause of Temperance was not at all responsible for slavery, and had no connexion [sic] with it" (Foner 42). In an open letter to Cox published in *The Liberator*, Douglass answered Cox's charges and systematically demonstrated how racist practices of white temperance advocates and their objection to Douglass's speech reflected the proslavery stance of the American Temperance movement. At the root of the delegates' objections, Douglass maintained, was their refusal to accept him as their equal. He boldly confronted Cox, stating, "the truth probably is, that you felt both yourself and your country severely rebuked by my presence there; and, besides this, it was undoubtedly painful to you to be placed on the same platform, on a level with a Negro, a fugitive slave" (Foner 43). Without disregarding certain racist and pro-slavery factions in the temperance movement, Douglass identified the relation between the degradation of enslavement and intemperance, between freedom of self-control – denied by slavery – and the loss of self-control caused by drunkenness. As Donald Yacovone demonstrates, African American antislavery and temperance advocates almost never overlooked the relations between enslavement and drunkenness (286). Temperance activism in African American communities did not equate intemperance with slavery in the reductive manner seen in mainstream temperance tracts.

For African Americans, abolition was rooted in the principle of human equality and the belief that slavery denied the right to equal treatment before the law. Many of these abolitionists held that by embracing high moral virtues, American society would begin to accept Black equality. Thus temperance commitment was a natural, if not required, companion to antislavery advocacy. In conjunction with establishing abolitionist societies, free northern Blacks formed temperance societies that recognized their responsibilities to enslaved African Americans. The preamble and constitution of the Temperance Society of the Coloured People of the City of Pittsburgh and Vicinity begins,

> Believing that moderate drinking leads the way to all the drunkenness in our land and the world – that total abstinence from intoxicating liquors, is the only perfect safeguard for the temperate – and the only hope for the intemperate – and that the future prospects of the two and a half millions of our brethren who are now groaning in our own country, beneath the iron hand of the oppressor, will depend materially upon the state of morals among the free people of colour, we the undersigned, coloured inhabitants of the city of Pittsburgh and vicinity, pledge ourselves neither to drink, nor buy, nor sell, nor give away any intoxicating liquor, except when rendered necessary as a medicine and prescribed by a physician, when it is to be obtained as such.[4]

The members of this society – who elected a twenty-five-year-old Martin R. Delany as their recording secretary during the second annual meeting in 1837 – understood the relation of their quasi-free status with that of enslaved African Americans and recognized their responsibility to support not only abolition but to be and offer models of moral virtue as well.[5] Delany's participation in this organization is significant because, as one of the most committed Black nationalists of the nineteenth century whose lithographic image became a model for virtuous Black masculinity, it underscores the intersections of race, gender, abolition, and temperance.

Among the many titles and occupations Delany held are "journalist, editor, doctor, scientist, inventor, customs inspector, orator, politician and novelist" (Gilroy 19). Perhaps the position of Major of the U. S. Army during the Civil War was the one with greatest impact visually as a result of the postcard portrait made by Abraham Bogardus of Delany in full military regalia promoted and distributed by *The Weekly Anglo African* in 1865 (Fig 2).[6] According to Maurice O. Wallace, the numerous reproductions of this image served to establish the morality and virtue of African American men. "Owing to the redoubled effect of standardization created by Delany's dress and pose and the potential, implicit in the announcement of *The Weekly Anglo African*, for the serial reproduction of the Bogardus carte in perpetuity," Wallace contends, "the Delany portrait came to portray not an exceptional man but a typical one, general and reproducible by others. The carte distilled broad, [B]lack masculine ambition into a single image and helped to shape a specific form of [B]lack masculine ideality" (75).

Like the constitutional values of the Pittsburgh temperance society of which Delany was a founding member, this portrait conveyed the conviction "that the future prospects of the two and a half millions of our brethren who are now groaning in our own country, beneath the iron hand of the oppressor, will depend materially upon the state of morals among the free people of colour" (*Proceedings*). The lithograph conveys honorable manliness and leadership qualities through not only Delany's military dress uniform but the natural setting, tents and infantry man, which suggests Delany's leadership ability and control of nature, other men, and himself. In her study of masculine gender and the discourse of civilization in late nineteenth- and early twentieth-century America, Gail Bederman finds that "By about 1890, the discourse of civilization had taken ona very specific set of meanings which revolved around three factors: race, gender, and millennial assumptions about human evolutionary progress" (25). While Bederman's work focuses on the late nineteenth century, she shows that this discourse had its origins in early nineteenth-century gender ideals. "Ever since the middle class had begun to define itself as a class in the early nineteenth century," Bederman maintains, "ideals of gender and of 'manliness' had been central to middle-class consciousness [...]. By gaining the manly strength to control him-

Fig 2. Martin R. Delany (c. 1865). Permission from the National Portrait Gallerv. Smithsonian Institution

self, a man gained strength, as well as the duty, to protect and direct those weaker than himself: his wife, his children, or his employees" (11-12). The representation of manliness in Delany's portrait – compounded with his clearly black skin (a fact he proudly heralded) signals his appropriation of masculine discourse, and simultaneously his challenge to the racial assumptions of that discourse. Although many years separate Delany's service as secretary of the Pittsburgh temperance society and his military service, the emphasis on the rights and responsibilities of Black masculinity was a staple in Delany's social reform work and contributed to the African American temperance cause.

With the exception of the 1859 short story "The Two Offers" by Frances E. W. Harper, antebellum literary works written by African Americans subsumed temperance rhetoric within protest narratives focused on antislavery and racial equality agenda.[7] Faced with the charge of Black moral degeneracy and inferiority used to justify slavery and racial violence and discrimination, African American temperance activists had to develop arguments to support the anti-drink cause without reinscribing racial pejoratives that marked Blacks as inherently deviant and immoral.

Perhaps for this reason African American temperance works feature intemperate whites who provide a negative contrast to morally upstanding Blacks. Robert S. Levine points out that in Frank J. Webb's *The Garies and Their Friends* (1857), "There are no scenes of inebriated blacks giving up the bottle, no discussions of Temperance. In Webb's novel, it is the whites, not the blacks, who are in dire need of Temperance reform, as the blacks generally are presented as industrious bourgeois capitalists" (352). Delany's *Blake, or the Huts of America* also contains a strong temperance subtext and depicts intemperate whites or alcohol used by nefarious characters to the detriment of African American interests. Similarly Douglass' 1853 novella, "The Heroic Slave," contains a rather explicit critique of drunkenness and racial constructions by juxtaposing the heroic figure of Madison Washington with the parasitic slothfulness of the tavern drunks.

Recognized as the first fictional work published by an African American, the novella recapitulates the slave rebellion led by Washington aboard the *Creole*, a vessel carrying 134 slaves bound for New Orleans slave markets. As his name indicates, Washington's resistance parallels the acts of American Revolutionary war heroes. William Andrews notes, "It seems clear that Douglass wanted not only to place Washington on the stage of history but to give him an extensive speaking part so that he could articulate himself in a fashion befitting true nobility of mind and spirit [...]. Douglass is determined to show that his [B]lack hero does not act merely on impulse but only as a consequence of rigorous self-examination and high-minded purpose" (13). Washington has a "heart full of honest manliness" and is described throughout the novella as a heroic figure both physically and mentally ("Heroic Slave" 45). Although Washington is the leader of a rebellion, Douglass does not emphasize his physical aggression. Richard Yarborough points out that "because the white sailor through whose eyes we witness the revolt is conveniently knocked unconscious at the outset of the uprising, in 'The Heroic Slave' we see Washington neither commit nor directly urge acts of physical violence whatsoever" (175). Douglass constructs the text in this manner, Yarborough argues, because he was sensitive to the values and expectations of his white audience who "might experience some discomfort with the means adopted by his slave hero to win his freedom" (175). Thus while Washington's physical power is apparent, his heroism rests on qualities of manliness that include control: control of language, the self, and others. His command of language is as heroic as his physicality. Tom Grant, the first mate of the *Creole*, asserts, "He seldom spake [sic] to any one, and when he did speak, it was with the utmost propriety. His words were well chosen, and his pronunciation equal to that of any schoolmaster. It was a mystery to us where he got his knowledge of language" (65). Language and physicality notwithstanding, Washington's self-control is the bedrock of his heroic masculinity. Indeed, his capacity to control himself and others repeatedly saves lives and cultivates followers. After his encounter with Washington, Grant, a veteran of such work vows to avoid slave ships, declaring, "I felt myself in the presence of a superior man; one who, had he been a white man, I would have followed willingly and gladly in any honorable enterprise" (68). This statement is reminiscent of Delany's Bogardus carte in that Washington's leadership presents a picture of manly ideality that challenges racial and gender assumptions. The white patrons of the tavern where the slave coffle with Washington stops the night before sailing on the *Creole* lack such honor and self-control.

In the four-part novella, Douglass uses a significant portion of Part III to detail the disrepair of the tavern and the dissipation of its white inhabitants. He writes, "It would not be proper here to give the reader any idea of the vulgarity and dark profanity which rolled, as 'a sweet morsel,' under these corrupt tongues. A more brutal set of creatures, perhaps, never congregated" (52). Their intemperance, racist language and raucous behavior further underscore Washington's manliness. Spatially, Washington remains outside the tavern, in the alley behind the building; a marginalization that both reprises Douglass's experience with the American Temperance delegation in London and marks Washington's commitment to temperance by virtue of his masculine ideality. Like Cox the patrons cannot envision a Black man as their equal. Moreover, their intemperate behavior practiced inside the tavern signals unmanliness because the patrons lack self-control. For Douglass temperance concerns more than abstinence from alcoholic beverages; temperance entails governing the self and recognizing every human's capacity for and right to self-governance. It is, therefore, intimately connected to equality and antislavery. His letter to Cox suggests one cannot be fully committed to the temperance cause and hold or tolerate racist ideology and inequality. Temperance is, then, secondary to equality and justice and cannot be realized without them. For this reason, abolition and racial equality were at the forefront of Douglass's temperance advocacy.

For many antebellum activists, who used moral suasion and emotional appeals as their tools of trade, temperance went hand-and-hand with other causes such as prison reform and women's rights. Northern temperance activists initially maintained this approach to reform immediately following the Civil War. Harold Thompson observes, "Unlike Southerners, northern reformers and missionaries to the freedmen viewed temperance as part of a comprehensive moral reform agenda for the nation that combined one-on-one moral suasion tactics with proactive governmental policies [...]. Because of slavery, however, southern antebellum temperance reformers fought to divorce their cause from abolitionism, with which it was closely associated in the North" (76). Even after Emancipation, the southern white reformer stance reflected the relationship between slavery and temperance. Most mainstream temperance organizations with strong southern ties increasingly began to focus on legislative measures to realize prohibition. Unfortunately, this political approach was used to facilitate Black disfranchisement and racial discrimination. Prior to the Civil War, African American temperance activists were located largely in the North and their activism concentrated on free Blacks living in northern areas. By the 1850s temperance advocacy was so widespread that "among [B]lacks abstinence from intoxicating beverages had become normative for all except those at the lowest economic level so the success of the movement eventually undercut its reason for being" (Thompson 90). Nevertheless, African Americans continued to support the cause through memberships in societies, lectures and oratory, church resolutions, and writing. During the Reconstruction and post-Reconstruction periods, African Americans in the South embraced temperance reform via Black churches and educational institutions. In his study of temperance advocacy in post-bellum Atlanta, Thompson asserts "the centrality of clergy and missionary school alumni" in Black temperance reform movements. He suggests these advocates "viewed a temperate lifestyle as beneficial to the race for a wide variety of reasons, not the least being the fact [that] the money not used for liquor could go into purchasing homes and property, thereby improving their well being and presumably white perceptions of them" (22). Temperance writing by African Americans during this period underscores Thompson's argument.

By 1876 when Frances Harper's novel *Sowing and Reaping: A Temperance Story* was serialized in the *Christian Recorder*, the official organ of the African Methodist Episcopal church, political and economic enfranchisement, racial equality, and freedom from racial discrimination were constant concerns in the daily lives of African Americans. Yet like the rest of the nation, temperance consciousness and concerns continued to mount in Black communities throughout the latter half of the nineteenth century. In addition to temperance societies, fraternal orders adopted anti-drink agendas and practices. The Independent Order of Good Templars was the largest and most visible temperance fraternal society in the 1870s and 1880s. Unlike many other fraternal societies, the Good Templars accepted members regardless of race and gender, although the non-white and female members had to meet certain qualifications. Despite the fact that they had organized and become members of fraternal societies since the late eighteenth century, African American participation and acceptance by their white counterparts had been fraught with difficulty.[8] David M. Fahey documents what he calls the "Great Schism" of 1876-1886 between the British and American lodges of the Good Templars, as a result of the American lodges refusing to racially integrate local, state, or Grand Lodges.[9] William Wells Brown, the most well-known African American Good Templar, worked tirelessly organizing lodges in Virginia, West Virginia and Tennessee. Although these lodges aimed for integrated membership, Brown admitted they were "more or less coloured persons [some being of mixed race], the whites holding aloof of course" (Fahey 114). Many lodges organized in African American communities failed to thrive primarily because members lacked sufficient funds to purchase charters and the requisite resources to sustain the lodge (staffing, meeting venues, and ritual books).

Continuing in the tradition established by their antebellum predecessors, post-Reconstruction African American women and men embraced temperance as part of the larger work of racial uplift, seeing it as "contributing to moral and material self-betterment" (Fahey 107). Black temperance activism had a high sense of purpose that not only considered the welfare of immediate members and communities but ultimately regarded the progress of the race as a whole as dependent on the ability of its reform efforts to bring about social, political, and economic justice. However, linking the anti-drink cause to political action in the late nineteenth century proved just as difficult as the slavery-temperance connection Douglass asserted before emancipation. Contrary to their white counterparts who increasingly agitated in favor of legislative measures to ban alcohol, many African American temperance advocates preferred to concentrate on social reformation. Although a few African Americans associated with the National Prohibition Party (NPP), most did not. African Americans shunned the NPP largely because "southern white prohibitionists, who were mostly middle and lower class whites, supported disfranchisement of [B]lacks" (Thompson 13). These prohibitionists believed Black voters were used to support the political agenda of a few wealthy whites who controlled the Democratic Party. Because many white prohibitionists advocated Black disenfranchisement, Fahey contends, "[B]lack Templars in the South for the most part remained detached from any political agitation for prohibition of the sale of drink" (123). While the politics of prohibition discouraged African American involvement, the politics of race and gender remained such that temperance work demanded African Americans infuse the struggle for racial equality into their temperance activism in subtle and profound ways.

Frances E. W. Harper's temperance writings are renowned for this inconspicuous infusion of racial concerns in an anti-drink narrative. In fact, the most notable quality of her temperance texts is the absence of racial markers. This inconspicuousness is found in both her poetry and prose and conveys Harper's sagacious comprehension of the dynamics of temperance activism vis-à-vis American race and gender politics. Harper's earliest known temperance writings are found in her second book, *Poems on Miscellaneous Subjects*, a collection of poems and prose writings published in 1854. This volume enjoyed multiple printings and a second edition was published in 1857. The collection reflects Harper's social and religious consciousness, especially concerning the wrongs of slavery and the hypocrisy inherent in using biblical texts to support slavery. Additionally, poems in this volume addressed equal rights for African Americans and women, temperance and support of radical resistance to slavery. Her poem "The Drunkard's Child" establishes what would be Harper's literary paradigm for temperance literature: the anticipated (and often unfulfilled) arrival of a drunkard at the deathbed of a loved one and racially ambiguous character descriptions such as "pale" skin and "marble brow." It is this ambiguity that distinguishes Harper's anti-drink fiction from that of her African American contemporaries, including Douglass, as well as from her own writings (fiction and nonfiction) on other topics – slavery and abolition, women's rights, and even religious and moral reform – in which she explicitly represents characters as African American. In *Beginnings: Intention and Method*, Edward Said offers the idea that beginnings are precipitated by social, historical, and even psychological conditions and that a writer's intention and method determine a beginning which is "a complex act of knowledge, experience, and art" (17). Given race, gender and class inequities in the nineteenth century and the mainstream temperance movement's indifference toward, purposeful disregard of, and often resistance to African Americans, Harper's intentions to foster temperance in African American communities and address race problems in temperance movement literature are accomplished by creating racially indeterminate characters and performing the "complex act of knowledge, experience and art" Said identifies. Racial indeterminacy acts as a lacuna that opens the text for multiple and varied engagements by different reading communities. "By creating racially ambivalent characters in *Sowing and Reaping*," contends Carolyn Sorisio, "Harper opens up the debate as to which bodies are ungovernable and who is capable of self-rule in the Reconstruction era" (94). Moreover, indeterminacy allows Harper to proffer a radical integrationist vision of America in which communities, though class stratified, are peopled by individuals whose race is insignificant to the context of the narrative. This is not to suggest that Harper creates a naïve world in which race is of no consequence or individuals are "color-blind." Her prolonged struggle for abolition and civil rights and against racial discrimination negates that charge.[10] What I am suggesting is that racial indeterminacy allowed Harper's readers both not to be preoccupied with race and, when it is considered, to realize the very instability of racial categories, and thus the inappropriateness of them as well.

Debra J. Rosenthal argues Harper's "deracialized discourse" normalized blackness for readers who encountered these texts in the original publication venues of the *Anglo-African* and the *Christian Recorder*. "Such self-reflection," Rosenthal contends, "as the norm or default race removes the black experience from the realm of the invisible and returns black Americans to the center, where the triumphs and foibles of personhood are more important than surface skin color" (156). Without disputing Rosenthal, I contend that racial indeterminacy in *Sowing and Reaping* allowed Harper to speak to and write for multiple audiences. The general African American readership of the *Christian Recorder* certainly may have accepted the novel's characters as Black without any apparent self-reflection; as such this audience was Harper's most obvious target. Nevertheless, Harper appeals to another audience, an audience of readers engaged in and familiar with the mainstream temperance movement and social reform who are cognizant of historical and contemporaneous circumstances of these movements.

While typical readers may have accepted Harper's deracialized discourse to normalize Blackness, historically conscious and politically astute readers would have recognized Harper's association and appropriation of real-life figures in what P. Gabrielle Foreman calls "histotextuality" – that is, a method of radicalizing the text by "homonymically connecting her characters to historical personages her African American and acculturated audience would know" (331). Neither of these audiences is privileged over the other; they are simultaneously and equally spoken to through narrative constructions. With histotextuality Harper addresses these "[s]eparate though perhaps overlapping cultures and communities, and readers of cultures [...]; they brought differing needs, desires and interpretive capacities to the same text" (Foreman 332). Histotextuality in Harper's 1892 historical novel *Iola Leroy*, Foreman argues, is achieved through the adoption of the name "Iola" for the novel's heroine, that name being the pseudonym used by Ida B. Wells, the most noted and militant anti-lynching activist in the 1890s. "By entitling her novel *Iola Leroy* and incorporating other historical figures as well," Foreman maintains, "Harper situates her coded explorations firmly in the context of the volatile decade in which she wrote" (332). Histotextuality proves to be a salient literary device for Harper.

Predating *Iola Leroy* by sixteen years, *Sowing and Reaping*, too, has histotextual features that situate the novel in radical temperance and racial politics. However, whereas Harper alludes to a radical African American life through the name of her protagonists in *Iola Leroy*, in *Sowing and Reaping* she appropriates a real-life white figure to radicalize the text, speak to different audiences simultaneously, and destabilize racial assumptions readers might make. In particular, Harper creates the character of Josiah (Joe) Gough, a drunkard who abuses his wife but is led to reformation by the heroine, Belle Gordon. Joe takes the temperance pledge and eventually finds a decent job and becomes a temperance advocate, giving speeches at prayer meetings. The real-life temperance activist John B. Gough is the referent for Harper's Joe Gough. John Gough was the most well-known temperance activist who came out of the Washingtonian brand of temperance reform in the 1840s.

The Washingtonian movement began in Baltimore when six drinking men decided to take the pledge against consumption of alcoholic beverages and formed a society to support their pledges and promote temperance, the Washington Temperance Society of Baltimore. This group quickly became known as the Washingtonians and "gained one hundred thousand members by 1841 and half a million two years later" (Reynolds 26). While the original members were working-class whites, the Washingtonians appealed to mass audiences across class, gender, and religious categories. Prior to this movement, temperance societies and proponents formed largely among the elite businessmen, religious persons, and social reformers who were intent on sobering up workers, congregants and constituencies for greater industrial and economic output and social control. In short, these were disinterested reformers reforming others. By contrast, Washingtonians focused on self-reform. They were made up of reformed drinkers and non-drinkers, employers and employees, members of the working and middle class, and clergy and laymen. Washingtonians adopted the philosophical approach of experiential testimonial for moral suasion against intemperance. Presented in the forum of experience meetings, reformed drunkards related harrowing experiences during drinking binges with the rationalization that drinkers would identify with their reformed fellows' experiences – experiences that traditional temperance reformers lacked – and turn from their wicked ways. Ian R. Tyrrell concludes, "The success of the experience meetings and the insatiable demand for experienced speakers suggested that the strategy was both realistic and effective" (163). It was John Gough who became the movement's chief spokesperson.

Known as the "poet of the d.t.'s" and "an erstwhile actor, a gifted singer, a master of mimicry who once had cadged his drinks with barroom burlesque, Gough blended tearful testimony with oratorical thunder and dialect humor into a brew so potent that scores of listeners at every stop were driven to their feet and swept down the aisles to sign the pledge" (Crowley, 118). First published in 1845, Gough's *Autobiography* was the most widely read and significant temperance narrative, going through thirty-one reprintings by 1853.[11] While many white temperance advocates eschewed discussions of abolition and slavery and, in fact, largely excluded Blacks from white temperance organizations, Gough was a known antislavery sympathizer.[12] Although Douglass quotes him as declaring "Whatever may be the title, my lecture is always on Temperance" (*Life and Times* 374), Gough's 1870 revised and expanded *Autobiography and Personal Recollections* devotes several pages to his temperance experiences and activism in Virginia before emancipation and explicitly espouses an antislavery position. In Lynchburg, Virginia, Gough barely avoided being lynched because he was accused of being an abolitionist. He told the gathered mob, "I have been threatened with whipping, with being run into the river with vitriol in my face, and I have been called an abolitionist. Now just hear me when I say that there is no gentleman here, whose opinion is worth having, who would not despise me heartily if I were not. You all know I am, and you knew it when you sent for me; but you engaged me to speak on Temperance, and I came for that purpose" (216-217). Gough's antislavery sentiment notwithstanding, he and other temperance activists were strongly criticized by African American temperance advocates like Douglass for ignoring abolitionist issues and refusing to speak publicly on behalf of the cause. By 1870 the Washington Temperance Society was defunct and Gough had become involved in the larger mainstream temperance movement, in which he could now express his personal opinions on slavery without fearing the repercussions.

Although mainstream temperance organizations and activists were not generally regarded as champions of racial equality, Gough's narrative and Harper's use of his name suggest closer ties, or, at the very least, Harper's desire for closer ties between African American communities and temperance reform. If racial ambiguity normalized blackness, as Rosenthal contends, John Gough's whiteness destabilizes the assumption that Joe Gough is Black – and by extension, his family's race and that of the rest of the community – so that racial categorization becomes moot. Readers conscious of the John Gough-Joe Gough link are forced to interrogate their racial assumptions. When he is introduced to readers, Harper's Joe Gough corresponds to John Gough's self-assessment, "a disgrace – a living, walking disgrace" (*Autobiography and Personal Recollections* 127). Unlike John Gough, Joe is largely a silent character; his condition is revealed through the dialogue between his wife and other temperate characters. Without employing the "dark" temperance conventions found in earlier temperance writings, Harper depicts Joe's depths of degradation in his wife's voice.[13] Joe's bouts with delirium tremens and his ultimate abusive act of shearing his wife's hair for liquor money are related in a manner that is at once unsettling and pathetic. Mary Gough – perhaps not coincidentally also the name of John Gough's wife – who struggles to feed and shelter her children while maintaining fidelity to Joe, represents not just the voice of a drunkard's wife; rather, she is the voice of exploited working-class women. While silence does not feminize Joe, it does highlight Mary's gendered position.

Although she is physically weak and work-worn, Mary poses questions that challenge Belle Gordon spiritually, morally, and politically. In fact, Mary becomes the figure that challenges the reader's consciousness with respect to: economic disparities between working class and middle- and upper middle-class groups; spiritual faith in theory and practice; and legislative prohibition versus moral suasion. When Belle suggests soliciting work for Mary from Belle's friend Mrs. Roberts and asks if Mary knows her, Mary states, "I know her and have worked for her" (129). After Belle expounds upon Roberts' religious faith and righteousness, Mary relates her work experience with Roberts' exploitative employment practices. In response to Belle's disbelief and assertion that Roberts pays her dressmaker well, Mary observes that some wealthy people can be misers: "I have seen people save twenty-five or fifty cents in dealing with poor people, who would squander ten times as much on some luxury of the table or wardrobe. I often find that meanness and extravagance go hand in hand" (131). While Mary's position may have represented that of many readers who struggled to gain economic sustenance and stability in spite of unfair wages, her testimony regarding worker exploitation by self-righteous and pious members of the more affluent classes enlightens Belle Gordon and Harper's middle-class and upper-middle-class readers who mistake lavishness for generosity, piety for faith, and hypocrisy for justice and humanity. Having recently returned from her tour of the South in which she visited and resided with poor families living in homes without windows or the smallest fire for heat and light, Harper understood poverty in ways many middle-class Americans, particularly in the North, did not.[14] For someone like Harper who gave not just her time, voice and pen but also considerable amounts of money to the causes of social justice, temperance, suffrage, and education, raising the consciousness and eliciting the compassion of readers was only the first step in social reform. The next step was action, inside and outside the home; Harper's proactive stance encourages readers' active engagement in the temperance cause.

Sowing and Reaping demands action and Mary Gough's voice is a catalyst for political action. After describing the horrors of being a drunkard's wife, she asks, "Miss Gordon, do you think the men who make our laws ever stop to consider the misery, crime and destruction that flow out of the liquor traffic?" (132) With this question, Harper defines the limitations of moral suasion. Mary's question raises the issue of legislative prohibition, an issue once popular in the early 1850s Maine Law legislation but which witnessed a decline in popular support by 1856.[15] The mid-1870s once again saw growing support for prohibition, and Harper was, as always, at the forefront of the political discourse. Mrs. Gladstone, who speaks for middle-class women on suffrage and temperance, is the novel's most explicit proponent for prohibition. "I want women to possess power as well as influence," she declares to the younger women in her circle, "I want every Christian woman as she passes by a grogshop or liquor saloon, to feel that she has on her heart a burden of responsibility for its existence, I hold my dear that a nation as well as an individual should have a conscience, and on this liquor question there is room for woman's conscience not merely as a persuasive influence but as an enlightened and aggressive power" (161). If Mary's question discursively opens the door to legal prohibition, Mrs. Gladstone locates women decisively on the threshold of legislative reform. Again, moral suasion is not enough; Harper insists women's Christian and social responsibilities extend to agitation and political power. Significantly, Harper juxtaposes "influence" and "power" to highlight the near emptiness of "influence." Michel Foucault observes law as "the very form of power, and that power always [has] to be exercised in the form of law" (88). Thus Harper's juxtaposition serves the political end of demanding women's enfranchisement. As the archetypical drunkard's wife, Mary attempts to influence Joe but is powerless to change him or the laws that facilitate his intemperance. Her inquiry appeals to legislators for help without challenging the status quo of male dominance. Mrs. Gladstone, conversely, speaks of women "possess[ing] power" through suffrage and effecting radical social change in legal structures and political systems.

Perhaps, like other critics, Harper's use of Gough's name is a critique of his lack of explicit antislavery advocacy. However, given the contemporary moment in which *Sowing and Reaping* is written, there is the more likely possibility that Harper's histotextual action had meaning for contemporary temperance organizations' organizing and activism among African American communities. Organizing in African American communities in 1876 by the Women's Christian Temperance Union (WCTU) was minimal. Founded two years earlier, the WCTU became the largest women's organization in the late nineteenth century, engaging in vigorous organizing and campaigning on local, state and national levels. Northern local "unions" were racially integrated, while many white women in southern unions insisted on strict segregationist policies. In fact, rejecting subordination to white unions, African American women in North Carolina seceded from their state organization and formed a second statewide union "North Carolina No. 2" that was independently affiliated with the national WCTU. These women adamantly demanded racial equality, reflected in their name. "When one of the committee suggested that we call it State W.C.T.U. No. 2," their president, Mrs. M. J. O'Connell explained, "we gladly accepted the suggestion. We cautiously avoided using the word *colored*, for that would exclude any white sisters who might wish to work with us; in other words, we wanted it distinctly understood that we had no race prejudice, for we believe *all* men are *equal*."[16] Although it is unclear exactly when Harper became a WCTU member, by 1883 she held the position of Superintendent of Work among Colored People in the North. Her initial skepticism of WCTU racial acceptance is evident in her essay, "The Woman's Christian Temperance Union and the Colored Woman." She writes, "For years I knew very little of its proceedings, and was not sure that colored comradeship was very desirable" (205). Harper's laudatory praise for the WCTU in this essay does not negate her criticism of the national organization's failure to adequately support administrative and organizational efforts in African American communities. In her 1894 report to the National WCTU convention, Harper castigates the national organization for neglecting Black communities and WCTU members working in those communities: "Appropriation should be made to carry on the work among colored people, not as a matter of charity but as a means of self-defense for the country" ("Mrs. Harper's Report").[17] Connecting temperance organizing among African Americans to the issue of national security, Harper identifies this organizing as a act of "self-defense for the country" and calls on the WCTU to live up to its "do everything" policy of social reform through agitation, education and legislation. Implicit in this call is a demand for acknowledgement of the crucial significance of African Americans to the nation and the very same power Mrs. Gladstone seeks for women, regardless of race.

Ultimately, the indeterminable race of characters in *Sowing and Reaping* is central to the novel's social reformation message. Whether to normalize blackness or to offer historical referents whose race creates opportunities for social and organizational criticism, Harper's use of racial indeterminacy makes it possible for her to address not only social crises caused by intemperance but also women's need to gain power in order to remedy these crises. Thus, racial ambiguities in temperance narratives function as a means to address quandaries of racism and racial indifference in the mainstream temperance movement. Correspondingly, emphasizing temperance, manliness, and civility in Black males, in the manner of Delany and Douglass, challenged mainstream gender and race constructions. Because the consequences of drunkenness affected all American lives, African American activists could use the temperance cause and its rhetoric to argue for racial equality. Carla L. Peterson suggests that if the characters in *Sowing and Reaping* "are not racialized it is because temperance transcends racial categorization. Hence the characters are to be imagined not as either white or black but as both/and" (45). While not disputing the merit of Peterson's suggestion, I posit that temperance literature's transcendence of race facilitated claims for equality and justice. Because intemperance was indiscriminate, the very thing that affected everyone was used to dispute racial inequality. Black activists engaged temperance rhetoric to re-articulate racial and gender constructs, countering racial and gender prejudice and demonstrating African Americans and women's virtue, honor, and intelligence.

The history of the temperance movement and its relationship to Black communities demonstrates African Americans had cause to be uncomfortable with and critical of organized mainstream anti-drink movements. The always already presence of racial inequality in America forced African Americans to recognize that combating the ill-effects of strong drink required they establish temperance projects and organizations devoted to a complex consciousness of social reform and justice; they understood that they had to work race and gender in order to work temperance.

I am indebted to the editors, Hanna Wallinger and John Gruesser, for their cogent comments and suggestions on earlier drafts of this essay. This work is much improved because of their efforts. Some parts of this essay were published in my article "Sowing Seeds in an Untilled Field: Temperance and Race, Indeterminacy and Recovery in

Frances E. W. Harper's *Sowing and Reaping*" in *Legacy: A Journal of American Women Writers* 24 (2007): 207-24.

[1] For a thorough discussion of early African American temperance activism see Donald Yacovone.

[2] Other temperance illustrations were not above exploiting racial stereotypes and caricatures. *The Drunkard's Reform* featured a set of six pictorial vignettes depicting the sufferings and hardships of a drunkard's family and his eventual redemption resulting in the family's prosperity. Tracts like *The Drunkard's Reform* appropriated and contributed to the prevailing racial discourses with saloon depictions of Black male dandies and kerchief-headed guzzling Black females. See Jimerson 30-31.

[3] As quoted in Hamilton 259.

[4] The society's preamble and constitution are published as part of the *Proceedings* of the Second Annual Meeting of the Temperance Society of the Coloured People of the City of Pittsburgh and Vicinity. This publication also includes the standing rules and annual report. See Proceedings.

[5] Although the society's published proceedings list the recording secretary as "M. R. Delaney," clearly this is the same Martin R. Delany given documented evidence of his residence in Pittsburgh from 1831 to at least 1847 and his association with the minister Lewis Woodson who is listed in the proceedings as the corresponding secretary. See Ellison and Metcalf 155.

[6] Although the Smithsonian Institute National Portrait Gallery is uncertain about the date of this image, Maurice O. Wallace concludes that the portrait only could have been made after Delany's officer's commission was issued in February 1865 and before the appearance of the portrait in *The Weekly Anglo African* a few weeks later. See Wallace 73.

[7] The lack of racial identifying markers among the characters differentiates "The Two Offers" from other antebellum texts by African Americans.

[8] The first Black order of Freemasons, African Lodge No. 459, received its charter in 1784 from a fellow lodge in England "after nine fruitless years of petitioning white American lodges from all across the colonies" (Wallace 55).

[9] Grand Lodges were comprised of a group of local or state lodges in a certain region. "Grand Lodges enjoyed enormous authority in their jurisdictions," asserts David M. Fahey, "whether the geographical area was a state or a province or a historic nation such as England or an independent country" (17).

[10] I am not arguing here that race does not matter. Adopting a color-blind approach naively disregards history, culture and politics and makes groups defined and situated by race invisible. However, Harper's nineteenth-century radical integrationist politics viewed racial difference from the standpoint of oppression, what Lani Guiner calls the "fears of difference" (4). This standpoint can be equally limiting. Guinier and Gerald Torres maintain, as opposed to the invisibility color-blindness engenders, race-consciousness in which one is cognizant of oppression and group solidarity offers empowerment through resistance to domination and fosters democratic politics.

[11] Coincidentally, 1845 marks the year of the first publication of both Gough's *An Autobiography* and Frederick Douglass' *Narrative of the Life of Frederick Douglass, An American Slave.* Calling Gough's narrative the classic text of the movement, John

W. Crowley notes this coincidence and asks, "What, if anything, do these texts reveal about the interrelationship of temperance and abolition?" (116). Crowley suggests temperance narrative accounts of "slaves to the bottle seem [...] to have had a subtle bearing on the representation of bondage by Douglass and, it may well be, by other writers of slave narratives" (129).

[12] White intolerance for African American temperance activism was so strident that in 1842 a parade of Black temperance society members was attacked and many Black homes and churches burned in a three-day assault by Irish Americans in Philadelphia. David Roediger points out that although major Irish nationalists and temperance organizers in Ireland supported and petitioned for freedom and racial equality, Irish Americans summarily rejected this petition and continually committed violence against Blacks (134-136).

[13] David S. Reynolds categorizes temperance discourse in four groups: conventional, dark, ironic, and transcendental. Dark temperance sensationalized drunken debauchery, hallucinations caused by delirium tremens, and violence to the point of engendering readers' titillation. Rosenthal suggests Harper avoids the dark temperance form through narrative distance and didacticism. See Reynolds 22-28 and Rosenthal 158-159.

[14] In her letters from the South published in William Still's *The Underground Rail Road*, Harper details many instances of planters' exploitation of ex-slaves. She documents racial violence and voter intimidation as well as living conditions that were little better than those experienced during slavery. She witnessed workers whose contracts with employers were ignored; one was paid fifteen bushels of corn for two years' labor. See Still 768-773.

[15] Dubbed the "Maine Law" because it was first enacted in Maine in 1851, state laws against the sale and consumption of alcohol gained widespread support by 1855. Ian Tyrrell points out that middle-class temperance reformers supported prohibition before 1851, however, not until the failure of licensing laws did prohibition gain mass support. Maine Laws fell out of favor because enforcement proved to be costly without sufficient political and civic infrastructures. See Tyrrell 252-315.

[16] This situation was not unique to North Carolina. Alabama and Georgia also had two state organizations, the second of which admitted both African American and white members. Harper argues these situations offer the WCTU "one of the grandest opportunities that God ever pressed into the hands of the womanhood of any country." See "The Woman's Christian Temperance Union and the Colored Woman" 206. For more of O'Connell's remarks, see O'Connell "North Carolina No.2."

[17] Although she was no longer a national superintendent, Harper continued to organize in northern African American communities. Her report to the national convention was published in the *New Haven Register*. See "Mrs. Harper's Report."

Works Cited

Andrews, William. Introduction. Andrews 7-21.

—, ed. *Three Classic African American Novels*. New York: Mentor, 1990.

Bederman, Gail. *Manliness and Civilization: A Cultural History of Gender and Race in the United States, 1880-1917*. Chicago: U of Chicago P, 1995.

Crowley, John W. "Slaves to the Bottle: Gough's *Autobiography* and Douglass' *Narrative*." Reynolds and Rosenthal 115-35.

Delany, Martin. *Blake, or the Huts of America*. 1859. Boston: Beacon, 1970.

Douglass, Frederick. "The Heroic Slave." 1853. Andrews 23-69.

—. *Life and Times of Frederick Douglass*. 1892. New York: Macmillan, 1962.

Ellison, Curtis W., and E. W. Metcalf, Jr. *William Wells Brown and Martin R. Delany: A Reference Guide*. Boston: Hall, 1978.

Fahey, David M. *Temperance and Racism: John Bull, Johnny Reb, and the Good Templars*. Lexington: U of Kentucky P, 1996.

Foner, Philip S. *Frederick Douglass: Selected Speeches and Writings*. Chicago: Lawrence, 1999.

Foreman, P. Gabrielle. "'Reading Aright': White Slavery, Black Referents and the Strategy of Histotextuality in *Iola Leroy*." *Yale Journal of Criticism* 10.2 (1997): 327-54.

Foster, Frances Smith. Introduction. *A Brighter Coming Day: A Frances Ellen Watkins Harper Reader*. By Frances E. W. Harper. New York: Feminist, 1990. 3-40.

Foucault, Michel. *The History of Sexuality: Volume I: An Introduction*. New York: Vintage, 1990.

Gilroy, Paul. *The Black Atlantic: Modernity and Double Consciousness*. Cambridge: Harvard UP, 1993.

Gough, John B. *Autobiography and Personal Recollections of John B. Gough, with Twenty-Six Years' Experience as a Public Speaker*. Springfield: Bill, 1870.

Guinier, Lani and Gerald Torres. *The Miner's Canary: Enlisting Race, Resisting Power, Transforming Democracy*. Cambridge: Harvard UP, 2002.

Hamilton, Cynthia S. "*Dred*: Intemperate Slavery." *Journal of American Studies*. 34 (2000). 257-77.

Harper, Frances E. W. *Sowing and Reaping, A Temperance Story*. 1876-77. *Minnie's Sacrifice, Sowing and Reaping, Trial and Triumph: Three Re-*

discovered Novels by Frances E. W. Harper. Ed. Frances Smith Foster. Boston: Beacon, 1994.

—. "The Drunkard's Child." *A Brighter Coming Day: A Frances Ellen Watkins Harper Reader*. Ed. Frances Smith Foster. New York: Feminist, 1990. 63-64.

—. "The Woman's Christian Temperance Union and the Colored Woman." 1888. *Discarded Legacy: Politics and Poetics of Frances E.W. Harper*. Ed. Melba Joyce Boyd. Detroit: Wayne State UP, 1994. 203-07.

Jimerson, Randall C., Francis X. Blouin, and Charles A. Isetts. *Guide to the Microfilm Edition of Temperance and Prohibition Papers*. Ann Arbor: U of Michigan P, 1977.

Levine, Robert S. "Disturbing Boundaries: Temperance, Black Elevation, and Violence in Frank J. Webb's *The Garies and Their Friends*." *Prospects: An Annual Journal of American Cultural Studies* 19 (1994): 349-73.

Martin Robison Delany. National Portrait Gallery, Smithsonian Institution, Washington, D. C.

"Mrs. Harper's Report." *New Haven Register*. 21 November 1894. *African Americans and the Women's Christian Temperance Union*. 12 December 2006 <http://www.alexanderstreet6.com/WASM/wasmrestricted/wctu2/doc10.htm>.

O'Connell, M. J. "North Carolina No. 2." *African Americans and the Women's Christian Temperance Union*. 13 December 2006 <http://www.alexanderstreet6.com/WASM/wasmrestricted/wctu2/doc8.htm>.

Peterson, Carla L. "Frances Harper, Charlotte Forten, and African American Literary Reconstruction." *Challenging Boundaries: Gender and Periodization*. Ed. Joyce W. Warren and Margaret Dickie. Athens: U of Georgia P, 2000. 39-61.

Proceedings of the Second Annual Meeting of the Temperance Society of the Coloured People of the City of Pittsburgh and Vicinity. Pittsburgh: Anderson, 1837.

Reynolds, David S. "Black Cats and Delirium Tremens: Temperance and the American Renaissance." Reynolds and Rosenthal 22-59.

Reynolds, David S., and Debra J. Rosenthal. *The Serpent in the Cup: Temperance in American Literature*. Amherst: U of Massachusetts P, 1997.

Roediger, David R. *The Wages of Whiteness: Race and the Making of the American Working Class*. London: Verso, 1991.

Rosenthal, Debra J. "Deracialized Discourse: Temperance and Racial Ambiguity in Harper's 'The Two Offers' and *Sowing and Reaping*." Reynolds and Rosenthal 153-64.

Said, Edward. *Beginnings: Intention and Method.* New York: Columbia UP, 1985.

Sinclair, Andrew. *Prohibition: The Era of Excess*. Boston: Little, 1962.

—. *Going into Captivity*. Sinclair 58.

Sorisio, Carolyn. *Fleshing Out America: Race, Gender, and the Politics of the Body in American Literature, 1833-1879*. Athens: U of Georgia P, 2002.

Still, William. *The Underground Rail Road.* 1872. New York: Arno, 1968.

Thompson, Harold Paul. *Race, Temperance, and Prohibition in the Postbellum South: Black Atlanta, 1865-1890.* Diss. Emory University, 2005. *Dissertations & Theses: Full Text*. ProQuest. University of Alabama Libraries, Tuscaloosa, AL. 21 May 2008 <http://www.proquest.com/>.

Tyrrell, Ian R. *Sobering Up: From Temperance to Prohibition in Antebellum America, 1800-1860*. Westport: Greenwood, 1979.

Wallace, Maurice O. *Constructing the Black Masculine: Identity and Ideality in African American Men's Literature and Culture, 1775-1995*. Durham: Duke UP, 2002.

"Women's Temperance Meeting." *New York Weekly Tribune*. 12 Feb. 1853. 11 November 2006 <http://www.artstor.org/artstor/ViewImages?id=4iFLcDwwJloLyk%2Bez9%2BQA%3D%3D&userId=hDRAfDw%3D&cid=gDND>.

Yacovone, Donald. "The Transformation of the Black Temperance Movement, 1827-1854: An Interpretation." *Journal of the Early Republic* 9 (1988): 281-97.

Yarborough, Richard. "Race, Violence, and Manhood: The Masculine Ideal in Frederick Douglass's 'The Heroic Slave.'" *Frederick Douglass: New Literary and Historical Essays*. Ed. Eric J. Sundquist. New York: Cambridge UP, 1990. 166-188.

"'Course I Knows Dem Feet!": Minstrelsy and Subversion in Pauline E. Hopkins's *Slaves' Escape; or the Underground Railroad*

Jessica Metzler

Despite Pauline E. Hopkins's notable influence as a playwright, singer, editor, journalist, activist, and novelist, the volume of scholarship on her life and work remains relatively small, even given the steady increase in Hopkins scholarship over the past twenty years. Ann Allen Shockley's 1972 essay, "Pauline Elizabeth Hopkins: A Biographical Excursion Into Obscurity," first brought notice to Hopkins's marginality, yet critical attention to her work remained sparse until 1988 when the Schomburg Library of Nineteenth-Century Black Women Writers republished an edition of her most widely-known novel, *Contending Forces* (1900) and her serialized works, originally published in the *Colored American Magazine* between 1901 and 1903, in the *Magazine Novels*, bringing a new visibility to Hopkins's position as a long-neglected turn-of-the-century African American woman novelist. More recently, *The Unruly Voice: Rediscovering Pauline Elizabeth Hopkins*, a 1996 collection of critical essays edited by John Cullen Gruesser, and Hanna Wallinger's 2005 volume, *Pauline E. Hopkins: A Literary Biography*, have shed further light upon Hopkins's life and work, while Ira Dworkin's 2007 anthology of Hopkins's nonfiction work, *Daughter of the Revolution: The Major Nonfiction Works of Pauline E. Hopkins*, offers access to many of her hard-to-find essays, articles, and personal correspondence from her tenure as an editor and contributor to the *Colored American Magazine*. This recent critical attention has examined much of Hopkins's work, yet her turn as a dramatist remains underexplored.

Although Hopkins is acknowledged as the first black American woman playwright, scholars of nineteenth-century musical theater usually only note Hopkins's plays in reference to the high profile black theater stars who appeared in them, such as Sam Lucas and the Hyers Sisters (Peterson 125). Similarly, literary scholars focus nearly exclusively on Hopkins's novels with the notable exception of Martha Patterson's essay "Remaking the Minstrel: Pauline Hopkins's *Peculiar Sam* and the Post-Reconstruction Black Subject." At first glance, it is not difficult to imagine why little critical commentary about Hopkins's 1879 musical drama, *Slaves' Escape; or, the Underground Railroad*, exists or why the manuscript languishes unpublished in the archives of Fisk University where Hopkins's papers reside. *Slaves' Escape* is, after all, a play rife with minstrel stereotypes easily dismissed as juvenilia. Given the current visibility of and interest in Hopkins's fiction, nonfiction, and biography, why unearth this buried manuscript that seemingly traffics in racist tropes? This essay argues that the significance of *Slaves' Escape* as a work rests in the multiple sites of transition it evinces in terms of both its historical context and Hopkins's corpus. A reconstruction of the play's performance history makes the transitional, conflicted nature of Hopkins's nineteenth-century audience visible – an audience struggling with class conflict and changing cultural and racial ideologies. The play's narrative representations of blackness as well as its staging and costuming situate the work within a transitional moment in Hopkins's career, while the play's subversive approach to racial stereotypes provides glimpses of Hopkins's future activist work both as an editor of the *Colored American Magazine* and as a fiction writer devoted to the task of racial uplift. Finally, *Slaves' Escape* serves as a material link between nineteenth-century blackface performance (and the "blacks in blackface" phenomenon it spawned near the turn of the century) and the emergence of politically progressive early twentieth-century black musical theater by Bob Cole, J. Rosamond Johnson, James Weldon Johnson, and Will Marion Cook, artists whose work was explicitly concerned with issues of racial representation. As the product of a specific moment in African American musical theater history, *Slaves' Escape* works both within and against a blackface tradition. At its core, the play reflects the volatile negotiations of racial difference occurring within a nineteenth-century audience.

Recent scholarly work that seeks to reexamine the history of blackface performance's roots allows for a better understanding of the relationship between Hopkins's play, blackface minstrelsy, and nineteenth-century audiences. Eric Lott's influential discussion of blackface minstrelsy in *Love and Theft: Blackface Minstrelsy and the American Working Class* greatly informs this reading of Hopkins's work. Lott's characterization of minstrelsy as a contested cultural site of racial interaction, negotiation, and appropriation predicated upon simultaneous feelings of desire and revulsion toward the other helps to identify the subversive elements of Hopkins's work. Similarly, W.T. Lhamon's reading of the origins of blackface performance as a mode of expressing "mixed feelings of identification and fascination" among working-class audiences and his formulation of the "blackface lore cycle" as a continually moving cultural force in which representations of blackness become markers of cultural exchange in *Raising Cain: Blackface Performance from Jim Crow to Hip Hop* offers a new way of critically engaging Hopkins's oft-neglected text (1988). I analyze *Slaves' Escape* not in spite of the various minstrel devices it employs, but rather because of the specific, frequently subversive, cultural work these depictions do. From the hardened racism of blackface minstrelsy in the 1850s came the formation of black minstrel troupes after the Civil War, troupes that still enacted the racist stereotypes created by their white predecessors. *Slaves' Escape* emerged from this legacy in 1879, during the height of "colored minstrel" popularity, and after white minstrelsy had begun to veer towards a vaudevillian character, as historian Robert Toll describes in his chronology of early nineteenth-century minstrel shows in the seminal 1974 work, *Blacking Up: The Minstrel Show in Nineteenth-Century America* (195-203). I examine *Slaves' Escape*'s liminal position within its specific historical and cultural context as a way of shedding light on this period of Hopkins's work and demonstrating the need for further critical attention to it.

Unmistakably linked to its minstrel roots in its use of heavy dialect and stereotypical characterizations, *Slaves' Escape* documents the travels and travails of a group of slaves during their "flight to freedom" via the Underground Railroad. The action begins when Virginia (Jinny) faces a forced marriage to Jim, the cruel overseer. Seeking to avoid the match, Jinny and Sam, her sweetheart, decide to run away. Sam's mother, Mammy, and sister, Juno, join their flight to Canada with Jim in close pursuit. During their journey, the group finds aid through the help of an abolitionist figure, Quaker John, and adds Uncle Caesar, an old friend of Mammy's, to their number at a stop along the way. After a series of captures, near captures, and escapes, they finally find freedom through a dramatic river crossing into Canada that is clearly reminiscent of the nineteenth-century's most famous river crossing – Eliza's escape across the icy Ohio River in Harriet Beecher Stowe's *Uncle Tom's Cabin* (1852). While two known versions of Hopkins's play were performed and are still extant (an unpublished three-act version entitled *Slaves' Escape; or, the Underground Railroad* and a published four-act version, *Peculiar Sam; or, the Underground Railroad*), I have chosen to work with *Slaves' Escape*, the unpublished version, rather than with the different and more widely available *Peculiar Sam*, which was published in 1991 in *The Roots of African American Drama*, an anthology edited by Leo Hamalian and James V. Hatch. I do so in light of the fact that *Slaves' Escape* was more extensively publicized, and was seen by larger Boston summer theater audiences during its run than *Peculiar Sam*'s smaller Midwestern tour. Piecing together information from various sources, including newspaper advertisements and the reviews and programs found in Pauline E. Hopkins's scrapbook, I am able to show the significant instances when the unpublished *Slaves' Escape* hit the boards and provide a comprehensive performance history of the play (see table 1). Using this reconstructed history, I analyze the importance of Hopkins's play within its specific cultural context and examine the effect of venue changes on the performance.

The original handwritten manuscripts of both scripts reside in the Pauline E. Hopkins papers in Fisk University Library's Special Collections, in Nashville, Tennessee. The papers house a typed manuscript of *Peculiar Sam* as well. Some confusion surrounds the production history of the play as both versions were performed, yet each of the manuscripts bears the date 1879. The differences between the typed and handwritten copies of *Peculiar Sam* are negligible and the typescript version was published as *Peculiar*

Sam, or the Underground Railroad "a musical drama in four acts" in Hamalian and Hatch's 1991 volume. Three years later, in 1994, Eileen Southern published a reproduction of *Peculiar Sam*'s handwritten manuscript in *African American Theater*, a volume in a series on Nineteenth-Century American Musical Theater. In her introduction to the volume, which also includes the script and score for the Hyers Sisters production *Out of Bondage* (1876), Southern states that the handwritten *Peculiar Sam* script constitutes the original version performed by Sprague's Underground Railroad Company from March 1879 until *Slaves' Escape* debuted on the East Coast on 8 December 1879: "The Hopkins play that made its East Coast premiere [...] differed considerably from the original copyrighted version. The title had been changed to *The Slaves' Escape, or, the Underground Railroad*, the four acts compressed into three, the plot altered in some details, and two characters added" (xxiv). This different three-act version Southern describes is the unpublished manuscript considered in this essay (*Slaves' Escape* hereafter). Southern regards the four-act published version (*Peculiar Sam*) as the original, which reaffirms Shockley's assertion that Hopkins "began her writing pursuits as a playwright, composing a four-act musical drama, *Peculiar Sam; or, the Underground Railroad* [...]. Later modified to three acts, it was presented as *Slaves' Escape; or the Underground Railroad* at the Oakland Garden by the Hopkins Colored Troubadours" (289). Yet Southern's assertion contradicts Hatch and Hamalian's claim in their headnote to *Peculiar Sam* that the published version constitutes a revision of the three-act original, *Slaves' Escape*: "Possibly to distinguish the title from Brown's [William Wells Brown's play *The Escape*], Hopkins in her revision called the play *Peculiar Sam*" (97). Archival evidence in the form of newspaper clippings and programs from Hopkins's scrapbook supports Southern's argument that the Z.W. Sprague company performed the published four-act version, *Peculiar Sam*, in a 1879 Midwestern tour, yet this same evidence also shows that *Slaves' Escape*, the unpublished three-act version, was the play seen by much larger audiences in Boston from 1879-1881 and received more publicity than the *Peculiar Sam* tour. The differences in the script and staging between *Peculiar Sam* and its shortened revision, *Slaves' Escape*, are substantial. Structurally, the addition of an opening scene and deletion of the fourth act works to alter the tone of the play from jovial to somber, while the addition of two characters and changes in characterization and dialogue deliver pointed ethical and political messages in the drama's revised representation of religion and gender. Other important changes appear to be venue-related, including the addition of an afterpiece. I focus on *Slaves' Escape*'s six-day 5-10 July 1880 run at Boston's Oakland Garden throughout this essay, in order to better facilitate a discussion of venue and audience.

The opening scene of *Slaves' Escape* that viewers encountered at the Oakland Garden on 5 July 1880 was a large-scale plantation spectacle involving a "mansion in distance, set cotton bushes with cotton, slaves picking, immediately in front [...] seated with cotton in baskets" according to stage directions.[1] The chorus' opening song began the show, at the close of which the overseer "saunters on R speaks roughly, cracks whip, slaves work diligently, one groans as if struck." This opening plantation scene mirrors the elaborate "scenic sets" used by early minstrel companies (Wittke 143), yet Hopkins replaces the traditional representations of slaves as happy with their lot with depictions of the cruelties of slavery and the overseer immediately takes on a menacing character. The effect of the addition of this carefully crafted opening scene, complete with five solemn songs and no dialogue, has a twofold effect: the play initially seems closer to a standard minstrel show performance in its use of a large scenic set depicting "old time plantation life," yet this similarity is tempered by creating a somber tone quite unlike the comic dancing that propels the opening scene of *Peculiar Sam. Slaves' Escape* begins with a chorus singing "Daniel," presumably the common spiritual titled "Didn't my Lord deliver Daniel" about the Lord's salvation as a gift to the oppressed, against the background sound of the overseer's whip.[2] Although the curtain on *Peculiar Sam* may also have parted to an offstage chorus' rendition of "Daniel," the spirited jig that opens the first scene of this version surely undermines whatever dramatic effect the spiritual might have had. The initial portrait of the overseer who "speaks roughly" and "cracks [his] whip" foregrounds Jim's cruel presence in *Slaves' Escape*. This script portrays the overseer as an inhumane mulatto who becomes emblematic of white authority and control. The jarring contrast between the introduction of a common minstrel device – the plantation set – and an emphasis on slaves who seem the very antithesis of minstrelsy's jolly caricatures gives us an initial insight into the subversive nature of Hopkins's play. *Slaves' Escape* employs and simultaneously undermines minstrel show tropes that would have been easily recognizable as such to a nineteenth-century audience, given the form's domination of the popular stage for the better part of the century.

Beyond the addition of this opening scene, *Slaves' Escape* further revises *Peculiar Sam* by omitting its fourth act, which constitutes a significant structural recentering of the narrative. *Peculiar Sam*'s fourth act, set in Canada after Reconstruction, shows Mammy and Caesar as an elderly married couple nostalgic for "massa" and the old plantation, while Sam, who has lost his thick minstrel dialect, appears as a recently elected Congressman. The scene's action occurs when overseer Jim, now a Massachusetts lawyer, arrives to "be frien's 'long wif you" and releases Virginia from their sham wedding vows so she can marry Sam (122). In a stark contrast, *Slaves' Escape* ends with a dramatic tableau of all the characters escaping on a boat across the river to freedom while Quaker John holds Jim at bay with a pistol. The deletion of this fourth act also distances the play from the Hyers Sisters' production of *Out of Bondage*, which has a similar plot that also ends with the younger characters achieving affluence in the North during Reconstruction, but was a skeleton play designed to showcase the talents of its cast through music and dance numbers. Although the 1880 Boston productions of *Slaves' Escape* maintained their connection to black minstrel troupes and musicals through performances by Sam Lucas, a noted black minstrel performer, and the Hyers Sisters, the removal of the fourth act asserts the primacy of narrative over spectacle and stresses a politically progressive message in diverting the show's focus from slapstick comedy to melodramatic plot twists. Sam's announcement at the end of *Peculiar Sam* as he dances to a plantation chorus of "Golden Slippers," "Ladies and gentlemen, I hope you will excuse me for laying aside the dignity of an elected M.C., and allow me to appear before you once more as peculiar Sam of the old underground railroad," forms a sharp contrast with the dramatic tableau that ends *Slaves' Escape* (123). The removal of the fourth act changes the tone and, indeed, the very message of the play. The jovial ending of *Peculiar Sam* disavows several of the political undercurrents that *Slaves' Escape* recuperates in its revision. Sam adopts an educated "whiteness" in the fourth act of *Peculiar Sam* so different from his character as a slave in the first three acts that he must lay aside the "dignity" of this persona in order to behave in what is by comparison an embarrassing spectacle. The deletion of the fourth act eliminates the problematic privileging of this performance of "whiteness." Thus, while the fourth act of *Peculiar Sam* serves as an interesting basis for a discussion of historical Reconstruction portrayals, evidence suggests Boston theatergoers never saw it.[3]

Slaves' Escape's introduction of the Quaker John character places the show at an even further remove from *Out of Bondage* by tackling serious questions of religious faith, evoking thoughts of somber performances of *Uncle Tom's Cabin* rather than comic minstrel acts or the popular "Tom Shows" of the time that included various minstrel devices and bore little resemblance to Stowe's drama. Quaker John's character, an "educated negro," becomes emblematic of the black Christianity to which Mammy and Jinny adhere with unblinking faith, a religion that reaffirms the intrinsic value of humanity and promises deliverance from oppression. *Slaves' Escape* juxtaposes Mammy and Jinny's spiritual faith with Juno's symbolic representation of paganism, and Quaker John's exaggerated speech patterns emphasize this disjuncture. In referring to Jim and Sam as "James" and "Samuel," Quaker John underscores the biblical origins of their names while simultaneously bringing the non-Christian origins of Juno's name into sharp relief. As the goddess of marriage and family and a protector of women in Roman mythology, Juno becomes the symbolic guardian of female sexuality who calls into question the legitimacy of Jinny and Jim's marriage: "only thing they done in the worl' was, Marse he say, 'Jim does you want to marry Jinny?' Jim he say yas, course Jim say yas. Marse he say, 'Jinny you want to marry Jim?' Jinny her say 'no' course Jinny say no, what Jinny want igernunt old Jim. Marse say, 'Well, you is man an' wife, and Lor' hab mussy on you soul.' Dat no kin' ob wedding." Juno's recollection in this passage correlates forced marriage ("Dat no kin' ob wedding") with death by framing the Master's pronouncement in the language of a death sentence – may the lord have mercy on your soul. This connection between death and forced marriage, and by extension rape, is one part of Juno's depiction of miscegenation as the result of sexual victimization of black female slaves by white slave owners. The most striking example of Juno's stance on miscegenation occurs in her recognition of the Master's gun in Sam's hands in act two as she exclaims, "Why I know all 'bout shootin' dat gun. I used to go up into Missee room, and shoot dat ol' gun at de bedstead, an' Marse he wonder how dat bedstead come full o' holes." While comic, these lines reveal Juno's anger toward the sexuality of "Marse" and "Missee," a serious subject for this "Topsy-like" character, as she was billed. In this respect, the play anticipates both Hopkins's later focus on questions of "mixed blood" in many of her novels, and her use of symbolic or mythological names, particularly in her *Contending Forces* character Sappho Clark.[4]

Juno's symbolic paganism also points to the racism inherent in white Christianity. It is Juno who co-opts the role of preacher in a camp meeting scene (a scene that appears only in *Slaves' Escape*, and not *Peculiar Sam*), and who later voices her discontentment with white Christianity:

> JUNO. Dar aint no use tryin' to be like white folks, we's just made fer nuthin' but igerrant slabes, an' I don't b'lieve God wants nuthin' to do wit us no how.
> MAMMY. You Juno, hish, fer we's all His chillren, an He lubs us all jes de same.
> JUNO. But Mammy dey say dat angels am all white! How's I gwine to be a angel mammy? I don't believe God wants eny black angels, 'deed I don't!
> MAMMY. Why chile, we's all to be washed in a powerful riber, an' arter dat, we'll all be white.
> JUNO. Golly! Den I wants to be washed now, so's to be sure.

Again, humor contains a deeply subversive racial ideology that questioned postbellum white epistemology. Mammy's assertion that physical blackness can be washed off – that race is a completely external or socially constructed attribute – expresses a belief that directly contradicted racist ideas of inherent black inferiority at the time, even as it seems to advocate assimilation as the key to salvation. Indeed, the river Mammy mentions symbolically corresponds to the river the party crosses at the end of the play when they find freedom and race becomes a non-issue in the play's vision of Canada as a utopia.

Peculiar Sam dampens the subversive aspects of Juno's character, as its fourth act undermines Juno's powerful stance on black female sexual victimization. The action in *Peculiar Sam*'s fourth act, as previously noted, revolves around Jim's return to free Jinny from their wedding vows, "Chile, I kno's dat warnt no weddin', de law wouldn't 'low it nohow," Jim says to a relieved Jinny (122). The action in this act privileges white legal authority, still represented by Jim's overseer character turned lawyer who declares their marriage invalid under the law, over Juno's intuitive and common sense observation from the beginning that "Dat no kin' ob wedding." In *Peculiar Sam*, Jinny abides by these illegal vows, refusing to marry Sam while she still believes herself married to Jim, until Jim, who remarries and has children, takes it upon himself to release her. Act IV further weakens Juno's position as a guardian of black female sexuality as she puts down the gun she had been pointing at Jim (the same symbol of a violent male sexuality she once used to penetrate the Master's bed frame) and laughs when Jim says he has merely come to be friends with them. In this act, Juno's goddess-like potency becomes subjugated to white authority and the law. By excising the fourth act, Hopkins ensured attention to the serious issues raised by Juno's comic character. This revision anticipates both Hopkins's later editorial work with the *Colored American Magazine* and the concerns of her fiction by highlighting the role of religion in racial persecution, and refuting common nineteenth-century portrayals of black women as lascivious and sexually indiscriminate. This concern with the representation of black female sexuality would become prominent in her novels and in fiction by later generations of black women writers.

Thus *Slaves' Escape* differed significantly from *Peculiar Sam* in its structure and narrative content when the show played its six-day run at Oakland Garden. Oakland Garden was a popular outdoor venue for the summer theater of the time; this open-air setting allowed productions to make use of a large lawn, the natural foliage of the garden and a lake, while a pavilion provided a smaller stage. Considered a "minor venue" in Boston theater history, what we know of the space available to performers and audiences comes primarily from reviews of shows produced there. Several years after *Slaves' Escape* appeared, Sam Lucas, who had become the first black performer to play the role of Uncle Tom in an 1878 production of *Uncle Tom's Cabin*, reprised his role at Oakland Garden productions in 1886 and 1888 according to Boston newspaper reviews (Williams 19). A review of a 9 August 1886 show reads:

> The performance of "Uncle Tom's Cabin" at Oakland Garden last evening was a very successful one and was largely attended. It was produced on the lawn and lake, and the blending of the artificial with the natural was so perfect as to represent a realistic picture such as could not be produced on the stage. In the background were the trees of the garden, festooned with Southern moss, forming a most natural setting to Uncle Tom's cabin, the slaves' quarters and St. Clair's mansion. To the left of the picture the lake was utilized to represent the river, and the floating ice on which Eliza, with her child, escapes in safety to the land of freedom, was quite effective.[5]

This plantation-like setting facilitated the highly publicized afterpiece to *Slaves' Escape* some years before. A 5 July 1880 *Boston Globe* advertisement enticed spectators to view the "COTTON PLANTATION SCENE on the Lawn [...] and the Entire Company in a Grand PLANTATION FESTIVAL," followed by a "working representation of the boats ROBT. E. LEE and the NATCHEZ on the MISSISSIPPI RIVER, concluding with the LARGEST DISPLAY OF FIREWORKS ever presented." Such a spectacle dwarfed even the grand opening scene of the production. This "famed plantation scene" on the lawn was not unique to the production of *Slaves' Escape*, nor does it appear in Hopkins's script, but was a regular occurrence at Oakland Garden; a similarly advertised event usually followed minstrel performances at the venue and continued in subsequent seasons.[6]

In the month preceding the debut of *Slaves' Escape*, "Haverly's Colored Carnival" (also billed as "Haverly's Genuine Colored Minstrels" or as a "Carnival of Negro Minstrelsy") performed at Oakland Garden with Sam Lucas and Billy Kersands – another enormously popular black minstrel performer. A June 21st *Boston Globe* advertisement promised, "After the performance in the Pavilion will be presented on the lawn a realistic COTTON PLANTATION [...] introducing the entire Company." On 3 July, two days before the premiere of *Slaves' Escape*, the Corinne Opera Company advertised "The Great Plantation Scene on the Lawn, introducing the entire Company, including the Hyers Sisters Combination and Sam Lucas" in the *Globe*. In August of that summer when Haverly's Genuine Colored Minstrels again played Oakland Garden, ads for "The Great Plantation Scene on the Lawn, at 10:15, with Sam Lucas In his Great Character of Uncle Pete" appeared.[7] The "Cotton Plantation Scene" thus operated firmly within minstrel show traditions as a grand finale that called upon the talents of the entire company, yet as a venue-specific addition it further highlights *Slaves' Escape*'s status as a show produced squarely between blackface minstrel shows starring Sam Lucas and serious productions of *Uncle Tom's Cabin* on the same stage. Lucas's attempts to break out of blackface and into serious dramatic performances, which his roles in *Slaves' Escape* and productions of *Uncle Tom's Cabin* were meant to aid, would continue with appearances in Bob Cole and Billy Johnson's *A Trip to Coontown* (1897) (Riis, *Just Before Jazz* 77). *Slaves' Escape*, like its star performer, drew from blackface traditions while simultaneously subverting them. The work proceeded from minstrel shows, but also anticipated Cole's work, which would signal a definite divide between minstrelsy and the black musical theater of the early twentieth century.

The advertising similarities between "Haverly's Colored Carnival" and *Slaves' Escape*, when combined with the billed appearance of famous black minstrel stars Sam Lucas in the title role and the Hyers Sisters Combination as accompaniment, allows us to see why audiences attending a performance of Hopkins's play might well have expected to witness a formulaic "colored minstrel" production. Instead, they witnessed a cleverly cloaked protest drama. These Oakland Garden audiences defied homogeneity: blacks and whites, locals and tourists, the upper class Boston elite and lower class workers alike came, saw, and were entertained by Hopkins's play. According to Toll, "black minstrels drew primarily black common people" (227). While the presence of black minstrel stars Sam Lucas and the Hyers Sisters certainly would have drawn what Toll characterizes as the "black common people," an 8 July 1880 piece on "The Summer Stage" in the *Boston Globe* noted the nature of Hopkins's theatergoers in this way: "The character of the audiences at the Oakland, where 'Escaped from Bondage,' [an alternate title for *Slaves' Escape*] with the famous plantation scene is nightly presented, is of the best." "Character" serves as a polite term for class in this white newspaper review, and most certainly refers to a white upper class audience. Another review in the *Home Journal* reiterates these sentiments: "The popularity of this admirably managed place of recreation and amusement [Oakland Garden] is constantly on the increase with the best classes of our citizens and visitors to Boston."[8] The convergence of different races and classes in the audience has particular relevance when viewing *Slaves' Escape* in relation to Lhamon's blackface lore cycle. Lhamon asserts that the folk origins of a lore cycle exist within an underclass until they gain popularity beyond group borders (77-78). Toll's description of a large black underclass audience for black minstrel shows corresponds with a similar "folk" popularity, while the mixed audience watching Hopkins's genre-blending production seems to indicate the very early beginnings of a move toward the mass popularity of black performance and controlled commercialization that would occur in the mid-twentieth century (Lhamon 80-81). These diverse audiences saw a musical that defied simple comparisons, a show that had as much in common with demeaning minstrel shows as it did with serious dramatic productions of *Uncle Tom's Cabin*, and a show that turned many conventions of both inside out.

A further understanding of the mindset of *Slaves' Escape*'s audience members during the summer of 1880 – an audience simultaneously drawn to and repelled by blackness – may be gained by a perusal of the *Boston Globe* for those months. White cast performances of *Uncle Tom's Cabin* were well attended by Boston theater audiences at Hooley's South End Theatre during the week of 2 May 1880 ("The Drama"). May 2nd also saw the Louisiana jubilee singers perform before an "enthusiastic audience"; a *Globe* review of the performance stated, "No better exemplification of the peculiar plantation music which the southern negroes have created could be asked than this excellent entertainment."[9] From 14-28 June, Haverly's Genuine Colored Minstrels featuring Sam Lucas, Billy Kersands, and Tom McIntosh played their two-week run at the Oakland Garden. An advertisement in the *Globe* promised a "Carnival of Negro Minstrelsy" and "An unprecedented Minstrel revival. The Largest Company in Existence. Reproducing all the salient elements of Plantation Life. Comprising a Monster Minstrel Achievement. Plantation Acts; Cotton-field Sketches; Flat-boat Frolics; Barn-yard scenes; Banjo Performances; Comic Dance Diversions; Burlesque Jig Dancing;

Unique Negro Melodies."[10] Henry T. Sampson succinctly explains the common advertising strategy of labeling "colored minstrels" as "genuine" and thus worthy of patronage in this way: "Minstrelsy, created by white men in blackface who purported to give a true delineation of slave amusements on the Southern plantations, provided a natural vehicle by which Blacks could gain access to American show business. Who else could give a more natural and authentic portrayal of slaves' lives than former slaves – real Negroes, the genuine article!" (*Ghost Walks* 4) Thus black performers found themselves typecast before they began their careers; the haunting effects of which Toll emphasizes: "since they inherited the white-created stereotypes and could make only minor modifications in them, black minstrels in effect added credibility to these images by making it seem that Negroes actually behaved like minstrelsy's black caricatures" (196). Following these "colored minstrel" performances by one week at Oakland Garden, *Slaves' Escape* offered entertainment that drew from this legacy while simultaneously rejecting it.

Eric Lott fully examines this phenomenon in *Love and Theft.* In his analysis of blackface minstrelsy, Lott asserts: "Minstrel performers often attempted to repress through ridicule the real interest in black cultural practices they nonetheless betrayed – minstrelsy's mixed erotic economy of celebration and exploitation [...]. It was cross-racial desire that coupled a nearly insupportable fascination and a self-protective derision with respect to black people and their cultural practices, and that made blackface minstrelsy less a sign of absolute white power and control than of panic, anxiety, terror, and pleasure" (6). This "cross-racial desire" helps account for *Slaves' Escape*'s wide audience. A white fascination with blackness drove audiences to Oakland Garden that week, where they were met with a play that did not conform to expectations and were faced instead with a show that refused to be neatly categorized.

The rest of the *Boston Globe*'s content that day reveals prevailing attitudes toward race and miscegenation at the time. A sensationalized story entitled, "Blood Will Tell, Especially When It Happens to be Black Blood" appeared the morning of *Slaves' Escape*'s Oakland Garden premiere. The story details the surprise of a young white husband whose wife gives birth to "an infant with a dark skin, thick full lips, and a head covered with genuine wool, in short, a child with Unmistakable African Blood in its veins." The doctor gave the woman's mother two possible explanations for the baby's appearance: "The first is too painful and horrible to mention," referring, of course, to the suggestion that the baby's father was not the husband, but a black man, and the second, that the woman's blood "is of mixed purity." The mother breaks down and admits that she had adopted her daughter, who was fair enough to pass for white, from a dying black woman. The story ends with the woman's mother telling her son-in-law the truth about his wife: "[He] was beside himself with rage and grief. The unfortunate young wife has not yet been told the whole truth, the child having been taken into the country, where it is cared for by kind, respectable people, and as yet no other steps have been taken, though it is understood that the lawyers advise a separation, so the end of the cruel story cannot be told at present." The striking juxtaposition between this horror tale of miscegenation with its underlying fear of black male sexuality, and lavish advertisements for entertaining "Cotton Plantation Scenes" and "Grand Plantation Festivals," perfectly illustrates a white public's conflicted attitude toward blackness – one of both fascination and repulsion.

When the 5 July 1880 advertisement promised the customary grand plantation scene and declared, "This Afternoon and Evening, HOPKINS' COLORED TROUBADOURS in the Great Musical Drama, ESCAPE FROM SLAVERY, introducing SAM LUCAS and the HYERS SISTERS COMBINATION," the stage was certainly set for Hopkins's play to be received as another "colored minstrel" performance, yet we must question why the anticipation of such a spectacle would draw a large audience. While it is impossible to gauge the exact number of people in the audience, the performance was large enough to garner the attention of newspaper reviewers whose columns appear in Hopkins's scrapbook. A review Hopkins attributes to the *Boston Herald* notes, "The attendance at this well-known place of amusement [Oakland Garden] yesterday was probably as large as ever seen here, and it is estimated that 10,000 persons visited the garden during the day and evening. The seats in the pavilion were all secured long before the commencement of the performance, and the standing room was filled to overflowing at an early hour. The display of fireworks was probably as fine as any exhibited in Boston. The plantation festival continues to remain a great attraction," while another clipping attributed to the *Home Journal* states, "An extra performance [of *Slaves' Escape*] was given on the 5th, and in the evening there was an usually brilliant display of fireworks. No less than ten thousand people visited the garden on that day." Although it is unlikely that all 10,000 visitors saw Hopkins's play, a standing-room only crowd still constituted a significant audience, and attendance at the "plantation festival" following the performance was likely much larger.

These audience members witnessed the start of Hopkins's tendency toward "deconstructing racial stereotypes" that appears throughout her body of work, as Elizabeth Ammons characterizes it in her afterward to *The Unruly Voice* (217). As Wallinger notes in a discussion of the *Peculiar Sam* version of the play, it "anticipates the deviation from norms and the negotiations with character depiction, plot construction, and the use of tradition as well as her concessions to the taste of her audience, all of which determine the later and more famous stages of Hopkins's career. She uses the minstrel model, exposes its ridiculous hyperbole, and subverts it with her own message" (36). Produced alongside black minstrel productions such as *Out of Bondage* and the various Georgia Minstrel and Haverly Minstrel performances, which merely reinscribed negative stereotypes without any pretense of subverting or deconstructing them, Hopkins's play adopted established minstrel elements out of necessity. In the theater climate of the time, an interrogation of racist stereotypes could only be mounted under the guise of giving the audience what it expected to see – blacks acting as caricatures in a predictable format. Although *Slaves' Escape* followed a logical, narrative format rather than minstrelsy's tripartite form, a multitude of similarities between the play and minstrel shows are still evident. In fact, the play's linear narrative structure within an external minstrel shell served as another inversion of convention, subverting what Lott identifies as an "early emphasis [...] on what film theorists have called spectacle rather than on narrative" (140). "The first minstrel shows," he goes on to explain, "put narrative to a variety of uses, but relied first and foremost on the objectification of black characters" (140). *Slaves' Escape* foregrounds narrative and resists such objectification, yet the play's parallels to a formulaic minstrel show are evident and speak to the legacy of both white and black minstrelsy it emerged from. In addition to the opening plantation scene and spectacle-driven afterpiece, the play seems at times to provide the well-known minstrel roles of interlocutor, middle man, and end men.[11] Carl Wittke describes the "first part" of a minstrel performance as "a well-coordinated program of songs and jokes, and lively repartee between the endmen and the middleman" (36). This description fits scene two in which Sam and Juno comically argue over the fact that no one ever takes her to Uncle Eph's to learn dancing.[12] At one point Sam threatens, "Gal if you don't keep dat mouf still, I'll smack all de taste out of it." When Sam finally promises to take her, she excitedly proclaims, "Go ahead ol' boy, kin jes tear de house down if you want to." Stage directions indicate that she "Shins round O round" and Juno, Sam, Pete, and Pomp begin a musical number. The stage directions further instruct: "Solo, quartette, chorus, merges into walk-around, with banjo, bones, and tambo, banjoist seated astride of table." Hopkins's manuscript notes the song "Climbing Golden Stairs" in combination with a walk-around – which Toll identifies as a common minstrel dance (44). After the walk-around, the joking continues as Sam vows to marry Jinny "de Lor' bein' willin' an de weather permittin'." Pete rejoins with "Taint no use Sam, you's got to do as marser say, you hyard what de preacher tol us, dat it were hard fer a mule to kick 'gin a brick wall. Now boy you is de mule an' slavery am de wall an' 'taint no use to kick agin' it," and exits laughing. This comic scene replete with joking and jig dancing would certainly have brought traditional minstrel shows to mind.

Likewise, the musical selections for act one vary from performance to performance, but draw heavily upon spirituals and minstrel shows of the time and included: "Good Bye Old Cabin Home," "Dem Silver Slippers," "De's Bones," "Old Time Things," and "Suwannee River."[13] Tom McIntosh, a popular black actor who toured with half a dozen minstrel troupes, performed “Dem Silver Slippers” in Boston with Haverly’s Genuine Colored Minstrels around the same time *Slaves’ Escape* was produced.[14] This song is likely related to James Bland’s minstrel song, “Oh! Dem Golden Slippers,” which is noted at the end of *Peculiar Sam*’s handwritten manuscript.[15] C.A. White composed “Good Bye Old Cabin Home” for the Hyers Sisters who performed it in *Out of Bondage* (Riis, *Just Before Jazz* 10). A possibly similar minstrel song entitled “The Old Cabin Home,” was also in use at the time.[16] “Suwannee River,” related to “Down on the Swanee River,” and Stephen Foster’s “Old Folks at Home,” is another song with definite links to minstrelsy.[17] These familiar, popular songs served to draw the audience into the stage spectacle while masking other, subversive aspects of the play.

Slaves’ Escape deliberately employs several textual, visual, and musical minstrel devices, which it then generally undermines and subverts thematically.[18] With the exception of Virginia, an educated house slave, and Quaker John, an “educated Negro,” all characters speak in a thick minstrel dialect, including Jim, the mulatto overseer. The program’s description of the lead character, Sam, as a “peculiar fellow,” exemplifies Hopkins’s subversive use of language and dialect. Use of the loaded word “peculiar” occurred often and in many different contexts during the mid to late nineteenth-century: slavery was a “peculiar institution,” instruments used in minstrel shows were described as being of a “peculiar nature,” a review of a Boston minstrel performance cites the “peculiar plantation music,” and so forth.[19] Wittke describes minstrel stereotypes in the following ways: “The stage Negro loved watermelons and ate them in a *peculiar* way [...]. In minstrelsy, the Negro type [...] always was distinguished by an unusually large mouth and a *peculiar* kind of broad grin [emphasis added]” (8). In *Slaves’ Escape*, the use of the word “peculiar,” normally a condescending term used in white speech and print to marginalize the other and to create a linguistic barrier between whiteness and blackness, constitutes a site of linguistic contestation. When applied to Sam, “peculiar” does not signify the strangeness or oddness of a foreign curiosity. Sam’s “peculiarity” does not rest on any abnormalities seen as characteristic of slave behavior, but rather on his rebellious actions and revolutionary tendencies. After act two, scene two’s altercation between Sam and overseer Jim over Jinny, during which Jim openly flaunts his power and states his wish to have Sam “tied to the whippin’ post,” sell him South, and “take de res’ ob it out o’ Jinny,” Sam’s physical attack on Jim is treated dismissively by Juno: “O [it’s] nuthin’ only Sam’s been showin’ de oberseer how ’culiar he is, dat’s all.” Sam’s “peculiarity” in this scene derives from his desire to fight and overthrow the overseer, the representation of white control, rather than an inherently othered inferiority – a significant inversion of the term.

Jim’s character, who serves as the symbol of white authority throughout the play, presents another compelling example of inverted stereotypes. Jim’s costuming directions instruct that he wear “immense false feet” in all scenes.[20] Lott characterizes the dehumanizing use of oversized clothing such as "enormous shooting collars and shoes several sizes too big" as having "the infantilizing effect of arresting 'black' people in the early stages of development" (143). Although her audience would have expected such "infantilizing" of a slave character, Hopkins's use of large feet on the overseer's character acts as a deliberate inversion of a racist stereotype. The large feet allow the slaves to mock the symbol of white authority and control – the half-white, cruel overseer, and engage the audience in such mockery as well. Indeed, Jim's conspicuous feet cause him trouble throughout the course of the play. In act two, scene one, when Jim wears a sheet to impersonate a ghost and scare Sam, his feet give him away: "I know dem feet! 'course I knows dem feet!" Sam exclaims, "[*looks at them again*] Dem's de same pair o' feet. I know dey is, kase dem feet never growed on no oder fellar but Jim in de worl'." Realizing the nature of the disguise, Sam then captures Jim. The large feet – now symbols of bumbling white incompetence – allow Sam to triumph and regain control of the situation. They also instantly reverse the common minstrel trope of the "superstitious negro" who constantly fears ghosts. Jim's enormous feet again serve as a liability for him and a source of amusement for the audience the second time Sam points a pistol at Jim and captures him in act three: "Drap dat knife mister, Fect if you don't I'll shoot, yas right into the most convenient place [...] 'deed I is, Ise gwine to shoot you right froo dem feet." Since the feet function as symbols of white power, shooting them literally cripples both Jim and the white establishment. As an inversion of racist stereotypes, the threat of shooting the large feet becomes the threat of killing the ugly stereotype.

Costuming further affected the complex representation of race in *Slaves' Escape* by working against two-dimensional stereotypical portrayals of blackness. Jim and Sam are both specified to be mulattoes (Jim in the cast description, and Sam by his own account). Furthermore, the costume list for one performance specifies that Sam have a "Very Fair complexion," an effect that would have necessitated the use of makeup if the actor were dark-skinned. Sam's comic antics and malapropisms represent a stereotypical "blackness," as inscribed by white minstrelsy. Yet here it is a blackness in whiteface. In contrast, Jim's character represents white authority, and symbolic "whiteness." He disavows his "blackness" by fulfilling the white role of overseer and declaring, "neber could bar free niggers no how," as he voices his murderous intentions toward Quaker John. The confrontations between Sam and Jim mirror a conflicted white public's attitude toward race, a struggle over the "permeability of the color line," Lott describes (6). While Jim becomes an obvious symbol of faceless whiteness when he dons a white sheet to disguise himself as a ghost, he simultaneously turns into an object of ridicule when his large feet stick out from beneath the sheet.[21] Sam triumphs over, captures, and robs this whiteness to the approval of a mixed audience. The audience's internal struggle intensifies as it sympathizes and roots for

Sam – the clear protagonist, even as he embodies racial contradiction and a public fear of miscegenation, the theme foregrounded throughout the text by Juno's character.

In 1879, Hopkins took the racist and degrading stereotypes of blackness that populated the nineteenth-century American stage and turned them to her own uses in a way that W.T. Lhamon in *Raising Cain* describes as a fundamental characteristic of a "lore cycle." He examines spatial and temporal relationships between race and performance in order to facilitate an analysis of the shifting and mutable cultural currency given to blackface performance from the eighteenth century to the present, and identifies cultural lore as "the basic gestures of all expressive behavior, from moans to narratives, signs to paintings, steps to dances" (69). When disparate cultural groups or classes come into contact with one another these "casual gestures of ordinary life [...] become tokens of transfer in marketplaces and other informal theatres where stress is stirred among miscellaneous populations meeting each other" (76). Lhamon posits a trans-historical theory of what he dubs "the blackface lore cycle" – a term that describes the historical turns by which "The cultural symbolism of blackface performance [...] is sometimes disdained, other times fetishized, sometimes buried, other times enhanced and elaborated. Along the way it has absorbed its warped intentions, folding them also into its effects" (66). Tracing the inversions of meaning and the cyclical nature of blackface lore from early T.D. Rice minstrel shows in the 1830s, to the racist and degrading minstrelsy of the 1850s, to the popularity of black performance in 1950s popular culture, *Raising Cain* outlines a cyclical movement made possible by the way "all the groups that participate in a lore cycle try to turn its gestures to their own uses" (76). It is in this act of appropriation that we may locate Hopkins's play. As a response to the blackface minstrelsy of post-civil war theater circuits, *Slaves' Escape* constitutes a material link between "blacks in blackface" performance and the progressive black musical theater of the early twentieth century. *Slaves' Escape*'s subversive use of minstrel conventions remains Hopkins's significant contribution to a black musical theater tradition. In 1879-1881, when *Slaves' Escape* was performed, Hopkins's unique production featured an all-black cast and a cohesive narrative structure that turned minstrel stereotypes against themselves. In terms of the blackface lore cycle, this positions *Slaves' Escape* as a precursor to the black musical theater of the early twentieth century created by Bob Cole, Billy Johnson, Will Marion Cook, and the Johnson brothers, J. Rosamond and James Weldon.

In *More Than Just Minstrel Shows: The Rise of Black Musical Theatre at the Turn of the Century*, Thomas Riis credits Bob Cole and Billy Johnson with staging the first black musical comedy, *A Trip to Coontown,* in September 1897 and documenting the ways in which Cole worked to refute black minstrel stereotypes: "A final sign of Cole's challenge to minstrelsy in *A Trip to Coontown* was his inclusion, just before the finale, of 'No Coons

Allowed!,' as direct a protest song as one can find in the musical theatre of the day. The text of the verse tells of a young man taking his date to the 'swellest place in town,' only to find a sign over the door reading 'No coons allowed!'" (15). *A Trip to Coontown* also saw Cole don whiteface makeup to portray "Willie Wayside" a tramp in the show. A review in the *New York Times* offered this dubious praise of Cole's performance: "Bob Cole, who plays Willie Wayside, the tramp, and in a white make-up which makes it almost impossible to guess his particular tint [...] showed last night that he is capable of playing any white part far better than most Negro comedians play black ones."[22] This reviewer's attitude toward performing race centers on the question of legitimacy. Even as the review affirms the effectiveness of blacks parodying whiteness, it simultaneously champions the legitimacy of whites to perform blackness. While *A Trip to Coontown* is often cited as the beginning of the rise of a black musical theater that strove to challenge inherited minstrel stereotypes, this trend is easily observed in Hopkins's *Slaves' Escape* eighteen years earlier.

Cole himself wrote about the state of black theater in a 1902 article for *Colored American Magazine* during Hopkins's time as an editor there, as he was working on *In Dahomey*, the first full-length black musical comedy to hit Broadway.[23] In his article, "The Negro and the Stage," which took the role of drama in race relations as its subject, Cole denounced the current state of American theater stating, "I am sorry to announce that I find the American dramatists making severe usages of the Negro in their plays. They either use the Negro as villain, or part villain in every instance with but few exceptions. And this has done a great deal to aid in keeping alive racial prejudices" (303). Cole further states his belief that "the greatest dramas of Negro life will be written by the Negroes themselves" (305). James Weldon Johnson also notes Cole's activist views in his autobiography, *Along This Way*: "Cole was the most versatile man in the group and a true artist [...]. [T]here was an element of pro-Negro propaganda in all his efforts" (173). This "element of pro-Negro propaganda," aptly describes Hopkins's work long before Cole and Johnson's collaborative efforts.

The collaboration between Cole, Jesse Shipp, Cook, and the Johnson brothers that resulted in the production of *In Dahomey* functioned as a decisive split from an earlier minstrel tradition. As producers, the company diligently worked to avoid perpetuating minstrel stereotypes. Although certain elements of the tradition remained, Cole and the Johnson brothers consciously made the decision to do away with most of these. According to Riis: "Many minstrel conventions were absent and most of the cast members did not don burnt cork, but audiences surely understood *In Dahomey* as a continuation of the older tradition. [...] Yet many positive messages about blackness and Africanness were embedded in the songs and book of *In Dahomey* [...]. While there are minstrel elements in the show's script – the opening stump speech [...], for example – such conventions are just as frequently foregone" (*Music and Scripts* 24-8). Hopkins's play, which similarly uses minstrel elements to subvert dominant racist stereotypes, stands here as an important link between blackface minstrel shows and turn-of-the-century black musical theater. *Slaves' Escape; or, The Underground Railroad* leapt into public consciousness at a critical moment in time. The late 1870s and early 1880s were a transitional period in the blackface lore cycle. Still hobbled by the racist caricatures of 1850s white minstrelsy, black minstrel troupes performed and reinscribed these stereotypes almost uniformly until *Slaves' Escape*. The cultural forces that compelled Hopkins to include racially subversive elements – and mixed audiences to applaud them – would inform a new generation of black composers and playwrights eighteen years later and the rise of twentieth-century black musical theater generally. By virtue of her pivotal place in black musical theater history, Hopkins and her dramatic works merit critical recognition and further study.

TABLE 1

Production History for *Slaves' Escape; or the Underground Railroad*

Date/Venue	Title/Version	Company
March 24, 1879 / Opera House, Rockford, Illinois	*The Flight for Freedom** / four-act version	Sprague's Underground Railroad Company
March 28, 1879 / Opera House, Racine, Wisconsin	*The Flight for Freedom* / four-act version	Sprague's Underground Railroad Company
March 31-April 2, 1879 / Grand Opera House, Milwaukee, Wisconsin	*The Flight for Freedom* / four-act version	Sprague's Underground Railroad Company
April 18-19, 1879 / Opera House, St. Paul, Minnesota**	*The Flight for Freedom* / four-act version	Sprague's Underground Railroad Company
N/D / Buffalo, New York	*The Flight for Freedom* / four-act version	Sprague's Underground Railroad Company
December 8, 1879 / Boston Union Opera House, Boston, Massachusetts	*The Slaves' Escape; or the Underground Railroad* / three-act version	Hopkins' Colored Troubadours
July 5-10, 1880 / Oakland Garden, Boston, Massachusetts	*Escape from Slavery; or the Underground Railroad* / three-act version	Hopkins' Colored Troubadours
September 29, 1881 / Boston Music Hall, Boston, Massachusetts	*The Flight for Freedom; or the Underground Railroad* / three-act version	Hopkins' Colored Troubadours

TABLE 2

Cast Listings for *Slaves' Escape; or the Underground Railroad*

Date	Title/Version	Cast	
March-April, 1879	*The Flight for Freedom* / four-act version	Performed by Sprague's Underground Railroad Company, starring Sam Lucas as Sam	
December 8, 1879	*The Slaves' Escape; or the Underground Railroad* / three-act version	Sam	Al. Holden
		Uncle Caesar	Mr. Rollins
		Pomp	George Tolliver
		Virginia	Pauline E. Hopkins
		Mammy	Sarah Allen Hopkins***
		Jim	William A. Hopkins***
		Juno	S. Williams
		Quaker John	Paul Desmond
July 5-10, 1880	*Escape from Slavery; or the Underground Railroad* / three-act version	Sam	Sam Lucas
		Jim	William A. Hopkins
		Uncle Caesar	WM. Cummings
		Pete	WM. Cummings
		Quaker John	Thos. Scottron
		Pomp	G. W. Paine
		Augustus	Fred Lyons
		Virginia	P. E. Hopkins
		Juno	S. Williams
		Mammy	S. A. Hopkins
		With the Hyers Sisters' Company	
September 29, 1881	*The Flight for Freedom; or the Underground Railroad* / three-act version	Sam	Frank Nelson
		Jim	William A. Hopkins
		Uncle Caesar	George Deamus / George Simonds
		Pete	George Deamus
		Quaker John	T. Scottron
		Pomp	George Wally
		Augustus	George Simonds
		Mammy	Sarah Allen Hopkins
		Juno	S. Williams
		Virginia	Pauline E. Hopkins
		With the Hopkins Troubadour Quartette: Pauline E. Hopkins, Adah Hector, William S. Copeland, George Wally	

Sources: Advertisements, *The Milwaukee Sentinel* 28 March-2 April 1879; Reviews, *The Milwaukee Sentinel* 1-2 April 1879; Review, *Daily Register* [Rockford, IL] 25 March 1879; Review, *Daily Herald* [Racine, WI] 29 March 1879; Review, *Buffalo Daily Courier* n.d., Scrapbook, Pauline E. Hopkins papers, Fisk University Library Special Collections, Nashville; Review, *Boston Globe* 9 December 1879; Advertisements, *Boston Globe*, 3-11 July 1879; Review, *Boston Herald* 6 July 1880; Scrapbook Program, Pauline E. Hopkins Papers, Fisk University Library Special Collections, Nashville.

*During the Sprague Tour, performances of the play were billed as both *The Flight for Freedom* and *The Underground Railroad*. The complete title may have been: *The Flight for Freedom; Or the Underground Railroad*.

** Southern names this venue as the "opera-hall" of the Boston Young Men's Christian Union in *African American Theater*, xxiv.

*** Sarah Allen Hopkins and William A. Hopkins were Pauline E. Hopkins's mother and stepfather.

I wish to thank W.T. Lhamon for his generous comments and insightful criticisms of this piece. I am also grateful for the helpful advice and encouragement I received from Leigh Edwards, Hanna Wallinger, Malin Pereira, John Gruesser, and Jim Adams. I appreciate as well the time John Graziano, James Hatch, and Annette Fern took to answer my queries. Finally, I wish to thank Beth Howse, Fisk University's Special Collections Librarian, for her gracious assistance as I completed the archival research that led to this article.

[1] All quotations from *Slaves' Escape* are taken from the unpublished, unpaginated bound manuscript located in the Pauline E. Hopkins Papers, Fisk University Library Special Collections, Nashville, TN.

[2] Music and lyrics to "Didn't my Lord deliver Daniel" can be found in Southern, 145-146.

[3] For a discussion on the fourth act of *Peculiar Sam* and Reconstruction see Patterson, 13-23.

[4] For a discussion of the symbolic function of Sappho's name see Carby, *Reconstructing Womanhood*, 142-144.

[5] Unsigned Review, Unidentified Boston Paper, 10 August 1886. *Uncle Tom's Cabin & American Culture: A Multi-Media Archive*. Dir. Stephen Railton. 2007. University of Virginia. 14 September 2007. <http://www.iath.virginia.edu/utc/>.

[6] "The Summer Stage," *Boston Globe*, 3 July 1880.

[7] Advertisement, *Boston Globe*, 21 August 1880.

[8] Review, *Home Journal* 10 July 1880, Scrapbook, Pauline E. Hopkins papers, Fisk University Library Special Collections, Nashville.

[9] Review, *Boston Globe* 3 May 1880.

[10] Advertisement, *Boston Globe* 14 June 1880.

[11] Detailed descriptions of the minstrel show format are given in Toll, Wittke 136-142, and Engle xvi-xix. For a lengthy description of black minstrel shows, see Toll 195-233, and Sampson, *Blacks in Blackface* 1-3.

[12] The mention of Uncle Eph's cabin in this scene is notable as well. While "Uncle Eph" appeared as a character in the Hyers Sisters' *Out of Bondage*, the figure itself preceded the play by at least five years. On 6 November 1871, Bryant's Minstrels performed "Uncle Eph's Dream: An Original Negro Sketch, In Two Scenes and Two Tableaux," and performances continued through at least 1874. This minstrel figure became a stock character – the "old darky," an ex-slave, played in blackface, who nostalgically longs for the old plantation life. He mourns the loss of his former "massa," bemoaning the fact that "we got no more massas now; de poor old slaves will hab to look out for demselves." Uncle Eph fulfills this archetype in *Out of Bondage*, as a member of an older generation with mixed or negative feelings about Reconstruction. The mention of this stock minstrel figure in *Slaves' Escape* serves to remind audiences of the minstrel tradition the play operates within. Uncle Eph becomes an unseen character, sharing the stage with characters that ultimately reject the myth of a happy plantation life he represents (DeWitt 55-61).

[13] Scrapbook Programs, 5 July 1880 and 21 September 1881, Pauline E. Hopkins Papers, Fisk University Library Special Collections, Nashville.

[14] Review, *Boston Globe* 17 August 1880.

[15] Hopkins, *Peculiar Sam* MS., reprinted in Southern. The music and lyrics to James Bland's song appear in *Minstrel Songs, Old and New*, 195-197. They have also been reprinted in Southern, who lists "Dem Golden Slippers" among the musical numbers for *Peculiar Sam*, 203-205.

[16] Words and Music found in *Minstrel Songs, Old and New* 202-203.

[17] Sampson, *The Ghost Walks* 24. Words and Music to "Old Folks at Home" can be found in *Minstrel Songs, Old and New* 3-5, and are also reprinted in Southern 195-196.

[18] Patterson notes, "Hopkins works to subvert the racist ideology of the dominant minstrel show tradition by granting subjectivity and social mobility to those characters who resist appropriation by the slave master" and reads Sam, the lead character, as a trickster figure who, following Henry Louis Gates' formulation in *The Signifying Monkey*, "signifies upon the racist tropes of white minstrelsy" (13-14). While Patterson's essay offers a compelling look at the fourth act of *Peculiar Sam* in terms of Reconstruction and black subjectivity, my focus here is on the revised version of the play, titled *Slaves' Escape*, which contains only three acts and eliminates the fourth act Patterson discusses.

[19] Review, *Boston Globe* 2 May 1880; Sampson 2.

[20] Hopkins, *Peculiar Sam* TS.

[21] Some scholars equate the donning of the white sheet with the actions of the Ku Klux Klan. See Patterson, 20.

[22] Review, *New York Times* 16 April 1898 (qtd. in Sampson, *The Ghost Walks* 149, 151).

[23] *In Dahomey*'s Broadway premiere occurred on 18 February 1903 and starred the famous comedy duo, Bert Williams and George Walker. See Riis, *Music and Scripts*, xii.

WORKS CITED

Ammons, Elizabeth. "Afterword: *Winona*, Bakhtin, and Hopkins in the Twenty-first Century." Gruesser 211-219.

Bradford, Joseph. *Out of Bondage*. 1876. Rpt. *African American Theater*. Ed. Eileen Southern. New York: Garland, 1994.

Carby, Hazel. Introduction. *The Magazine Novels of Pauline Hopkins*. New York: Oxford UP, 1988. xxix-xlvii.

—. *Reconstructing Womanhood*: *The Emergence of the Afro-American Woman Novelist*. New York: Oxford UP, 1987.

Cole, Bob. "The Negro and the Stage." *Colored American Magazine* 4.3 (1902): 303.

DeWitt, Robert M. "Uncle Eph's Dream." Engle 55-61.

"The Drama." *Boston Globe*. 2 May 1880. n. p.

Engle, Gary D., ed. *This Grotesque Essence: Plays from the American Minstrel Stage*. Baton Rouge: Louisiana State UP, 1978.

Gruesser, John Cullen, ed. *The Unruly Voice: Rediscovering Pauline Elizabeth Hopkins*. Urbana: U of Illinois Press, 1996.

Hamalian, Leo, and James V. Hatch, ed. *The Roots of African American Drama*. Detroit: Wayne State UP, 1991.

Hill, Errol G. and James V. Hatch. *A History of African American Theatre*. Cambridge: Cambridge UP, 2003.

Hopkins, Pauline Elizabeth. *Contending Forces: A Romance Illustrative of Negro Life North and South*. 1900. New York: Oxford UP, 1988.

—. *Daughter of the Revolution: The Major Nonfiction Works of Pauline E. Hopkins*. Ed. Ira Dworkin. New Brunswick: Rutgers UP, 2007.

—. Letter to W.M. Trotter, 16 April 1905. *Colored American Magazine* Correspondence folder, Fisk University Library Special Collections, Nashville.

—. *The Magazine Novels of Pauline Hopkins*. New York: Oxford UP, 1988.

—. *Peculiar Sam, or, the Underground Railroad*. Hamalian and Hatch 100-123.

—. *Peculiar Sam* MS. Southern 117-205.

—. *Peculiar Sam* TS, Pauline E. Hopkins Papers, Fisk University Library Special Collections, Nashville.

—. *Slaves' Escape; or, The Underground Railroad*. MS, Pauline E. Hopkins Papers, Fisk University Library Special Collections, Nashville.

Lhamon, W.T. *Raising Cain: Blackface Performance from Jim Crow to Hip Hop*. Cambridge: Harvard UP, 1998.

Lott, Eric. *Love and Theft: Blackface Minstrelsy and the American Working Class*. New York: Oxford UP, 1993.

Minstrel Songs, Old and New. Boston, 1882.

Patterson, Martha. "Remaking the Minstrel: Pauline Hopkins's *Peculiar Sam* and the Post-Reconstruction Black Subject." *Black Women Playwrights: Visions on the American Stage*. Ed. Carol P. Marsh-Lockett. New York: Garland, 1999. 13-23.

Peterson, Bernard L. *Profiles of African American Stage Performers and Theater People, 1816 – 1960*. Westport: Greenwood, 2001.

Riis, Thomas L. "*In Dahomey* in Text and Performance." *The Music and Scripts of* In Dahomey. Ed. Thomas L. Riis. Madison: A-R Editions, 1996. xiii-xlvi.

—. *Just Before Jazz: Black Musical Theater in New York, 1890-1915*. Washington: Smithsonian, 1989.

—. *More Than Just Minstrel Shows: The Rise of Black Musical Theatre at the Turn of the Century*. Brooklyn: Institute for Studies in American Music, 1992.

Sampson, Henry T. *Blacks in Blackface: A Source Book on Early Black Musical Shows*. Metuchen: Scarecrow, 1980.

—. *The Ghost Walks: A Chronological History of Blacks in Show Business, 1865-1910*. Metuchen: Scarecrow, 1988.

Shockley, Ann Allen. "Pauline Elizabeth Hopkins: A Biographical Excursion into Obscurity." *Phylon* 33.1 (1972): 22-26.

Southern, Eileen. *African American Theater*. New York: Garland, 1994.

Stowe, Harriet Beecher. *Uncle Tom's Cabin or, Life Among the Lowly*. 1852. New York: Penguin, 1986.

Toll, Robert. *Blacking Up: The Minstrel Show in Nineteenth-Century America*. New York: Oxford UP, 1974.

Wallinger, Hanna. *Pauline E. Hopkins: A Literary Biography*. Athens: U of Georgia Press, 2005.

Williams, Judith. "Uncle Tom's Women." *African American Performance and Theater History: A Critical Reader*. Ed. Henry J. Elam, Jr. and David Krasner. New York: Oxford UP, 2001. 19-39.

Wittke, Carl. *Tambo and Bones: A History of the American Minstrel Stage*. 1930. Westport: Greenwood, 1968.

"All Things Work Together for Good": Pauline Hopkins's Race Woman and the Gospel of Success

Alisha R. Knight

In August 1899 a controversy erupted during the second biennial National Association of Colored Women (NACW) convention in Chicago when Josephine St. Pierre Ruffin challenged Mary Church Terrell's election to a second term as NACW president. Ruffin and fellow delegates from the Boston-based Woman's Era Club made allegations of disorganization and ballot tampering. After the convention, once Ruffin's attempt to be elected as the NACW's second president failed, the Woman's Era Club appointed an ad hoc committee to draft resolutions of censure against the Association. The Woman's Era Club, which considered itself the authoritative "mother club of the NACW," disapproved of "the conduct of all the business sessions of that convention, [and] the high-handed, unparliamentary rulings of the presiding officer [Terrell], and the unconstitutional elections" ("Report" 1). Pauline Elizabeth Hopkins, who at this time was an up and coming novelist and journalist, was a member of the Woman's Era Club and served as this committee's secretary. Considering the nature of this position, it is safe to assume Hopkins was responsible for drafting the resolutions, which were unanimously adopted by the club, including the recommendation that the Woman's Era Club "withdraw all affiliation with the National Association until such a time as that organization is presided over by constitutionally elected officers" ("Report" 1). Although the resolutions were approved by the club members, at Ruffin's request they were "laid upon the table for a more careful consideration, and consultation with other clubs in the Federation" ("Report" 1). The ad hoc committee assented on the condition that their censures be printed in *The National Notes* (the NACW's newsletter) and the *New York Age*.[1]

Hopkins's participation in what has been called "Mrs. Ruffin's Attacks" illuminates the political interactions that took place between Hopkins and prominent club women.[2] While Hopkins's own activity with the black woman's club movement has already been noted by Hazel Carby and others, little attention has been given to the direct influence club women, namely Josephine St. Pierre Ruffin, had on Hopkins's literary endeavors. Humanitarian, women's rights advocate, and founder of the *Woman's Era*, a national newspaper for African American women, and the Woman's Era Club, Ruffin was a member of Boston's African American upper class and the widow of George Lewis Ruffin, the first African American to graduate from Harvard Law School and one of the first appointed black judges in the nation. Rodger

Streitmatter characterizes Ruffin as a resourceful woman who was "financially secure and had a national reputation for her organizational ability and philanthropic endeavors" (64). Mrs. Willis's character in Hopkins's first novel, *Contending Forces*, is a powerful club woman, "the brilliant widow of a bright Negro politician," and just one literary manifestation of Hopkins's interactions with Ruffin (143). Published in 1900, *Contending Forces* was actually completed in 1899, the same year as the contested NACW elections. Mrs. Willis multitasks, overseeing young women in Ma Smith's sewing-circle and using a blackboard to review recent events pertinent to the black community. Afterward, Mrs. Willis leads a formal discussion on "The place which the virtuous woman occupies in upbuilding a race" (148). Unfortunately, Mrs. Willis's characterization has been routinely underrated, notwithstanding Siobhan Somerville's assertion that her conversation with Sappho "has an important function in the narrative, as it piques the reader's appetite for the divulgence of Saphho's secret while deferring its exposure" (155). Mrs. Willis is present in only one chapter and *Contending Forces'* narrator makes ambiguous statements about her motives, but a close reading reveals Hopkins does not share her narrator's sentiments. Albeit a secondary character, Mrs. Willis plays a positive and pivotal role in *Contending Forces*, serving as a black woman's success archetype that, prior to 1900, had been absent from American literature.

A number of literary critics mistakenly assume Hopkins's portrayal of Mrs. Willis is intended to diminish the influence of ambitious black women. Richard Yarborough provides a primary example of this assumption in his introduction to the Oxford edition of *Contending Forces*. Here he argues that Hopkins's feelings toward Mrs. Willis are ambivalent: "Obviously attracted to this woman's strength of mind and forthright feminism, Hopkins seems somewhat unsettled, however, by the extraordinary extent of Willis's driving ambition" (Yarborough xl). By adding an endnote to suggest that Mrs. Willis "may" be modeled after Ruffin, Yarborough implies that Hopkins's conflicted attitude toward this fictive character is indicative of her feelings about the character's historical counterpart (xlvi). Yarborough's statement, and those of critics who have followed his lead, presume Hopkins's authorial voice and the narrator are one and the same. I, on the other hand, agree with Thomas Cassidy's admonishment that "it is a mistake to identify the narrator of *Contending Forces* with Pauline Hopkins" (662). There is no reason not to connect Mrs. Willis to the real life Ruffin, and, as Hanna Wallinger notes, "It may be assumed that Hopkins's Boston readers recognized Mrs. Willis as a thinly disguised Mrs. Ruffin and were amused at this" (106). Yet one must keep in mind that Mrs. Willis's actual presence in the novel can be more indicative of Hopkins's attitudes than comments offered by a narrator who Cassidy convincingly argues is "omniscient but unreliable" (661). More importantly, if one follows the common practice of reading *Contending Forces* squarely within the tradition of domestic and sentimental fiction, then, yes,

Mrs. Willis's intense ambition and other character traits position her on the margins of the nineteenth-century domestic sphere, leading readers to assume Hopkins intentionally casts her as an unsavory figure. Domestic fiction, however, is just one of the multiple literary genres that Hopkins employs in her work. Situating *Contending Forces,* especially the Sewing-Circle chapter, within the genre of success literature shows Hopkins's tone is less "unsettled" than previously presumed. Indeed, Hopkins adopts and adapts success literature in much of her fiction and journalism to promote a particular definition of success for African American women, which Josephine St. Pierre Ruffin and Mrs. Willis embody.

Over the past three decades, identifying sentimental forms in turn-of-the-century fiction has become a mainstay of literary criticism, and scholars habitually constrict discussions of Hopkins's work to this literary genre. According to Kate McCullough, for example, "literary critics agree that the post-Reconstruction fiction of African American women such as Hopkins and Frances E.W. Harper reflects a desire to 'uplift' the race by offering self-representations that refuted the multiple received stereotypes of African American women. Critics have also agreed that to this end these authors use the vehicle of the sentimental novel, producing heroines who celebrate domesticity, marriage, and motherhood, and who reflect a dominant white model of virtuous womanhood" (22-23). Ironically, sentimental novels do not typically compel readers to seek "explicit expression of their outrage at racial oppression" but instead "[fulfill] the expectations of their first public audience for pleasurable reading in plots affirming the social meaning to which it generally [subscribes]" (Tate 6). In this sense, sentimental novels alone would have been ill-suited for the purposes of a race woman like Hopkins. Domestic fiction, even when it is reconstituted by black women writers, still circumscribes upward-climbing women within a domestic sphere. Politically active black women like Ruffin explicitly opposed being limited to domestic spaces as a means of achieving progress. For example, in the first issue of *Woman's Era*, Ruffin argues, "the stumbling block in the way of even the most cultured colored woman is the narrowness of her environment" ("Greeting" 8). Here, as Francesca Sawaya explains, "Ruffin relies on assumptions about progressive civilization much like [white women activists] to criticize the narrowness of both domesticity and 'culture' in a racist society. Black women, she writes, are forced by segregation to exist in a 'circumscribed sphere' the use of the word *sphere* suggesting a kind of enforced domesticity" (40). Other black women, including Hopkins, offer more implicit statements against the suitability of prescribed domestic spheres for all women. I agree with McCullough that "Hopkins used sentimental forms in part because they were among the culturally available and familiar forms of her time; that is, her audience would have known how to read the sentimental signifiers in her work – an important goal given the didactic aim of *Contending Forces*" (24); however, she also drew upon success literature which was equally popular during this time period, with its own set of signifiers that readers would have recognized.

During the late nineteenth and early twentieth centuries, the phrase "self-made man" invoked the image of an autonomous male who became wealthy and powerful through his hard work, shrewd judgment, and ambition. According to Richard Weiss, "Tradition has it that every American child receives, as part of his birthright, the freedom to mold his own life. [...] The belief that all men, in accordance with certain rules, but exclusively by their own efforts, can make of their lives what they will has been widely popularized for well over a century" (3). This scenario, generally referred to as the "gospel of success," has deep roots in United States culture. An entire genre of success literature, typically consisting of novels, advice guides, biographical and autobiographical works, correlates with this ideology. The figure of the self-made man is a common trope in "rags-to-riches," or more accurately "rags-to-respectability," narratives where a young hero moves from the country to the city, or from the gutter to the penthouse, in search of better employment opportunities. Once he secures entry-level employment, he incrementally works his way up from menial laborer to office manager or even corporate executive. Benjamin Franklin's *Autobiography* and various other fictional and nonfictional sketches of poor young boys working to become wealthy businessmen were read by working- and middle-class adults and children not only for motivation to better themselves, but also to escape the realities of economic hardship. From labor disputes to economic depression, the working- and middle-classes faced serious challenges during the Gilded Age. Hence, according to Paulette Kilmer, the success archetype offered people "a refuge from modernity" (3). Indeed, the American success myth and the trope of the self-made man served dual purposes in late nineteenth- and early twentieth-century society. On the one hand, they provided a model for lower- and middle-class citizens to aspire to although Post-Civil-War technological advancements like the telegraph and the transcontinental railroad contributed to the rapid development of the nation's major cities and to a shift from an agrarian to industrial economy and culture, "frequently, progress intensified the misery of the poor, even while raising their standard of living" (Kilmer 4). Even though new industrial centers offered job opportunities, labor conditions were often hard. The growing steel industry, for example, was "the showpiece of American progress"; and yet, "labor conditions in the steel industry were exceedingly harsh. For less than subsistence wages, workers put in twelve-hour days and seven-day weeks" (Painter 110). In light of the limited opportunities for advancement that many workers faced, biographies of self-made men in popular magazines offered audiences real-life examples of men who rose from humble beginnings to respectable positions with increased wealth. On the other hand, the success myth also served to placate these same working- and middle-class individuals who were struggling in a capitalist society. As popular literature for the masses, "the 'rags-to-riches' tradition, by creating an illusion of opportunity, served as a social pacifier inimical to reform" (Weiss 7). Thus, stories about self-made men, offered readers an escape from their humdrum existences. "In fantasy," the working and middle classes "briefly attained the success that often eluded them in the real world" (Kilmer 3).

Many scholars have assumed that no one produced any success literature specifically for late nineteenth-century black audiences. Michael Denning, for example, assures us, "There were [...] no dime novels aimed at Blacks; and I have not found evidence of any Black readership" (30). Indeed, Richard Weiss claims that mainstream success literature targets native-born, Protestant, middle-class whites and that there is a "nativist bias" in these texts (116). Yet, various other sources indicate that the black working- and middle-class communities were just as hungry for success literature as whites, perhaps even more so. For example, Michael Fultz's article, "'The Morning Cometh': African American Periodicals, Education, and the Black Middle Class, 1900-1930," discusses how several early twentieth-century black journals, such as the *Colored American Magazine, The Voice of the Negro,* and *Alexander's Magazine*, address black higher education. Referring to members of the emerging black middle class, Fultz writes that "Among other traits, they were decidedly race conscious, and they forcefully advocated self-help, character-building, social uplift, and race patronage and solidarity" (130). Clearly turn-of-the-century blacks *were* concerned with success and progress, but literary and cultural historians tend to analyze these concerns within the parameters of race literature not success literature. Ultimately, the American gospel of success was as much a part of black culture as it was of white culture. Pauline Hopkins's fiction and biographical sketches are testimonies to this fact. Denning may not have found any popular literature aimed at black readers, but, as Hazel Carby contends, "Hopkins continued to write political fiction at the same time as she adopted popular fiction formulas and was the first Afro-American author to produce a black popular fiction that drew on the archetypes of dime novels and story papers" (144). Claudia Tate speculates that reading Hopkins's fictional texts "probably incited pleasure" for her audience "because they enabled these readers temporarily to escape oppression and gain access to a collective racial desire for enlarged social opportunity as full-fledged American citizens" (7). Indeed, one can seek "escape" by reading fiction, but Hopkins seeks to educate, not pacify her readership. Even as Hopkins acknowledges having "introduced [into *Contending Forces*] enough of the exquisitely droll humor peculiar to the Negro (a work like this would not be complete without it) to give a bright touch to an otherwise gruesome subject" (*Contending Forces* 16), her main objective in portraying lynching, mob violence and sexual exploitation is "to raise the stigma of degradation from [her] race" (13), hardly an escapist venture. For Hopkins, popular literature for the African American masses offers more than a momentary reprieve from the severe reality of living during the nadir. In the now frequently quoted preface to *Contending Forces*, she writes, "Fiction is of great value to any people as a preserver of manners and customs – religious, political and social. It is a record of growth and development from generation to generation" (13-14), expressing her commitment to using popular fiction to motivate black people to strive to succeed and to document their success.

Post-Reconstruction black leaders believed economic success achieved through racial solidarity and self-help would earn the black masses the respect of whites and the full benefits of United States citizenship. During this period, blacks increasingly viewed wealth as a sign of success and they adopted "the ideas of the gospel of wealth and Social Darwinism and applied them to their own racial situation" (Meier 23, 24). By the late nineteenth century, the typical definition of success included some form of affluence, eminence, respectability and social mobility, while personal virtues of the self-made man included "thrift, perseverance, loyalty, integrity, [and] honor" (Kilmer 6). Considering the political, social and economic condition of the majority of African Americans in the early 1900s, this paradigm does not adequately reflect their experiences because it does not factor in the impact of discrimination or racism on a black person's ability to earn a significant income or have access to the same social circles as white Americans. On the surface, Hopkins's definition of success appears the same as the traditional model in which an individual labors independently to achieve personal success. Hopkins introduces the element of racial uplift, however, that not only makes the success archetype more germane for African Americans, but also highlights the role social environment plays in one's ability to succeed in the United States. Hopkins's success archetype is ever mindful of the need to work cooperatively to ensure that the black individual *and* the black community achieve progress. By modifying the success paradigm in this way, she implicitly responds to white oppression and also offers African Americans an alternative success model that embraces African American culture. For example, in the "Famous Men of the Negro Race" series, Hopkins adopts and alters the traditional success formula and constructs a paradigm apropos of the African American experience by gauging the impact of race, racism and the black community on the life of a successful black man. In "Famous Men of the Negro Race," Hopkins subscribes to the concepts of affluence, eminence and social mobility; however, she revises the traditional definition of success by augmenting the meaning of social respectability to include freedom from racial discrimination. Rather than completely subscribing to the traditional definition of success, Hopkins deemphasizes the materialism and competition characteristic of the traditional model and places more emphasis on making social contributions to one's community. An examination of individual biographical sketches, and the series as a whole, reveals that Hopkins defines success not only in terms of the extent to which a man has been able to overcome hardship, increase his net worth, and acquire fame and social acceptance, but also by the degree to which he acts to help others. Furthermore, the level of social respectability Hopkins's successful man achieves revolves around his acceptance in white society. In the traditional model, conversely, a successful white man does not need to be socially accepted in black society. In light of the discordant social, economic and political climate of the United States at the turn of the century, it seems only fitting that Hopkins would choose to use her work to expose the race specific nature of the gospel of success.

There are some challenges to identifying a standard female model of success since there has not been as much scholarship in this area as there has been on male or generic success. As Karol Kelley notes in *Models for the Multitudes*, "Female paradigms present certain problems that male paradigms do not. There is no body of literature on feminine success, so female models are harder to find than male models" (30). Nonetheless, she posits that success for women is based on the premise that "In nineteenth-century America there were few occupations open to women which could offer them wealth or status" (xvii), and as such, motherhood, domesticity, sorority, and true womanhood are factors that have been used to measure a woman's achievements (xviii). In essence, the virtues of true womanhood that dominated American society from the 1820s to the 1860s, "piety, purity, submissiveness, and domesticity" (Welter 152), continued to create the conditions of success for the late nineteenth- and early twentieth-century woman (Decker 27). Indeed, according to Barbara Welter, without these virtues "no matter whether there was fame, achievement or wealth, all was ashes. With them she was promised happiness and power" (152). Interestingly, the expectations of true womanhood did evolve to the point where those who promoted success for women encouraged them to retain their traditional "feminine virtues," along with "a substitution of new elements in the cluster of qualities which comprised the ideal woman. Activity, assertiveness, intelligence, and independence replaced passivity, submission, ignorance, and dependence. [...] She would be seriously devoted to her work, as well as committed to her family. She would work to satisfy her own needs; yet her work would benefit society" (Ognibene 26-27). In short, the archetypal successful female can be described as a woman who either inherits or marries into money and keeps her feminine virtues intact. Some women did pursue a business enterprise, but because women were still expected to live in separate spheres from men and remain in the domestic space of the home, school or church, the self-made woman did not exist per se. Most successful women (with a few exceptions) at the turn of the twentieth century achieved influence and wealth through marriage to a successful man.

The thematic content of Hopkins's journalism in the *Colored American Magazine* exemplifies how she persists in applying and modifying the traditional American success myth to the unique social circumstances of the black middle-class community. In "Famous Women of the Negro Race," Hopkins endeavors to construct a separate black woman's paradigm for success by providing her reading audience with historical and contemporary figures worthy of emulation. The *Colored American Magazine*'s "Announcement for 1902" advertises Hopkins's project as "One of the most unique features ever printed by any magazine." Her notions about success echo Ruffin's concerns that "progressive colored women" are not living up to their full potential, "many of them warped and cramped for lack of opportunity" ("Address" 14): "Can the Negro woman learn anything? Is she capable of the highest mental culture? are questions which have been conclusively answered in this series of articles" (Hopkins, "Higher Education" 445). Defining success archetypes for black women becomes racialized; Hopkins adapts the standard model to defend their intellect and virtue in the first installment: "It is profitable, too, for us to appreciate the fact that the women of the race have always kept pace with every advance made, often leading the upward flight. [...] In writing of the attainments of a people it is important that the position of its women be carefully defined – whether endowed with traits of character fit for cultivation, bright intellects and broad humanitarianism, virtuous in all things, tender, loving and of deep religious convictions" ("Phenomenal Vocalists" 46). The cultivation of character and womanhood figure prominently among Hopkins's list of black female attainments. Arguing that black women have been "maligned and misunderstood" but are just as virtuous and gifted as white women, Hopkins offers her series as proof of their equality (46).

Based on the content of her "Famous Women" series, it is apparent that Hopkins measures a black woman's success by the extent to which she utilizes her artistic and intellectual talent to uplift the African American community. Hopkins's successful black woman is, ideally, a race woman who marries a successful man; simultaneously, the women she spotlights are particularly adept at their professions. Her subjects are vocalists, writers, educators, artists and club women who overcome hardship and humble beginnings to use their talents to help benefit and advance the causes of the black community. Hopkins informs readers, for example, that Elizabeth Greenfield had a broad vocal range and could play multiple instruments. She also sang for Queen Victoria while on tour abroad. Annie Pauline Pindell had a broad vocal range and sang in three languages. Phillis Wheatley's "style of writings is pure; her verses full of beauty and sublimity; her language chaste and elegant. Could she have lived a few years longer she would have been renowned as a poet" ("Some Literary Workers" 279). Frances E. W. Harper's intellectual gifts were respected by both whites and blacks: "her ability and labors were everywhere appreciated, and her meetings largely attended. She breakfasted with the Governor of Maine" ("Literary Workers Concluded" 367). Hopkins informs her readers that Mary Church Terrell was so highly respected as a public speaker that she was chosen to represent the white Equal Suffrage Association of Washington at the National Woman's Suffrage Association (370). Fanny Jackson, head of The Institute at Philadelphia, achieved success because "Her ability in governing this institution of learning has given her world-wide fame; she is respected by parents and guardians, and loved by her pupils" ("Educators" 46). Elizabeth Smith, another educator, was noteworthy for using "her wide influence among the young of both races for their elevation and advancement" ("Educators Continued" 126). Thus, achieving renown for one's talents also brings renown to the African American community.

It is not enough that these women are gifted; they use these gifts pragmatically. "If we possess any particular talent," Hopkins writes, "the first question which presents itself to the practical mind is, how this talent can best serve us as a pivot for wage-earning? This is a momentous question for the Negro race at this stage of our progress, when avenues for gathering cold American dollars are gradually lessening for us" ("Artists" 366). Wealth does not receive a lengthy discussion in this series, but Hopkins shows that she is aware of artists' need to earn a living so they can assist others. As an active participant in the black women's club movement, Hopkins devotes the most attention in these articles to black women's racial uplift activities. She contends that through service both individual women and the African American community can benefit and improve their social, economic and political status. "In the wonderful scheme of God's earthly government," she argues, "the doing of good to others is the direct means of achieving success in life for ourselves. All science, commerce, industry, spread blessings abroad, leading to fame and fortune if pursued for the benefits spread abroad" ("Higher Education" 446).

It is interesting that Hopkins, who never married, makes a point of showing how successful black women are both intelligent and married. In "Higher Education" she writes, "In reviewing the careers of these young women we must not fail to note one important fact: three of them have become the wives of progressive college men. Education has not caused these women to shirk the cares and responsibilities of private life; rather, we believe each feels the blessing which her example must be to the entire race. Education, with us, does not encourage celibacy but is developing pleasant homes and beautiful families" (450). Most of the women Hopkins includes in her series were married. Annie Pindell was married to Joseph Pindell, of a well-known Baltimore family. Gertrude Fortune Grimké, Fanny M. Jackson, Ida B. Wells and Frances E. W. Harper were married. Hopkins even gives an account of Mary Church and Judge Robert H. Terrell's wedding. One subject, Elizabeth Baker, "is particularly interesting to us by reason of the fame that has come to her husband" (449). Hopkins's agenda in her nonfiction thus differs slightly from her agenda in her fiction, where she critiques marriageability's central role in the traditional woman's success paradigm. Her journalism provides explicit models for black female readers to aspire to while also illustrating to white readers how intelligent and capable black women are. In her fiction, Hopkins's treatment of female success offers implicit critiques of the traditional archetype that merely judges all women according to the extent to which they have married a successful man. In *Contending Forces*, for example, black women achieve success both through matrimony with accomplished men (i.e., Sappho Clark and Dora Smith's unions with Will Smith and Arthur Lewis, respectively) and also through active participation in the club movement, which Mrs. Willis demonstrates.

A close examination of Mrs. Willis's function in *Contending Forces* reveals how highly Hopkins values women's ambition beyond the boundaries of childrearing and wedlock, principles which are antithetical to the narrator's. We see an early indication of this in a statement the narrator makes about women like Mrs. Willis inhabiting cities throughout the Eastern seaboard: "Mrs. Willis was a good example of a class of women of color that came into existence at the close of the Civil War. She was not a *rara avis,* but one of many possibilities which the future will develop from among the colored women of New England" (144). If we take this comment at face value, and trust the narrator's claim that Mrs. Willis is a common type of woman, then we should question why there are no other characters like her in the novel. Hopkins understands Mrs. Willis may well be a rarity to the majority of her readers. She assumes they know little about Mrs. Willis's class and enlightens them accordingly: "Even today it is erroneously believed that all racial development among colored people has taken place since emancipation. It is impossible of belief for some, that little circles of educated men and women of color have existed since the Revolutionary War. [...] Mrs. Willis was one from among these classes" (145). Moreover, there are instances when Mrs. Willis's character is cast quite favorably: "At sixty odd she was vigorous, well-preserved, broad and comfortable in appearance, with an aureole of white hair crowning a pleasant face" (145). She is in fine physical shape, the halo-like ring of white hair identifying her as a virtuous matron.

Hopkins uses the two phases of Mrs. Willis's adult life to represent two paths to black women's success. During the first phase, Mrs. Willis is devoted to her husband and his career while remaining at home raising their children: "She had loved her husband with a love ambitious for his advancement. His foot on the stairs mounting to the two-room tenement which constituted their home in the early years of married life, had sent a thrill to her very heart as she sat sewing baby clothes for the always expected addition to the family" (146). She encourages her husband to run for the state legislature, and although a career in politics is not his initial goal, her support helps him become more successful and wealthy. Mrs. Willis's marital life fits the pattern of late nineteenth-century middle-class women assigned to domestic spaces. Even though she is excluded from the business world, she still lives an accomplished life. As Jeffrey Louis Decker explains, "Because women took on the roles of virtuous mothers and supporting wives, entrepreneurial success was mediated through the achievements of men" (17). As a dutiful wife and mother, Mrs. Willis initially experiences financial and social success vicariously through her husband, but when he dies he does not pass on his wealth to her. The narrator does not indicate what has happened to her husband's fortune, only that: "Money, the sinews of living and social standing, she did not possess upon her husband's death" (Hopkins, *Contending Forces* 146). As a result, she enters the second phase of her life and leaves her domestic sphere to earn a living, demonstrating that neither her personal ambitions nor her prospects for success die with her husband. Widowhood, in fact, expands Mrs. Willis's opportunities for advancement. She looks for a means of supporting herself and decides to dedicate herself to "the great cause of the evolution of true womanhood in the work of the 'Woman Question' as embodied in marriage and suffrage" (146). In this way, she matches the profile of women who "became entrepreneurs only after a matrimonial crisis, such as the death or divorce of a husband" (Decker 17). There are some similarities between club work and entrepreneurship in terms of the drive and motivation one must have to be successful. Mrs. Willis, in fact, is characterized as a cunning entrepreneur: "Shrewd in business matters, many a subtle business man had been worsted by her apparent womanly weakness and charming simplicity" (Hopkins, *Contending Forces* 144).

Mrs. Willis's character models Hopkins's real-life expectation that "Beyond the common duties peculiar to woman's sphere, the colored woman must have an intimate knowledge of every question that agitates the councils of the world" ("Some Literary Workers" 277). Mrs. Willis represents an archetype of black female success through active participation in the club movement to benefit the race outside the home. "The guiding principle behind all the clubs was racial uplift through self-help," Deborah White notes (27-28). In Ma Smith's sewing-circle, young African American women use domestic skills to raise money to improve the church's finances. Discussing political events develops their intellectual abilities and Mrs. Willis's lecture further stresses their moral responsibility to themselves and others. According to Hopkins, a black woman has a particular duty to help the black community because of her "unique position" in society: "Upon the Negro woman lies a great responsibility – the broadening and deepening of her race, the teaching of youth to grasp present opportunities, and, greater than all, to help clear the moral atmosphere by inculcating a clearer appreciation of the Holy Word and its application to everyday living" ("Some Literary Workers" 277). Active participation in the women's club movement enabled black women to successfully live up to these expectations: "So, through the example of a few public-spirited women, the Negro woman has become ubiquitous in club life, over-flowing into all the avenues of self-help that are adopted by her white sisters as a means to the end of rising herself and 'lifting others as she climbs'" (Hopkins, "Club Life" 274).

Mrs. Willis is a successful advocate for black women. She helps form several colored women's clubs and becomes a powerful leader in her Boston community. Yet, there are some compromises she must make in her line of work since entrepreneurial women's "marketplace ambitions typically led to the diminishment of their domestic authority as wives and mothers" (Decker 18). Mrs. Willis pursues club work only after she has raised her children and supported her husband's political career. She is proud of having had a family, "It was her boast that she had made the fortunes of her family, and settled her children well in life"; yet, once she becomes a public figure, certain aspects of her domestic authority are weakened (Hopkins, *Contending Forces* 147). For example, she inadvertently repels at least one woman she hopes to inspire. Mrs. Willis's comments about the black woman's virtue attract Sappho's attention and compel her to talk with Mrs. Willis about her past: "For a moment the flood-gates of suppressed feeling flew open in the girl's heart, and she longed to lean her head on that motherly breast and unburden her sorrows there" (155). But then, all of a sudden, Sappho changes her mind and becomes reticent as "a wave of repulsion toward this woman and her effusiveness, so forced and insincere," keeps her from divulging her secret (155).

Yarborough calls attention to this scene to support his theory that Sappho's repulsion mirrors Hopkins's true position on Mrs. Willis's conduct. Other literary critics have followed Yarborough's lead. Siobhan Somerville argues that Mrs. Willis's portrayal "symbolized ambivalence about the possibility of women's solidarity" (154). Thomas Cassidy suggests, "Sappho's ambivalence toward her seems to reflect the narrator's. The problem with Mrs. Willis is that she is too slick" (666). Hanna Wallinger observes that Hopkins's portrayal of Mrs. Willis is "not totally positive. The heroine Sappho especially resents Mrs. Willis's attempt to meddle in her affairs, her effusive and inquisitive manner and her officiousness" (105). Apparently seizing on the narrator's comment that Mrs. Willis's designs for concentrating her efforts on the Woman Question are "conceived in selfishness" (Hopkins, *Contending Forces* 147), Claudia Tate goes as far as to argue that Mrs. Willis is a "successful but problematic professional woman": "She revises the traditional role of the retiring, reticent, widowed matron to become an outspoken race woman who attracts ambivalence precisely because she seeks self-authority rather than selflessness" (164). Selfless acts may be requisite of the sentimental matron, but not of the successful woman. What is more important to Hopkins is not how one's plans are conceived, but their outcome, which in Mrs. Willis's case, "bore glorious fruit in the formation of clubs of colored women banded together for charity, for study, for every reason under God's glorious heavens that can better the condition of mankind" (*Contending Forces* 147). Josephine St. Pierre Ruffin utilized this success rhetoric during an 1895 convention address when she identified issues "of especial interest to us as *colored* women," including not only children's education, vocational training for black youth, and moral education for the black community, but also black women's own "mental elevation and physical development" and the means "to make the most of our own, to some extent limited opportunities" ("Address" 14). Ruffin established a precedent for Mrs. Willis, who employs the same success rhetoric to encourage Sappho to "stand up for uplifting of the race and womanhood" (Hopkins, *Contending Forces* 156).

Mrs. Willis's "sheer force of will-power and indomitable pluck" (148) does challenge Hopkins to depict her as a believable and sympathetic character. Claudia Tate recognizes Mrs. Willis's unconventionality and argues Hopkins "could not resolve the discomfort of her contemporaries about female will to power," but "she could mitigate its effect by deploying what Fredric Jameson has called 'strategies of containment,' which is to say that she allows Sappho to voice and control the likely expression of her contemporaries' objections" (164). I think Hopkins ultimately mitigates this discomfort by drawing on the literary tradition of success instead of sentimentalism. When Sappho obsesses over how her past transgressions, committed under duress, will affect her marriageability, Mrs. Willis proclaims, "See here, my dear, I am a practical woman of the world" (156). Mrs. Willis draws from her sagacious understanding of human nature to assure Sappho that she need only "have faith and trust" in order to fulfill her duty to herself "and the good of those about [her]" (157). Our last image of Mrs. Willis is of her vanishing "in a crowd of other matrons" (157). Sappho is "impressed in spite of herself, by the woman's words," which leads the narrator to conclude: "There was evidently more in this woman than appeared upon the surface. [...] There are men and women whose seeming uselessness fit perfectly into the warp and woof of Destiny's web. All things work together for good" (157). Even though the narrator initially suggests that Mrs. Willis's mien renders her an ineffective mentor, in this final comment, the narrator unwittingly gives credence to Mrs. Willis's driving ambition, beneficent work, and sage advice. Hopkins's faith in the positive role Mrs. Willis's pragmatism plays in black women's lives as well as racial uplift movements is certainly more constant than the narrator's.

Hopkins broke new ground with Mrs. Willis's character. With the exception of Frances E.W. Harper's racially ambiguous Janette Alston in "The Two Offers" (1859), black women did not depict such forcefully independent and successful female characters in their fiction. Mrs. Willis's character serves as one of Hopkins's very first attempts to move beyond the parameters of sentimental literature to offer alternative models of success for black women. Hopkins is like other advocates who "dangled a dramatic vision of a successful woman before their audience and invited members of their audience to become that ideal" (Ognibene 159). By the conclusion of *Contending Forces,* Sappho has married "the noblest of men" and has succeeded in creating a family with Will and Alphonse (401). The "life of promise" she happily contemplates is not complete with matrimony and motherhood, however. Sappho, like Mrs. Willis before her, is destined to achieve eminence and respectability through matrimony *and* racial uplift: "United by love, chastened by sorrow and self-sacrifice, [Will and Sappho] planned to work together to bring joy to hearts crushed by despair" (401). One question remains: Would

Hopkins, who did not marry but rather followed Mrs. Willis's alternative path to success by concentrating her energies on her writing career and club activities, have considered herself a success? Her work on behalf of racial uplift, black women's clubs, and the *Colored American Magazine* qualify as successful achievements by her own standards.

[1] For more on the contested NACW elections, see Harley and Terrell.

[2] "Mrs. Ruffin's Attacks" is handwritten by an unknown person on the front page of *The National Notes* issue containing the Woman's Era Club's resolutions. A microfilm copy of this issue is located at Rutgers University.

WORKS CITED

"Announcement for 1902." *Colored American Magazine* 4.5 (April 1902): n.p.

Carby, Hazel V. *Reconstructing Womanhood: The Emergence of the Afro-American Woman Novelist.* New York: Oxford UP, 1987.

Cassidy, Thomas. "Contending Contexts: Pauline Hopkins's *Contending Forces*." *African American Review* 32.4 (1998): 661-672.

Decker, Jeffrey Louis. *Made in America: Self-Styled Success from Horatio Alger to Oprah Winfrey.* Minneapolis: U of Minnesota P, 1997.

Denning, Michael. *Mechanic Accents: Dime Novels and Working-Class Culture in America.* London: Verso, 1987.

Fultz, Michael. "'The Morning Cometh': African-American Periodicals, Education, and the Black Middle Class, 1900-1930." *Print Culture in a Diverse America.* Ed. James P. Danky and Wayne A. Wiegand. Urbana: U of Illinois P, 1998.

Harley, Sharon. "Mary Church Terrell: Genteel Militant." *Black Leaders of the Nineteenth Century.* Ed. Leon Litwack and August Meier. Urbana: U of Illinois P, 1988. 307-321.

Hopkins, Pauline E. *Contending Forces: A Romance Illustrative of Negro Life North and South.* 1900. New York: Oxford UP, 1988.

—. "Famous Women of the Negro Race. I. Phenomenal Vocalists." *Colored American Magazine* 4.1 (Nov. 1901): 45-53.

—. "Famous Women of the Negro Race. IV. Some Literary Workers." *Colored American Magazine* 4.4 (March 1902): 276-280.

—. "Famous Women of the Negro Race. V. Literary Workers (Concluded)." *Colored American Magazine* 4.5 (April 1902): 366-371.

—. "Famous Women of the Negro Race. VI. Educators." *Colored American Magazine* 5.1 (May 1902): 41-46.

—. "Famous Women of the Negro Race. VII. Educators (Continued)." *Colored American Magazine* 5.2 (June 1902): 125-130.

—. "Famous Women of the Negro Race. IX. Club Life Among Colored Women." *Colored American Magazine* 5.4 (August 1902): 273-277.

—. "Famous Women of the Negro Race. X. Artists." *Colored American Magazine* 5.5 (Sept. 1902): 362-367.

—. "Famous Women of the Negro Race. XII. Higher Education of Colored Women in White Schools and Colleges." *Colored American Magazine* 5.6 (October 1902): 445-450.

Kelley, Karol. *Models for the Multitudes: Social Values in the American Popular Novel, 1850-1920*. New York: Greenwood, 1987.

Kilmer, Paulette D. *The Fear of Sinking: The American Success Formula in the Gilded Age*. Knoxville: U of Tennessee P, 1996.

McCullough, Kate. "Slavery, Sexuality, and Genre: Pauline Hopkins and the Representation of Female Desire." *The Unruly Voice: Rediscovering Pauline Elizabeth Hopkins*. Ed. John Cullen Gruesser. Urbana: U of Illinois P, 1996. 21-49.

Meier, August. *Negro Thought in America, 1880-1915: Radical Ideologies in the Age of Booker T. Washington*. Ann Arbor: U of Michigan P, 1963.

Ognibene, Elaine R. "Women to Women: The Rhetoric of Success for Women, 1860-1920." Diss. Rensselaer Polytechnic Institute, 1979.

Painter, Nell Irvin. *Standing at Armageddon: The United States, 1877-1919*. New York: Norton, 1987.

"Report of the Woman's Era Club for 1899." *The National Association Notes*. 3.10 (April 1900): 1-2.

Ruffin, Josephine St. Pierre. "Address of Josephine St. P. Ruffin, President of Conference." *Woman's Era* Aug. 1895: 13-15. *Emory Woman Writers Resource Project at the Lewis H. Beck Center*. Emory University. 12 June 2007. <http://chaucer.library.emory.edu/wwrp>

—. "Greeting." *Woman's Era* 24 March 1894: 8. *Emory Woman Writers Resource Project at the Lewis H. Beck Center*. Emory University. 12 June 2007. <http://chaucer.library.emory.edu/wwrp>

Sawaya, Francesca. *Modern Women, Modern Work: Domesticity, Professionalism, and American Writing, 1890-1950*. Philadelphia: U of Pennsylvania P, 2004.

Somerville, Siobhan. "Passing through the Closet in Pauline E. Hopkins's *Contending Forces*." *American Literature* 69.1 (1997): 139-166.

Streitmatter, Rodger. *Raising Her Voice: African-American Women Journalists Who Changed History*. Lexington: UP of Kentucky, 1994.

Tate, Claudia. *Domestic Allegories of Political Desire: The Black Heroine's Text at the Turn of the Century*. New York: Oxford UP, 1992.

Terrell, Mary Church. *A Colored Woman in a White World*. New York: Hall, 1996.

Wallinger, Hanna. *Pauline E. Hopkins: A Literary Biography*. Athens: U of Georgia P, 2005.

Weiss, Richard. *The American Myth of Success: From Horatio Alger to Norman Vincent Peale*. New York: Basic, 1969.

Welter, Barbara. "The Cult of True Womanhood: 1820-1860." *American Quarterly* 18.2 (1966): 151-174.

White, Deborah Gray. *Too Heavy a Load: Black Women in Defense of Themselves 1894-1994*. New York: Norton, 1999.

Yarborough, Richard. Introduction. *Contending Forces: A Romance Illustrative of Negro Life North and South*. By Pauline Hopkins. New York: Oxford UP, 1988. xxvii-xlviii.

Elusive Autobiographical Performativity: Vicey Skipwith's Home Place and Sarah Parker Remond's Italian Retreat[1]

Angelita Reyes

> "If we don't name ourselves, we are nothing."
>
> Audre Lorde

> Memory is archival as a collection of tangible and intangible artifacts that include our discoveries in the context of history, culture, and intellect [...]. Memory invokes the things that were and the things that are not. Memory opposes history and embraces it with ordinary things and extraordinary artifacts.
>
> Angelita Reyes
>
> *Mothering ACROSS Cultures*

The latest book from the award-winning historian Martha Hodes, *The Sea Captain's Wife: A True Story of Love, Race, and War in the Nineteenth Century* (2006), creates an autobiographical narrative of Eunice Richardson Stone Connolly (1831-1877), an impoverished white woman from New England, who in 1869 married a wealthy sea captain, a man of color from the Cayman Islands. The sea captain, Smiley Connolly, was definitively "black" in the United States, but more or less "white" in the Caribbean. As Hodes puts it: "In the United States he was not white, but in the Caribbean he was not black" (Stasio 2006). Although interracial marriage was not illegal in Massachusetts at that time, marriage across racial boundaries was socially less accepted than in the Caribbean where prejudices were based on gradations of skin color and hierarchal phenotypes rather than on legal definitions of "race." A Civil War widow with two children, Eunice Richardson Stone Connolly escaped from her life of dire poverty in Massachusetts for respectability in the Caribbean. Ironically, Eunice had married up. Leaving her New England home and a life of adversity, Eunice went with Connolly to Grand Cayman Island where she lived the rest of her life in relative luxury and comfort. She died in 1877 without ever returning to Massachusetts.

From the book's romantic title to the creation of an autobiographical narrative with the cache of Richardson family letters that she discovered, Hodes merges the historian's archival and on-site investigations (she traveled to Grand Cayman Island) with the letters that Eunice Richardson Connolly wrote as the sea captain's wife. About her own journey in the discovery of evidence as a history detective, Hodes states, "Following every lead in a collection of family correspondence took me out to the open road, tracking down an intersection in a New England town, a house in a Gulf South city, even a particular expanse of sand on a Caribbean island" ("A House in Vermont"). Connolly's nineteenth-century self-representation – in this instance, epistolary autobiography – is located in her letters that indicate place, memory, and community that are elusive, fragmented, and at times obscure.

While there are the "grand themes" of rags to riches, interracial romance, race and racism, the Civil War, and sea travel in the Caribbean, I am fascinated with *The Sea Captain's Wife* because of the way in which Hodes reconstructs Connolly's autobiographical space through various archival artifacts such as public records, census data, ships' logs, and even weather reports, that engage reading, writing, and interpreting a particular woman's life in the nineteenth century. Yet *The Sea Captain's Wife* remains an elusive autobiography of collected letters. Hodes is involved in collaborating with Connolly's elusive autobiographical voice and, therefore, in delineating the boundaries of what constitutes an autobiographical text because "*what* has happened in this life is more immediately compelling than *how* it is being communicated and by *whom*" (Stone 234).

In contextualizing Connolly's epistolary writings, Hodes became a history sleuth like Jean Fagan Yellin who unveiled the context and extraordinary text of Harriet A. Jacobs's *Incidents in the Life of a Slave Girl*: *Written by Herself* (1861). Jacobs (1813-1897) was born into slavery and her literary autobiography is the account of that life in slavery and of her quest for freedom and dignity as a woman and mother. Yellin traced Jacobs's veiled background through archival research, public records, and clues from the published autobiography in order to bring back to life Jacobs's original autobiography that had slipped into oblivion. Hodes and Yellin privilege material artifacts (such as letters, public records, and natural environments) in their uncovering of circumstantial as well as historical evidence that documents the autobiographical presence of women who were both ordinary and extraordinary.

Harriet Jacobs delayed her escape to freedom for seven years secluded in the crawl space of her grandmother's house because of the imperative to safeguard her children; she also honed her literacy skills during those years as a fugitive slave in hiding. Eunice and the Richardson family were literate, but impoverished working class people and as Hodes explained in an interview, "working class correspondence was not saved. Prominent families saved their correspondence because they had a sense of their own significance. Working class families don't see themselves significant in the same way [...]. It's remarkable that the family saved Eunice's letters" (Stasio). Most nineteenth-century New Englanders learned how to read for religious reasons. Not only was the King James Bible central to education, but the "aim of the [secular] *New England Primer* [...] was to induce Bible literacy in children as a means to spiritual maturity" (Fessenden 7). For enslaved African Americans, on the other hand, reading and writing skills were often unattainable and when attained, literacy was a rite of passage; it was about the access, the loophole to writing oneself into humanity (Davis and Gates 185).

As I read Martha Hodes's captivating account of her own journey of discovery into the, at first, ordinary and then extraordinary life of Eunice Richardson Stone Connolly, I was intrigued by the seemingly unlimited power of literacy – the vital empowerment of the written word – that readily enables the historian to engage with discovery and to resurrect portraitures of autobiography. Martha Hodes and Jean Fagan Yellin filled in the spaces of their subjects' autobiographical portraitures through gender-oriented speculation and intriguing historical contexts. Yellin and Hodes interpreted and enabled the autobiographical "I" (through historical evidence and cultural speculation) when their subjects (Jacobs and Connolly) did not or chose not to do so.

At the same time that I was intrigued by the power of autobiographical literacy that could delineate female subjectivity, I also wondered about non-literate black women as historical subjects, creating autobiographical inscriptions. Is the autobiographical moment limited to discursive literacy? To echo benchmark paradigms coming out of 1980s black feminist discourse, if "all the women are white, all the blacks are men, but some of *them* are brave," how did some of the non-literate brave black women articulate the "richness they held" and name themselves by creating alternative autobiographical loopholes and retreats? (Hull, Scott and Smith; Walker 232).

This essay highlights the autobiographical acts of two nineteenth-century African American women, Vicey Skipwith (1856-1936) and Sarah Parker Remond (1824-1894) – the former, known in her rural Virginia environment; and the latter, prominent in national and international abolitionist and feminist communities. Vicey Skipwith, born into slavery on the eve of the Civil War, was non-literate, but counteracted hegemonic denials of black female agency by becoming a property owner in her community of freedpeople and former slaveholders after Reconstruction (1865-1877). She named herself through the powerful significance of land ownership in the American south. Sarah Parker Remond was born free in an affluent Salem, Massachusetts family. She was educated and at the end of the Civil War in 1866 (she was already in England) went to Italy where she attained a diploma in medicine. Thereafter, Italy offered an environment that enabled Remond to fulfill educational goals and personal achievement. Europe in general was no longer an imagined refuge of "desires" where she could only "for a time enjoy freedom," but a bona fide retreat for comfortable measures of freedom (Remond, "Sarah" 286). My focus on Remond's Italian years is an attempt to bring to the forefront through intertextual autobiographical traces the neglected period of Remond's life in Italy.[2]

The lives of these two African American women never crossed, but their propensity for expressions of gendered and racialized agency intersects in the context of how they inscribed autobiographical identity during the long nineteenth century. Despite the fact that Skipwith was born enslaved and Remond was born free, each was undeniably affected by slavery and abolition. Remond worked as an abolitionist on behalf of enslaved men and women like Skipwith. Both women were socially involved in different spheres of creating empowerment – loopholes and retreats – for themselves and their kin. Autobiographical loopholes and retreats, as will be discussed in this essay, signify transformations and transcendences of black female subjectivity. Remond ultimately located self-representation and "retreat" in Italy. On the other hand, property ownership was a "loophole" that provided Skipwith an economic and social opening for self-reliance. As a freedwoman and farmer, Skipwith could, for the first time, legally enter into a contract – the symbolic "signing" of her name – and even legally enter into a marriage contract. Slave marriages had not been legally recognized and slaves did not have the right to contract law. Remond and Skipwith inscribed autobiographical representations through alternative social and political acts and, indeed, named themselves because of their ambitions and aspirations. Therefore, within this essay autobiographical inscription as feminist performativity "defies generic stabilization" (Smith and Watson, *De/Colonizing* xviii) and pushes the boundaries constituting Audre Lorde's imperative that "if we don't name ourselves, we are nothing" (Hammon 19). Sidonie Smith and Julia Watson have long argued how "there are other modes of life story telling, both oral and written, to be recognized, other *genealogies* of life story telling to be chronicled, [...] to be factored into the making and unmaking of autobiographical subjects [...]" (*De/Colonizing* xviii, my emphasis). Such genealogies, which are often elusive, fragmented, or witnessed through indirect discourse, must include women who inscribed their lives beyond conventional literary autobiography.

Against the backdrop of slavery, abolition, the Civil War, and post-emancipation transitions that included social and political upheaval, Skipwith and Remond were both ordinary and extraordinary because of the ways in which they each defined and asserted black female agency and the sense of place. Moreover, despite any "contrary instincts" (Walker 235) regarding black female subjectivity, Skipwith gained ironic ascendancy by owning the very parcel of land on which she once had been enslaved as property. Despite contrary instincts, Remond became a physician and had an interracial marriage. Indeed, despite contrary instincts, Skipwith's dwelling – the antebellum log cabin – continues to stand well into the twenty-first century. The cabin is at the site of historical memory and national integrity (named on the Virginia Landmarks Register and the National Register of Historic Places), which "is an active rather than a passive response to the social, historical, and environmental conditions" of an African American setting (Singleton 13). In other words, through cultural and environmental transformation, a slave dwelling that used to be utilitarian can now be viewed as a dynamic cultural material artifact that resonates with history and autobiographical memory at the home place. What is the significance of the term "home place"?

Home place is a vernacular term used throughout the American south (by blacks and whites) to designate affinity to the land, the house, and memories of kinship and fictive kin, generated from the sense of belonging on the cultural landscape. A vernacular articulation of home place conveys associations of family and kinship connected to a familiar natural environment and to historical memory. The site of memory is a *space* for exploring attributes of autobiographical inscriptions where memory is "mixed, hybrid, mutant, bound intimately with life and death, with time and eternity; enveloped in a Möbius strip of the collective and the individual, the sacred and the profane, the immutable and the mobile" (Nora 25). The antebellum cabin property became a home place (no longer the slave quarters) at the site of memory produced by the acceleration of slavery and the realization of freedom.

The home place in the context of a specific cultural ethos is linked to the broad patterns of rural African Americans attempting to establish themselves as *American* citizens beyond the ratification of the Thirteenth Amendment. Skipwith's extant deed to the property and subsequent relevant public records that span a period of fifty-eight years embody the autobiographical as well as historical implication of land ownership. The concept of home place signifies house and property, but the image also embodies ancestral and descendant connections to oral histories, communal legacies, and the potential inheritance of land. Skipwith's antebellum log cabin is an architectural symbol of the home place that was transformed after the Civil War when freedmen and freedwomen established new sentiments and aspirations. While the antebellum cabin is acclaimed because of its material longevity and thus is an artifact of history that exemplifies cultural integrity, the contextual beginnings of the site elucidate Vicey Skipwith's naming of self. The former slave quarters transitioned into the home place of freedom and struggle outside and inside the memory of slavery and black female subjectivity. Skipwith and Remond experienced paradigmatic shifts – from black female subjectivity during slavery to negotiating liberty after slavery.

Pioneering twentieth-century literary scholars dealing with the intersectional paradigms of race, class, gender, sexuality, and citizenship, such as Gloria Anzaldúa, Françoise Lionnet, Shari Benstock, Frances Smith Foster, James Olney, Sidonie Smith, and Julia Watson, have revised significantly the genre of autobiography and pushed the boundaries of the autobiographical. Decidedly, autobiography is no longer viewed as "the retrospective narration of 'great' public lives" (Smith and Watson, *Interfaces* 8). Using intersectional theories that destabilized, diversified, and complicated formal autobiographical conventions, twentieth-century feminist scholars elevated women's autobiographical acts from the margins to the center of interdisciplinary inquiry, performance, and practice. At the same time, theorists and creators of autobiography questioned whether the term "autobiography" could accurately capture the varied intertextual ways of reading and writing self-representation: representation of episodes or events in a life may only be situational moments and not, in fact, the life. Smith and Watson advocate understanding how women in particular "have inscribed themselves textually, visually, or performatively" (*Interfaces* 9).

In his formation of ideas about autobiographical acts, subjectivity, and autobiographical performativity, Houston Baker, Jr. borrows from Elizabeth W. Bruss's notion of "speech acts" that intersect "context, conditions, and intentions of self-revelation" (Baker 260). While the raw materials of reading and writing were empowerment tools within the slave community, journals, letters, public records, petitions, oral-aural narratives, and material artifacts resonated with significance as part of the African American intertextual tradition in autobiographical performativity. Such private and public "texts" indicate the extent to which there are limitations in telling the life, but also reveal the push to go beyond conventional boundaries of self-revelation. Furthermore, as Bruss puts it, "[A]ll reading (or writing) involves us in choice: we choose to pursue a style or subject matter, to struggle with or against a design. We also choose [...] to take part in an interaction, and it is here that generic labels have their use. The genre does not tell us the style or construction of a text as much as how we should expect to take that 'style' or mode of construction – what force it should have for us" (qtd. in Baker 260). Performativity therefore pushes the boundaries of autobiographical expressions. Likewise, Smith and Watson further advance feminist autobiographical perspectives and maintain that "autobiographical telling is performative; it enacts the 'self' that it claims has given rise to an 'I.' And that 'I' is neither unified nor stable – it is fragmented, provisional, multiple, in process" (*Interfaces* 9). Smith and Watson contend that there are "multiple sites of the autobiographical not only *in* visual, aural, and textual media but *at* their intersections" of women's self-representation (*Interfaces* 21). As this essay highlights, material cultural artifacts such as an antebellum cabin are visual/textual interfaces associated with freedom, gendered autonomy, and the rights of citizenship.

While twentieth-century feminist literary scholars focused on expanding the scope and dynamics of women's autobiographical writing, feminist anthropologists, folklorists, historians, and archaeologists also explored alternative forms through which women create multiple sites for self-representation. Within feminist archaeology, for example, material cultural artifacts in women's communities are no longer interrogated as passive "reflections of cultural behavior" (Wilkie 10). Margaret Conkey, Joan Gero, Theresa A. Singleton, and Janet Spector are among the early group of feminist archaeologists and anthropologists who brought attention to transdisciplinary gender-and ethnicity-focused paradigms for interpreting and interrogating autobiographical identity within material culture. Addressing revised approaches to archaeological studies of culture and material artifacts, Singleton, noted scholar of African American archaeological studies, states, "Transcending and encompassing both representation and power relations is the theme of historiography, specifically how historical interpretations generated solely from written sources compare with those that incorporate analyses of material culture" (12).

Innovative archaeologists and anthropologists "abandoned methodologies that had been framed with static and functional analytical systems that attempted to pigeonhole artifacts' meanings into simple, unchanging categories" (Wilkie 10). At the archaeological and material cultural intersections of text and context, artifacts can inscribe "visual/textual self-portraiture [as] the sign of the autobiographical" (Smith and Watson, *Interfaces* 5). Building on the theoretical approaches of the aforementioned feminist scholars in literary, material, and cultural studies, I engage transdisciplinary approaches to explore how Vicey Skipwith and Sarah Parker Remond created and engaged visual/textual portraitures of autobiographical performativity.

Vicey Skipwith's Naming of Self at the Home Place

Restored and well-maintained antebellum plantation "big houses" associated with Anglo-American first families such as Monroe, Madison, Jefferson, and Randolph are visible and acclaimed throughout the Tidewater and Piedmont landscapes in Virginia. The stylized plantation houses of Berkeley, Monticello, and Montpelier, for example, reflect the history of planter-class families who created the foundations of Early America. In southern Virginia, the neoclassical stone design of Prestwould, the antebellum manor of Sir Peyton Skipwith (1740-1805) and Lady Jean Skipwith (1748-1826) is also a part of antebellum history and national memory.

Prestwould (like the other great plantations) has two histories. Whereas Sir Peyton Skipwith's Prestwould represents power, pride, and wealth grounded in the American industry for success enabled by slavery, the other history of Prestwould witnesses the enslaved people's ebb and flow of endurance, survival, and achievement, despite slavery. Whereas Prestwould's history has been well documented, we have only elusive glimpses into the history and culture of the enslaved people who lived in the "quarters." While the elegant architectural vestiges of the antebellum environment represent social and political achievements of an era, on adjacent landscapes there are vernacular architectural narratives – the deteriorated traces of the dwellings where African Virginians had once lived.[3] Despite the harshness of their lives beyond slavery, the freedmen and freedwoman "seemed to have drawn their coherence from the deep well-spring of a shared African American culture and its inventory of expressive forms [and] the creation of their own residential domains has been an achievement that has been consistently overlooked" (Vlach 230). Vicey Skipwith's antebellum cabin is a signifier – her visual/textual portraiture – of gendered achievement and self-representation.

Built of pine logs, the remarkably intact log cabin sits off a rural Virginia road, behind a canopy of young and middle-aged cedar, white ash, Spanish oak, and pine trees. This is an undisputed hinterland. The younger to middle-aged deciduous trees abound in serenity and summer breezes. There is calm and beauty among the variegated tree tops, but closer to the underbrush there is the livelihood of the grounded environment with its chiggers, fleas, and poisonous snakes. Coming from the road and winding in front of the cabin among the trees and wild flowers is the suggestion of a twentieth-century circular driveway, where there must have been a narrow nineteenth-century carriageway that was used for mules and wagons. The cabin has a side-gabled roof with a typical 16' x 20' one-room-with-loft interior floor plan.[4] There are small windows on the east, north and south walls. The exterior chimney of the west wall is built of fieldstone and cut blocks (with some mortar repairs probably early to mid-twentieth-century in date), with a brick stack laid in traditional American bond. The use of stones and bricks for the chimney reduced the possibility of fire. Prestwould's African Virginians brought stones for the cabin chimney from the same plantation quarry whose stones had been used to build the manor in the eighteenth century. The workmanship in shaping and fitting the stones shows considerable skill in masonry construction in comparison to similar log house chimneys from the same period in Mecklenburg County.

There had been a clearing or "house yard" around the cabin that fostered outdoor farm activities and family camaraderie. In prosperous years, Vicey would have had a pen for a few hogs. Scattered about are rusted twentieth-century farm tools. Most of the land is level, but there are several areas north of the cabin that slope down to one of the two creeks hidden among oaks and other hardwoods. The property is further interlaced with traces of footpaths indicating areas where Vicey Skipwith, with the help of family and neighbors, planted cash crops such as tobacco and corn; and garden produce such as collard greens and kale, beans, peas, potatoes, melons, cucumbers, and onions for self-sufficiency. There are fewer hardwoods here and the younger and second-growth pines indicate that this area had been regularly used for farming. Overall, the land has traces of tillage and human habitation. Blackberry bushes proliferate along the periphery of the setting and, according to adjacent property owners, still produce sweet fruit for easy picking during the hot summer months. The antebellum cabin as a cultural material artifact enables the Skipwith story to pass on at the site of memory and performativity.

We are familiar with the refrain "passing on" that Toni Morrison evokes through the double entendre of oral-aural meaning in her novel *Beloved.* The novel is based on a true story about a fugitive slave mother, Margaret Garner, who in 1856 killed her baby daughter rather than to allow the child to be returned to slavery. Morrison's readers must engage in historical memory and consider whether the Garner tragedy is a story to *pass* on as if we should forfeit remembering slavery's past. Or is this a story about an historical event to pass *on* – to interrogate and to convey to the next generation for empowerment from knowing about the past? While Margaret Garner was non-literate and died in slavery, she left fragments of her personal narrative with witnesses, in court transcripts, and interviews. An ordinary woman, Garner had an extraordinary story to pass *on*. Within the subjectivities of culture, history, and memory, Vicey Skipwith left a nineteenth-century story – implicating land ownership with race, gender, class, and the specificities of an intact antebellum vernacular dwelling – to pass on.

In the late spring of 1888, thirty-two year old Lovice "Vicey" Skipwith "closed" on her purchase of six and one-fifth acres of land in Mecklenburg County. Vicey Skipwith was listed in the 1870 U. S. Census – the first census to enumerate freedpeople – and she was among rural African American Virginians who had not yet taken flight from the plantation community. Her mother, Delia Skipwith Moody (ca. 1821-?) lived in a cluster of cabins further up the road from the intersection known as Cabin Point along with other lineages of African American Skipwiths, friends, and fictive kin in the census precinct called Gregory's Store. Born into slavery, Vicey Skipwith's mother, like many of the freedpeople from Prestwould, took the surname of her former slaveholders not so much as to identify with them, as to identify with the community and its natural environment. Naming was a part of the ethos of home place. There were "free negroes" among them as well – they were the African Americans who had been free before emancipation. Decidedly, there was longstanding identity, familiarity, and a sense of belonging within the network of rural roads and hamlets. Many of the people who had lived in Prestwould's slave cabins were still connected with the plantation as sharecroppers and day workers long after Reconstruction and into the early twentieth century. Vicey Skipwith had been one of those workers on the plantation until she became a property owner.

Although it was only June in that year of 1888, the early morning was already humid and hot in Mecklenburg County when Vicey Skipwith and her little entourage started out for the town of Boydton, the County Seat, where evidence of the important public transactions, and sometimes scandalous private incidents made public, which happened in the county, were kept. Vicey Skipwith was reluctant to go to the bustling town because she had to miss a day's work, but she wanted to make sure the claim was filed correctly in her name. It was an important day. She had to "hitch up the mule" and along with Brother Parker Sydnor, her sister, and three of her blood brothers, who supplied three other people to replace them for the day's work in Mr. Fulwar's tobacco field, she left the plantation. Boydton was eleven miles away and they traveled on the Old Plank Road. They were all dressed up as if they were going to church.

Vicey Skipwith would have been like any "first time home owner" thinking about her accomplishment and feeling good. Riding behind her in the wagon, her siblings may have been more boisterous. Brother Parker, young and handsome with his long naturally curly hair tied back into a pony tail, sat beside her, kept a man's poker face as he held the reins, and maintained the mule's steady pace to Boydton. Because of her past, she certainly may have felt humbled and in awe of her blessing. She wore her pink floral Sunday dress that she had made, with the white church hat that Miss Annie L discarded; and she carried her black "Sunday-go-meetin'" shoes in a sack until she got to Boydton; after dusting off her slender feet, she carefully put the shoes on.

The entourage, now quieter among themselves, headed for the back door of the court house. Vicey could not read or write. But there were people in the family who could. Her sister Celia Skipwith, the nanny for Miss Annie L's children at Prestwould, had some schooling and even wrote letters. And Brother Parker from just across the river in Halifax County in "The Forks" had gone to school soon after emancipation and so he was very good at those kinds of things. Some of his people lived in Bluestone and they had already intermarried with some of Vicey's people following emancipation when African Americans could both get married in church and record their marriages in the court house.

Mr. J. J. Crowder, the white man who had sold her the land – he had bought forty acres from Mr. Fulwar and now he was reselling parcels at a nice profit for himself – of course could read and write, but Vicey wanted at least one of her own people who could "cipher" and witness the moment when she finally claimed "a little piece of land" and could fix up the place for the future. She knew that she needed to *see* the proof of *her name on the land*, even if she could not read the proof. There had been no stretched out time for schooling for her when slavery was over and those people from the North came and told them they could go to school. She kept on working at the big house with Aunt Lucinda. Mr. Fulwar *liked* Aunt Lucinda and *gave* her one of Prestwould's cabins *before* emancipation. But these papers would remain in the court house *forever* – for everyone to know that she now owned Mr. Fulwar's old cabin along with six and one fifth acres of farm land. It seems that the irregular one-fifth acre ensured that the cabin was not on Mr. Hardy's property line or maybe that strange sounding cut was how the tree lines affected the "meted out" boundaries and when that happened there was not an even number for ciphering.[5]

And so, at the court house, she made her mark in front of the witnesses and the "paper" became a legal contract; at the court house, as her brothers silently watched with hats in hand, Celia and Brother Parker read to her that the "title was clear." The clerk wrote the words "fee simple" next to her name and Brother Parker said that meant that she had paid in full. At the court house, they had counted out the sixty-two dollars to Mr. Crowder. Thus, she "signed" her name and,

> On the first day of June eighteen hundred and eighty-eight, between J. J. Crowder & Margaret R. Crowder his wife of the county of Mecklenburg of the first part & Vicey Skipwith of the 2nd part, witnesseth that in consideration of the sum of sixty two dollars the said J. J. Crowder & Margaret R. Crowder his wife do grant unto the said Vicey Skipwith with General Warranty all their right title & interest in Six & one fifth acres of land in Mecklenburg County, known & surveyed on plat as lot no 3-and being a part of the Fulwar Skipwith tract. The said J. J. Crowder & Margaret R. Crowder his wife covenant that they have the right to convey the said land to the Grantee that they have done no act to encumber the said land that the Grantee

> shall have quiet possession of the said land, free from all encumbrances [...]. This land is to be taken from the 40 acre tract. (Deed Book 50, pp 68-69)

And, indeed, it was a remarkable day because someone who had been property could now own property.[6]

For the small parcel of land Vicey Skipwith paid a hard-earned $62.00 (plus the tax of fifty cents) – a large sum in 1888 for a woman who was a domestic cook and seasonal farm laborer at the Prestwould manor. Historical monetary values are often difficult to measure in comparative terms. Knowing that $62.00 in 1888 is equivalent to $1355.66 in 2008 helps us to understand the value of the six-acre property in historical and social terms and the significance of the dollar amount that Skipwith accumulated in a relatively short time after slavery. Located in the court house ledger, Skipwith's "signed" deed is autobiographical performativity in the intertextual records of nineteenth-century black female subjectivity. She enacted naming through the public "texts" of property ownership and the private text of the home place.

Cheryl I. Harris argues that race and property ownership in the United States were profoundly interrelated and contained inclusions of "income (such as revenues from leases, mortgages, and patent monopolies), and one's life, liberty and labor; [...] one's physical self was one's property. From this premise, one's labor, 'the work of his hands,' combined with those things found in the common to form property over which one could exercise ownership, control and dominion" (1735). Land ownership was undeniably central to privilege, slavery and success in colonial Virginia. In a letter published in Boydton's *The Tobacco Planter* on Christmas Day 1869, J. S. R. Burwell, one of the sons of the famous Burwell planter family in Virginia, lamented, "Our idea of a fortune was two plantations and a hundred negroes, out of debt, and a plenty of money" (Simpson 77). Burwell had not built the fine mansion before "his best property" (enslaved people) had been taken away. Chattel property ownership had been the profound right that enabled the *rites* of entitlement.

As a freedwoman, Vicey Skipwith had the right to her own labor on the land. Land ownership was a valued personal, social, and economic identity through which to name the self. Land ownership was more than a commodification of or entitlement to property. Land deeds, contracts, farm records, and tax revenues enabled the freedpeople to write themselves into existence, even if they remained non-literate. The freedpeople knew that land acquisition was ultimate security for themselves and for the next generation. Vicey Skipwith constructed new meaning at the home place site – a former slave quarter – and created agency in the interest of herself, kin, and community. How was Vicey Skipwith able to amass the capital necessary for purchasing farm land? How did she put into practice the "free labor ideal of property ownership"? (Faulkner 11).

The first generation of African Americans had to have the discipline of hard labor and thriftiness in order to accumulate enough capital to buy land. At the same time, there was the introduction of the sharecropping system in the south that steadily prevented thriftiness and savings, but maintained African American dependency and hard farm labor. Despite class and social distinctions, or perhaps because of such divisions, blacks and whites all knew each other in one way or another in the small community. Skipwith had learned to cook in the vast Prestwould kitchens. During Reconstruction, she would have sold country meals to workers at the market on Saturdays in the nearby town of Clarksville in order to supplement her farming income. And despite its drudgery, there was always white people's washing and ironing that she took in as did black women all over the south in order to make ends meet, and if at all possible to add to the savings for the parcel of land. When she was not working at the plantation house as a cook, therefore, she would have done the usual income-producing "women's work" – selling eggs, baking, taking in more laundry, sewing, and keeping a small vegetable garden.[7] With thriftiness and a measure of autonomy, Vicey Skipwith moved away from the debilitating system of sharecropping and renting by asserting control over where she bought commodities and what she consumed (Swann-Wright 99).

What other circumstances created the economic loophole that enabled Vicey Skipwith to purchase land? Fulwar Skipwith (1836-1900), the last antebellum owner of Prestwould, had descended into financial ruin during Reconstruction when there was no longer the free labor of slavery to work the plantation. Fulwar Skipwith was the grandson of Sir Peyton, the aforementioned eighteenth-century aristocratic builder of Prestwould. In order to divest the estate of his debts, Fulwar Skipwith sold off small parcels of land to both blacks and whites (women and men) who had cash to buy.[8] J. J. Crowder, a long-standing white plantation owner, had bought forty acres from Fulwar Skipwith in 1884. At profit, Crowder then sold parcels of the forty acres. Vicey Skipwith was among the farmers who benefited from her former slave master's insolvency – she seized the opportunity for economic and personal advancement. Most of the four million formerly enslaved African Americans were non-literate and could not write about their anxieties, fears, exaltations, confusion, and a host of other sentiments connected to the nebulous meaning of freedom. They created other means of telling their stories. Land ownership enabled Skipwith to name herself through the intertextuality of court documents, U. S. Census records, and oral histories that foregrounded her relationship to other land-owning proprietors (including former slaveholders).

The convergence of the antebellum cabin as a material cultural artifact with the historical inscriptions of Skipwith's land ownership represents visual/textual agency that encapsulates autobiographical performativity. Her performativity reflects what Audre Lorde would describe as a black woman's unique ownership of her own identity: "As a Black woman, I have to deal with identity or I don't exist at all. I can't depend on the world to name me kindly, because it never will [...]. So either I'm going to be defined by myself or not at all" (Hammon 19).

A cultural artifact with the legacy of inscriptions (subsequent public texts identifying Skipwith as the owner of a dwelling and six acres), the antebellum cabin functions as Skipwith's historical act of agency and autobiographical identity. In this instance, land ownership inscribed Vicey Skipwith's name at the site of memory. Skipwith successfully engendered herself into the social and economic system of land-owning citizenship despite any contrary instincts. Thus, with her purchase of fertile farm land with its already-built log cabin, Vicey Skipwith embarked on a new journey with vibrancy and determination (the old journey had been surviving slavery) that characterized property and home place proprietorship. Vicey Skipwith struggled for the rights of citizenship – as opposed to the privilege of citizenship – through the integrity of her own labor (not slave labor or sharecropping), the integrity of being able to have a legal marriage, and the integrity of home place land ownership.

"I shall be obliged to speak mostly Italian"

In 1887, a year before Vicey Skipwith enabled and defined her own sense of freedom and agency in southern Virginia, Frederick Douglass (1818-1895) went on an extended tour of Europe and Egypt with his second wife, née Helen Pitts. The Douglasses were in Rome on two different occasions in that year and visited the Remond sisters – Caroline, Sarah, and Maritche.[9] They intermittently stayed with Caroline Remond Putnam in her comfortable apartment at the Palazzo Moroni. Douglass wrote in his 1892 autobiography, *Life and Times of Frederick Douglass*, "Like myself, the Remond sisters with the exception of Caroline have grown quite old but in all of them I saw much of the fire of their eloquent brother Charles" (qtd. in McFeely 329). Douglass claimed that it had been an astonishing forty years since he had seen Sarah, his old, in the sense of cherished, abolitionist friend.

After spending several weeks in Italy, Douglass and his wife went to England and returned to the United States in the fall of 1887. While in England, Douglass received at least two letters from Sarah Parker Remond. In an extraordinary gem of a four-page letter (for the scholar/sleuth) dated 8 July 1887, Remond wrote to Douglass, "I shall be obliged to speak mostly Italian" because most of her English-speaking friends, including her sisters – "all of my kin took flight some time ago" – had left Rome during the very hot summer of 1887.[10] Remond's statement confirms her fluency in Italian and the extent to which she had created a comfortable domestic retreat, if not self-exile, in Italy. She knew the language and therefore she had intimate access to Italian culture, society – "no one knows Italy till they see it in summer, the beauty heightens with the heat" – and Italian politics. Remond also confirms that she and Douglass were in affable correspondence: "I have just received the promised and welcome letter dated July 2nd [...] it has been delayed till today, although the postmen know where I am. I hope you will receive this before you sail for America [...]. It will be useless for me to write to my friends, as you will be no longer in England. I write to you by return of the post and shall hope to hear again from you just as soon as you are rested after your ocean voyage." With a focus on what I will refer to as the Barberini letter, one of the uncovered visual/textual artifacts of Remond's epistolary autobiographical performativity in Italy, my discussion of Remond situates the trans-Atlantic context of Remond's life after the Civil War. Written in the summer of 1887 when Remond was residing in one of the city's busiest centers (the Piazza Barberini continues to be among the popular plazas in Rome), the Barberini letter contains the sentiments of the "Italian" Remond with references to social medicine, trans-Atlantic travel, and the environmental (society and location) sense of a home place.

Sarah Parker Remond. Unidentified photographer. From Portraits of American Abolitionists. Massachusetts Historical Society. Used with permission.

Remond resided at Piazza Barberini No. 6, *primo piano* (first floor), and despite the fact that she did not like the summer heat, she believed that it was good for her health. Remond's home was a welcoming place for British, European and American friends – "Mrs. Edmund and her father leave in a few days."[11] Remond created a retreat in Italy that offered levels of political engagement, personal achievement, and cultural comfort. Through her sense of belonging and knowledge of the aesthetic landscape of Rome, she described with familiarity the ancient hill gardens overlooking the city – "the lovely Pincio is always beautiful." Remond wrote that when walking among the Pincio gardens she frequently sought out "a shady nook even at the noon day hour when the fierce sun comes down with intense white heat. There is always a cool spot to be found." Constructed on one of the many hills of the city, the Pincio with its spectacular vistas is still an attraction in Rome's historical center.

While Vicey Skipwith took advantage of loopholes for self-reliance and advancement by inscribing her name on the public and vernacular texts of property ownership, Remond retreated to Italy and signed her name with the procurement of an Italian medical diploma, an Italian marriage, and overall personal fulfillment with her sisters at her side. Intrigued with many fragmented biographical references to this nineteenth-century African American woman who spoke Italian and who had studied medicine in Florence, I began searching for Remond's autobiographical traces in Italy.

Remond went to Italy in the midst of Italian unification, which had its ramifications well into the 1870s; and she associated with some of the controversial revolutionary figures of Italy's unification movement. While literary, cultural, and historical scholarship and critiques have emphasized and acclaimed Remond's abolitionist speeches and writings, and have made laudatory references to her obtaining a medical degree from one of Italy's well known hospital schools, Santa Maria Nuova in Florence, it is quite surprising that no study has focused on the cultural, medical, and social contexts of Remond's Italian years. Remond's extraordinary decision to immigrate to Italy reveals her fervor for Italian nationalism, feminist agency, and international friendships. Remond died in 1894, a year before her "dear friend Frederick Douglass" as she calls Douglass in the Barberini letter. By most contemporary accounts she was buried in Rome's Protestant Cemetery – *Cimitero Acattolico di Roma.*[12] During the last twenty-eight years of Remond's life, Rome, the exceedingly beautiful city, and Florence, the renowned center of culture, science and art, were her collective places of retreat. One of the main connections that Remond had with Italy as an intellectual and professional retreat was through her study and work at the renowned *Ospedale di Santa Maria Nuova*, Santa Maria Nuova hospital.

Remond's American audience learned about her medical accomplishments in 1868 with the announcement,

> Our first white women who completed a regular Medical education had to go to Europe to do it. It is not strange therefore that colored women are compelled to do so too. We are glad to see [...] that our gifted country woman, Miss Sarah P. Remond has availed herself of a long visit abroad to acquire a medical course of education. She has been in Europe for several years past, and during the last two years a medical student at Florence, Italy, in the largest hospital, the S. Maria Nuova. After a regular course of study and also of hospital practice, she has recently passed the necessary examinations, and received a diploma for professional medical practice. ("Colored")

The journalist was aware of Santa Maria Nuova's status and there was obvious approval regarding Remond's success in the medical field considering how *all* women were discriminated against in the American medical profession. In twenty-first century parlance, Santa Maria Nuova was a sustainability enterprise and serviced the principles of social justice, which is why it was a convivial sociopolitical niche for Remond. The hospital's medical and social philosophy reflected Remond's aspirations of social justice for herself, women, and less fortunate people in society. Undoubtedly, because of the hospital's social and medical creed, Remond was able to find a retreat for studying and achieving goals that she could not achieve in the United States.

Remond's parents, John and Nancy Remond, were "well-to-do free Negroes" in the seaport town of Salem, Massachusetts. Her father came to the United States from the Caribbean island of Curaçao when he was ten years old. Remond was the third generation of free-born Americans and her father rigorously maintained the "industry" of the family's businesses in Salem. According to Remond, "The coloured population [free born African Americans of Salem] was of an elevated character, and for industry, morality, and native intellect, would compare favourably with any class in the community" ("Sarah P. Remond" 282). The Remonds had a successful hair-dressing business that continued to operate through their descendants into the early twentieth century; and Nancy Remond, Sarah's mother, was a prosperous caterer and "accomplished fancy cake maker" (Porter, "The Remonds" 267). "With a foothold in food preparation, the family moved to supplying ships and local merchants with a variety of foodstuffs. The amazing array of items included ham from Virginia, smoked beef from Albany, cigars from Spain, wine from Lisbon and soy from India" (Coleman 175). With his large family in tow, John Remond was an "aristocrat of his profession" (Porter, "The Remonds" 266).

Besides their "habits of industry," John and Nancy Remond and their offspring were active in the abolitionist movement. They were friends of William Lloyd Garrison (1805-1879) and other famous white American abolitionists. Sarah and her siblings grew up amidst their parents' abolitionist activities and their home was a welcome place for interracial business ventures as well as friendships. Remond and her older brother Charles Lenox were excellent, well-informed speakers, and they both traveled to England, Scotland, and Ireland in the 1840s and late 1850s as workers for the abolitionist cause. During the height of her abolitionist activities and speaking engagements in England, Scotland and Ireland from 1859 through 1865, Remond was often described as "remarkably feminine," "well-toned," "noble," and "elegant." In one of her 1861 autobiographical narratives Remond wrote:

> My mother's aim seemed to be to strengthen her children, not only for the trials and duties of life, but also to enable them to meet the terrible pressure which prejudice against color would force upon them. Her discipline taught us that to be black was no crime, but an accident of birth. Our home discipline was what we needed, but it did not - could not - fit us for the scorn and contempt which met us on every hand when face to face with the world, where we met a community who hated all who were identified with an enslaved race. *My strongest desire through life has been to be educated.* We had from time to time been taught to read and write a little, but had received no regular instruction. Again and again my mother

> would endeavor to have us placed in some private school, but being colored we were refused. ("A Colored Lady Lecturer" 270, my emphasis)

Despite the fact that the Remond children were free-born in a prosperous African American family, they experienced prejudice and indignities that prevented them from having an advanced formal education that their economic class could afford. Remond frequently lamented that she did not have a solid educational foundation, which consistently affected her efforts for intellectual advancement. In 1858 she wrote, "I was in need of a good English education," and she had an "intense desire to visit England that [she] might for a time enjoy freedom" ("Sarah P. Remond" 285, 286).

From published letters and speeches, we know Remond's views regarding social justice and her belief in autonomy, citizenship, and human rights. There are a number of public incidents in which Remond opposed discrimination and asserted her civil and social rights in the United States and in England. One of the many publicized incidents concerns a passport issue when Remond was in England. She went to the American Legation (Embassy) in order to get her passport "viséd" for travel to France. The Legation denied travel permission on the grounds that "the indispensable qualification for an American passport that of 'United States citizenship' does not exist [for Remond], Miss Sarah P. Remond cannot be complied with" ("Disabilities"). Feisty in fighting for her rights and justice, Remond knew how to use the "power of the press" and publicized the discrimination that she had to endure from her own Embassy as an American citizen. Remond made public the correspondence between herself and the American diplomats in various British and American newspapers. In explicating the discrimination levied by the American representative, Benjamin Moran, she replied to his written denial of her American citizenship: "The purport of your communication is most extraordinary. You now lay down the rule that persons free-born in the United States, and who have been subjected in all their lives to the taxation and other burdens imposed upon American citizens, are to be deprived of their rights as such, merely because their complexions happen to be dark, and that they are to be refused the aid of Ministers of their country, whose salaries they contribute to pay. I remain Sir, your obedient servant" ("Disabilities"). These are amazing words of diplomatic gnash, "your obedient servant," interlocked with sophisticated political argument about "taxation" and "salaries they contribute to pay." Remond wanted the freedom to pursue her goals in a civil society not as a privilege, but as a human right. Because of the discrimination that she encountered from the long arm of official American diplomacy on foreign soil, Remond well understood that even free-born African Americans could not really be "free." Remond eventually had travel documents viséd through the British government and went to France.

Remond was an activist in such groups as the London Anti Slavery Society, the Glasgow Emancipation Society, and the Edinburgh Ladies Emancipation Society. In one of her famous anti-slavery speeches delivered in Warrington, England, Remond told the large and receptive crowd about the Margaret

Garner tragedy that had taken place in 1856. She unabashedly informed her audience, "Women are sold into slavery with cheeks like the lily and the rose, as well as those that might compare with the wing of the raven. They are exposed for sale, and subjected to the most shameful indignities. The more Anglo-Saxon blood that mingles with the blood of the slave, the more gold is poured out when the auctioneer has a woman for sale, because they are sold to be concubines for white Americans" ("Music Hall, Warrington England 24 January 1859"). Thus, early in her public oratory on behalf of enslaved women, Remond was acutely aware of the intersection of race, class and gender.

By the beginning of Reconstruction, Remond had already written several autobiographical narratives that were political and social in scope. She had been on the abolitionist lecture circuit throughout the British Isles and, by all contemporary accounts, Remond was a dynamic and endearing speaker. Her venues in England were generally "sold out" by today's criteria of success. She regularly corresponded with the *Anti-Slavery Advocate*, *Warrington Times*, the *Standard*, and the *Manchester Weekly* in England; and *The Liberator*, *The National Anti-Slavery Standard* and other abolitionist publications in the United States. When Remond immigrated to Italy, she was not only a distinguished international figure who had worked relentlessly for the abolition of slavery; she was well-known in British circles of class-oriented radicalism. As she worked for overall social justice, Remond associated with a diverse group of supportive British, Europeans, and Americans. Remond no doubt had learned about Italian hospitals and opportunities for studying medicine from Italian friends in England, among them being Giuseppe Mazzini (1805-1872), a radical Italian nationalist, who was a leading figure during *Risorgimento*.

Where are the traces of Remond's nineteenth-century retreats in Rome and Florence? Would I find any record of Remond's work and study in the archives of Santa Maria Nuova in Florence? How far would I have to walk along the centuries old, tangled, but serene pathways of the old section of the *Cimitero Acattolico di Roma* in trying to find her grave site that has been lost in time? Did Caroline or Maritche return to the United States or are they buried in the *Cimitero*? Remond may have converted to Catholicism as an Italian citizen, and, therefore, she may not be buried here – what English speakers call the Protestant Cemetery – after all. I know that Remond had walked these same streets of Rome more than a century ago where she, indeed, "charted her own course" among plazas and time-worn streets like the *Piazza di Spagna, Via Sistina, Via Veneto, Via San Nicolo di Tolentino, Via Fontanella*, and the *Piazza Barberini*.

Mid-nineteenth century Florence and Rome were dynamic gathering places for Anglo-American intellectuals and artists such as Margaret Foley, Nathaniel Hawthorne, Henry James, Harriet Beecher Stowe, William Wetmore Story, and Anne Whitney. There was also a small contingent of African Americans that included Eugene Warburg, Robert Scott Duncanson, the famous black-Native American sculptor Mary Edmonia Lewis, and the Remonds. African American expatriates in Italy might have realized that along with legal freedoms in the United States following the abolition of slavery, there would be the onslaught of legal segregation – Jim Crow – and therefore they remained in or immigrated to Italy. Italy was, indeed, a political, artistic, and social retreat. Fascinated with Italy, Frederick Douglass met "the small black expatriate community that found Rome a congenial political and aesthetic refuge from a racist United States," and he viewed the city as a "conjunction of mixed blood peoples (the Romans) [within] the rise of Western civilization" (Levine 220).

Remond arrived in Florence in August of 1866 with ambition and determination. In a letter to the *National Anti Slavery Standard* describing her extraordinary immigration to Italy via Switzerland she wrote, "After a long day's journey in the full moonlight of a summer night, I arrive at 'Firenze La Bella.' With some interest, I look around to see all that I can [...]. I am soon on my way to a hotel which had been highly recommended to me, and very soon I am in a most comfortable room" (Letter). Remond knew where she was going and what she wanted to do when she arrived in Italy. Thus Remond wrote to her American readers, "I am not here [in Florence] for pleasure, but for study" (Letter). Having traveled to Italy several times, Remond had entrée into Italian liberal political circles in England through her friendship with Mazzini, who had founded the Society of the Friends of Italy in England. What kind of medical facility led Sarah Parker Remond to pursue the next stage of self-representation in Florence?

While the medieval period of Florentine science and medicine could not compare to the flourishing Salerno "school" of medicine and scientific inquiry in southern Italy (Green 2001), Santa Maria Nuova has an impressive cultural and medical history. Folco di Ricovero Portinari, father of Dante's adored Beatrice, founded the hospital in 1288. Closely linked to the hospital's history was its *Scuola di Chirurgia*, School of Surgery, where distinguished physicians engaged in teaching hospital procedures. From the beginning of the Renaissance, the hospital was "exemplary even in the sophisticated institutional world of northern and central Italy" (Park and Henderson 170). An obstetrics school was added in 1762, and pharmaceutical chemistry laboratories in 1880. There was the integration of hospital practice into the licensing requirements of the Florentine Guild of Doctors with the creation of a formal school of surgery on the premises (Gentilcore; Granshaw and Porter).

With its classic Renaissance design, Santa Maria Nuova became a specialized medical institution. The hospital was not only the most remarkable charitable institution of its kind in Europe and described as "the first hospital among Christians," but it had an "unrivalled reputation as a medical center [...]. Santa Maria Nuova was arguably the first Western European hospital in the modern sense of the word, an institution organized along therapeutic lines and dedicated exclusively to the care of the sick, which was directed by members of the medical profession. [... Santa Maria Nuova] was governed by a constitution and regulations that were clearly religious in tone" (Park and Henderson 169).

From its founding, Santa Maria Nuova included women on the medical staff: "Women were empirically trained surgeons who had learned their craft through apprenticeship and experience, presumably in the hospital, rather than through a formal course of study" (Park and Henderson 186).[13]

I draw attention to Santa Maria Nuova as a visual/textual paradigm that reflects Remond's bold autobiographical moment of performativity – "I am not here for pleasure, but for study." Ann Whitney, one of the American sculptors living in Rome wrote in 1868 that Remond had attended a gathering in her home and, "Miss Remond, now a physician in Florence, was here that same eve, her handsome dark person set off by a broad gold chain wound round and round her head and a white shawl" (Letter to Sarah Whitney). Remond demonstrated an empowering sense of social responsibility and self-actualization when she successfully studied at one of the most renowned nineteenth-century medical facilities in Europe. In the Barberini letter, Remond alludes to natural medicinal cures for the bed-ridden or house-bound: "The summer months often cure invalids if they can be persuaded to try it, and lead the right kind of life. I have some interesting facts on this point." While Remond did not expand on the "interesting facts" for improving the health of invalids, she may well have been referring to her knowledge of medicinal herbal cures acquired at Santa Maria Nuova.

By the time that Remond married Lazzaro Pintor, an Italian from Sardinia, in 1877, she had a medical practice. Numerous contemporary scholars claim that Remond left Florence and relocated to Rome after the "failure of her marriage" to Pintor. The British abolitionist William Robson's 1879 reference to "Miss Remond [...] living in great poverty in Rome, her profession of medicine having been a failure" is also given validity by scholars who cite Remond's marriage as probable cause for the alleged poverty two years after her marriage (qtd. in Brownlee 32). Lazzaro Pintor could have died as opposed to abandoning his wife soon after the marriage. Frederick Douglass did not mention Pintor or Remond's possible widowhood when he wrote about his Rome visit with the Remond sisters. Indeed, the absence of a reference to a spouse is not sufficient evidence of a failed marriage. Moreover, in the nineteenth-century context of class- and gender-oriented decorum, Douglass would not have discussed publicly Remond's spouse or lack of a spouse. Certainly, as a widow, Remond would have been the exceedingly independent and elegant mistress of her own affairs with the respectability of having been married by the time that Douglass encountered her in Rome with her prosperous sisters.

Furthermore, Remond and Douglass shared a commonality regarding interracial marriage. When Frederick Douglass married Helen Pitts, a white American, two years after the death of his first wife, Anna Murray Douglass, in 1882, there was widespread controversy. African Americans and white Americans who opposed interracial marriage judged Helen Pitts Douglass, respectively, as the oppositional "white woman" or the debased woman. Viewed from the American side of the Atlantic, Remond's Italian marriage was interracial –

as opposed to cross-cultural – and sociopolitical attitudes may continue with predisposed interpretations about "interracial" unions. Significantly, Remond identified as a *signora* – whether widowed or abandoned – and signed her name "Sarah Remond Pintor" in the Barberini letter. That autonomous act is more than an epistolary signature. Defining herself as Sarah Remond Pintor signifies social status and honor. The signing – the naming – is an autograph that signifies unabashed self-representation. Decidedly, the status of *signora* affirms autobiographical performativity. As she expressively and graciously writes in the Barberini letter offers of future "chat[s] now and then on paper" with Douglass, Remond in her mature years appears as a *signora* content in Italy and at peace with herself. Moreover, by maintaining her family surname, she demonstrates that she had not given up her sense of identity as an African American and seems to have come to terms with being "an extraordinary black woman who had chosen exile over inequality" (Coleman 184).

In their waning years, Remond and Douglass had worldviews that went beyond categorical definitions of race as they explored questions of "race" outside the confines of racism and segregation in the United States. While Remond and Douglass understood that race (the social construct) was alive and well, they began to think beyond social definitions. In his post-emancipation writings, Douglass believed that humanity had to transcend the limitations and segregation of race. Influenced by his extensive travels in Europe, Greece, and Egypt, he positioned himself as a member of the only one "race" that exists – that of humanity (Levine 200). "Race" seems to have been just that for Remond and Douglass: a qualifying term and fluid paradigm. Yet they wrestled with the contradictions inherent in taking pride in race, the black race, even as they sought to move beyond racialized constructs and embrace ideas about the oneness of humanity. Remond and Douglass were kindred spirits ahead of their times. The Barberini letter is a reminder that there was a shared commonality between the two old friends that transcended race and abolitionist politics of the past: they enjoyed a measure of contentment, internationalism, and achievement as they both were moving towards the end of their extraordinary lives.

Vicey Skipwith and Sarah Remond Pintor

I began this study thinking about Eunice Richardson Stone Connolly's remarkable nineteenth-century story and the letters she wrote as the sea captain's wife. But non-literate women could not write themselves into conventional autobiography or epistolary naming and agency. In particular, were nineteenth-century black women without autobiography because they were supposed to be "without history" and "without paper" (Reyes 125), or because their lives became elusive and fleeting as they went about their extraordinary personal business? I encountered the nineteenth-century visual/textual portraiture of Vicey Skipwith on a southern Virginia landscape. And then I placed the elusive narrative of her quiet stature next to the transitory, but remarkable presence of Sarah Remond Pintor in Italy. They become kindred spirits in their elusive texts of autobiographical performativity.

Skipwith reflects the tenuous and often contradictory meaning of citizenship and freedom at the home place of a former plantation in rural Virginia. Skipwith's historical/personal/public autobiographical representation is located in the purchase of property that enabled self-reliance – the loophole – on the eve of nineteenth-century legal segregation. Thus, although Skipwith did not write a conventional autobiography, she names herself through property deeds, various public records related to property ownership, and oral history interventions that situate her relationship with the standing antebellum cabin at the site of the visual/textual home place – her multiple sites of autobiographical representation.

Sarah Remond Pintor lived the last twenty-eight years of her life in the urban environment of an expatriate retreat created in Italy. The extraordinary Barberini letter signifies one of the visual/textual artifacts of autobiographical performativity. I place the Barberini letter in the overarching context of the safe "retreat." Remond's Italian retreat enabled her accomplishments at Santa Maria Nuova and later in Rome. She articulated the moment of autobiographical performativity when she first arrived in Florence and announced, "I am not here for pleasure, but for study." Moreover, with the use of her married name, Remond claimed the identity of *signora*, which enabled the respectability and dignity that she always wanted.

Sidonie Smith and Julia Watson remind us that autobiographical narratives that push the boundaries through performativity invite "readers' collaboration in producing specific meanings for the 'life'" (*Interfaces* 11). Vicey Skipwith and Sarah Remond Pintor were ordinary and extraordinary women whose autobiographical acts invite us to push the boundaries.

[1] I take this opportunity to thank my research assistant, Danelle Mallen, Barrett Honors College, Arizona State University, for her splendid archival assistance with, and lively discussions about the Sarah Parker Remond project. For the sake of historical familiarity, I use Remond's family name. As I discuss, however, Remond signed her name "Pintor" after her 1877 marriage to Lazarro Pintor. The Vicey Skipwith research was featured in the multi-media exhibition, *Dynamic Journey: Transformations of Slavery-Era Spaces, Routes and Sounds* sponsored by the Herberger College of Fine Arts, Faculty Collaborative Research and Creative Activity grant, Arizona State University, 2007. I also take this opportunity to thank the Virginia Historical Society for its generous funding support in the 2007 Mellon Fellows Program that enabled the Vicey Skipwith research.

[2] The current research is part of the book-in-progress that highlights Sarah Parker Remond's Italian years from 1866-1894, *Sarah Parker Remond: A Life in Letters and Speeches*.

[3] While the designator "African American Virginians" refers to African Americans residing in the state of Virginia after the abolition of slavery, I use the term "African Virginian" to specify the status of enslaved people of African descent residing in Virginia before the abolition of slavery. My use of "African Virginian" is also a historical reference to the Middle Passage and its role in the formation of the African Diaspora in the Americas. While there were Northern and Southern communities of "free Negroes," I use the term "first generation" to denote the first generation of former slaves to experience freedom through the Emancipation Proclamation. The contemporary "first generation" designator refers to the children of foreign-immigrant parents who are born in the United States and have the birthright of American citizenship. Likewise, African Americans as "freedpeople" were, indeed, the first generation to experience citizenship as ratified in the 13th and 14th Amendments to the U. S. Constitution. The terms "freedpeople," "freedmen," or "freedwomen" refer to African Americans who obtained freedom through the constitutional acts. See Engs and Kerr-Ritchie.

[4] In 1860, Humberston Skipwith (1791-1863) owned 247 slaves at Prestwould sheltered in "33 houses." Vicey Skipwith's cabin is among the houses located in the "quarters." Space in this essay does not allow for a more detailed description of the cabin's interior. I thank the Virginia Department of Historic Resources for its valuable contribution to the architectural information herein included, Angelita Reyes, DHR File No. 058-5076. Unless otherwise indicated, subsequent information about the Vicey Skipwith property is from the DHR file. Not open to the public, the cabin's address is restricted.

[5] The acreage was not measured in a rectangular grid but in a diagonal position to the main road. Much of this kind of acreage irregularity was caused by the "metes and bounds method" of claiming land that was used between the land claimant and the surveyor in colonial Virginia – first walking the boundaries and counting paces and then bringing in the surveyor. The result "was a crazy-quilt pattern of irregularly shaped tracts that may be seen today throughout the area of Virginia [...]. By comparison with other patterns of land use, the Virginia system created a tangle of overlapping claims, based on ephemeral markers. It greatly encouraged litigation" (Fischer and Kelly 254).

[6] Dianne Swann-Wright describes in marked detail a similar land transaction where newly freed African Americans bought property: "When the Gregorys made marks beneath their neatly scripted names on the land deed, legalizing their purchase, their action stood for a remarkable feat. Their x's signified a change in their status from tenant farmers to landholders" (70)

[7] Jacqueline Jones states, "freedwomen perceived freedom to mean not a release from backbreaking labor, but rather the opportunity to labor on behalf of their own families and kin with the protected spheres of household and community" (78).

[8] Lynda Morgan, in *Emancipation in Virginia's Tobacco Belt, 1850-1870*, discusses former slaveholders who had to sell land because of the post-Civil War economy in Virginia (205-09).

[9] The Remonds were the sisters of the distinguished international abolitionist and friend of Douglass, Charles Lenox Remond (1810-1873). Charles Lenox Remond had been a member of the American Anti-Slavery Society, and had helped to form the New England Anti-Slavery Society. Douglass named his third son Charles Lenox Remond Douglass.

[10] Unless otherwise indicated, subsequent quotes are from the 8 July 1887 letter, Sarah Remond Pintor to Frederick Douglass.

[11] The semi-formal reference to "Mrs. Edmund and her father" may very well refer to the British wife and father-in-law of Edmund Quincy, Caroline's son. The famous American sculptor and author, William Wetmore Story (1819-1895) and his wife lived at the nearby Palazzo Barberini and their spacious apartment was a well known gathering place for American expatriates and artists (Nelson 143). The black-Native American sculptor Mary Edmonia Lewis had one of her studios near Piazza Barberini and knew the Remond sisters.

[12] The "Non-Catholic Cemetery" in Rome, *il Cimitero Acattolico di Roma*, aptly known as the Protestant Cemetery, dates to 1738. John Keats and Percy Bysshe Shelley are among the most famous English-speaking poets buried there. The cemetery was not only for Protestants, but it was the nineteenth-century burial place for non-Catholics, Jews, suicides, actors, and foreigners in Rome.

[13] In 1500, Henry VII of England requested and received the statutes of Santa Maria Nuova with the intent of building an English hospital on the Florentine model. The official document was "The Text of Francesco Portinari's Letter to Henry VII Incorporating Statutes for Santa Maria Nuova" (Park and Henderson 175-188).

Works Cited

Baker, Houston A., Jr. *The Journey Back: Issues in Black Literature and Criticism.* Chicago: U of Chicago P, 1980.

Benstock, Shari, ed. *The Private Self: Theory and Practice of Women's Autobiographical Writings.* Chapel Hill: U of North Carolina P, 1988.

Brownlee, Sibyl Ventress. "Out of the Abundance of the Heart: Sarah Ann Parker Remond's Quest for Freedom." *The Harrod Lecture Series.* XVI 1997-1998: 3-44.

Bruss, Elizabeth W. *Autobiographical Acts: The Changing Situation of a Literary Genre.* Baltimore: Johns Hopkins UP, 1976.

"Charles Lenox Remond" (obituary). *New York Times*, 26 December 1873. n.p.

Coleman, Willi. "'Like Hot Lead to Pour on the Americans …': Sarah Parker Remond – From Salem, Mass., to the British Isles." *Women's Rights and Transatlantic Antislavery in the Era of Emancipation.* Ed. Kathryn

Kish Sklar and James Brewer Stewart. New Haven: Yale UP, 2007: 173-188.

“Colored Women as Physicians.” *The Revolution.* 22 October 1868. n. p.

Davis, Charles T., and Henry Louis Gates, Jr., ed. *The Slave's Narrative.* London: Oxford UP, 1985.

Dittrick, Howard, M.D. “*History of the New England Female Medical College* by Frederick C. Waite.” *Bulletin of the Medical Library Association.* (1951) 39:4: 379-380.

Donnell, Alison. “When Writing the Other Is Being True to the Self: Jamaica Kincaid's *The Autobiography of My Mother.*” *Women's Lives into Print: The Theory, Practice and Writing of Feminist Auto/Biography.* Ed. Pauline Polkey. London: St. Martin's, 1999. 123–36.

Eighth U. S. Census 1860 Slave Schedule (22nd Regiment Mecklenburg County), Vol. 5 No. 653 Roll 1394, p. 10/76.

Engs, Robert F. *Freedom's First Generation: Black Hampton, Virginia 1861-1890.* New York: Fordham UP, 2004.

Faulkner, Carol. *Women's Radical Reconstruction: The Freedmen's Aid Movement.* Philadelphia: U of Pennsylvania P, 2004.

Fessenden, Tracy. *Culture and Redemption: Religion, the Secular, and American Literature.* Princeton: Princeton UP, 2006.

Fischer, David Hackett and James C. Kelly. *Bound Away: Virginia and the Westward Movement.* Charlottesville: UP of Virginia, 2000.

Foner, Eric. *Forever Free: The Story of Emancipation and Reconstruction.* New York: Knopf, 2005.

Foster, Frances Smith. *Written By Herself: Literary Production by African American Women, 1746-1892.* Bloomington: Indiana UP, 1991.

Gentilcore, David. *Healers and Healing in Early Modern Europe.* Manchester: Manchester UP, 1998.

Gero, Joan and Margaret Conkey, ed. *Engendering Archaeology: Women in Prehistory.* Oxford: Basil Blackwell, 1991.

Granshaw, Lindsay and Roy Porter, ed. *The Hospital in History.* New York: Routledge, 1989.

Green, Monica H. *The Trotula: A Medieval Compendium of Women's Medicine.* Philadelphia: U of Pennsylvania P, 2001.

Hammond, Karla. “An Interview with Audre Lorde.” *American Poetry Review* 9:2 (March/April 1980): 18-21.

Harris, Cheryl I. “Whiteness as Property.” *Harvard Law Review* 106 (1993): 8. 1707-1791.

Hodes, Martha. "A House in Vermont, A Caribbean Beach: Beckoned by Landscapes Beyond the Archive," *Common-Place*. www.common-place.org. Vol. 7 No. 4 July 2007. <http://www.common-place.org/vol-07/no-04/tales/>

—. *The Sea Captain's Wife: A True Story of Love, Race, and War in the Nineteenth Century*. New York: Norton, 2006.

Hull, Gloria T., Patricia Scott Bell, and Barbara Smith. *All the Women Are White, All the Blacks Are Men, But Some of Us Are Brave: Black Women's Studies*. Old Westbury: Feminist, 1982.

Jacobs, Harriet A. *Incidents in the Life of a Slave Girl, Written by Herself.* 1861. Ed. Jean Fagan Yellin. Cambridge: Harvard UP, 1987.

Jones, Jacqueline. *Labor of Love, Labor of Sorrow: Black Women, Work and the Family from Slavery to the Present*. New York: Basics, 1985.

Kerr-Ritchie, Jeffrey R. *Freedpeople in the Tobacco South Virginia, 1860–1900*. Chapel Hill: U of North Carolina P, 1999.

Levine, Robert S. "Road to Africa: Frederick Douglass's Rome." *African American Review* 34:2 (Summer, 2000): 217-231.

McFeely, William S. *Frederick Douglass*. New York: Norton, 1991.

Mecklenburg County Clerk's Office, Boydton, Virginia. Deed Book 50, 1888: 68-69.

Morgan, Lynda J. *Emancipation in Virginia's Tobacco Belt. 1850-1817.* Athens: U of Georgia P, 1992.

Morrison, Toni. *Beloved*. New York: Knopf, 1987.

Nelson, Charmaine A. *The Color of Stone: Sculpting the Black Female Subject in Nineteenth-Century America*. Minneapolis: U of Minnesota P, 2007.

Noether, Emiliana P. "Mazzini and the Radical Movement in Nineteenth Century Italy." *International Journal of Social Education*, 3 (April 1987): 59-72.

Nora, Pierre. "Between Memory and History: *Les Lieux de Mémoire*." *Representations* 29 (Spring 1989): 7-25.

Park, Katherine. "Healing the Poor: Hospitals and the Medical Assistance in Renaissance Florence." *Medicine and Charity Before the Welfare State*. Ed. Jonathan Barry and Colin Jones. London: Routledge, 1991. 26-45.

Park, Katherine, and John Henderson. "'The First Hospital Among Christians': The Ospedale di Santa Maria Nuova in Early Sixteenth-Century Florence." *Medical History* (1991) 35: 164-188.

Porter, Dorothy. "The Remonds of Salem, Massachusetts: A Nineteenth-Century Family Revisited." *Proceedings of the American Antiquarian Society* 95:2 (1985): 259-95.

—. "Sarah Remond." *Notable American Women 1607-1950: A Biographical Dictionary*. Ed. Edward T. James. Volume III. Cambridge: Harvard UP, 1971: 136-137.

—."Sarah Parker Remond, Abolitionist and Physician." *Journal of Negro History* 20.1 (1935): 287-93.

Remond [Pintor], Sarah Parker. Letter to Frederick Douglass, 8 July 1887. The Frederick Douglass Papers at the Library of Congress. <http://lcweb2.loc.gov/ ammem/doughtml/>

Remond, Sarah Parker. "A Colored Lady Lecturer." *English Woman's Journal*, 7 (June, 1861): 269-75.

—. "Colonization." *Freedman* 1 February 1866: 162-163.

—. "Disabilities of American Persons of Colour" [Letter to George Mifflin Dallas]. *Liberator* (17 February 1860) n. p.

—. "Disabilities of American Persons of Colour" [Letter to Sarah Parker Remond]. *Liberator* (17 February 1860) n. p.

—. Letter, *The Liberator*. 3 November 1866. n. p.

—. "The Negroes in the United States of America." (Address delivered in London, 1862, edited by Dorothy B. Porter). *Journal of Negro History* 27 (April 1942): 216-218.

—. "Sarah P. Remond." *Our Exemplars, Poor and Rich or Biographical Sketches of Men and Women*. Ed. Matthew Davenport Hill. London: Cassell, 1861. 276-286.

—. "Speech Delivered at the Music Hall, Warrington, England. 24 January 1859, *The Black Abolitionist Papers*. Vol. I *The British Isles, 1830-1865*. Ed. C. Peter Ripley. Chapel Hill: U of North Carolina P, 1985. 435-444.

Reyes, Angelita. *Mothering ACROSS Cultures: Postcolonial Representations*. Minneapolis: U of Minnesota P, 2002.

—. DHR File No. 058-5076. Virginia Department of Historic Resources. Richmond, Virginia. 2007.

Simpson, Alan. *The Legend of Carter's Grove and Other Mysteries: A Collection of Essays from Colonial Williamsburg*. Colonial Williamsburg: Colonial Williamsburg Foundation, 1993.

Singleton, Theresa A. "An Introduction to African-American Archaeology." *"I, Too, Am America": Archaeological Studies of African-American Life*. Ed. Theresa A. Singleton. Charlottesville: UP of Virginia, 1999. 1-17.

Smith, Sidonie, and Julia Watson, ed. *De/Colonizing the Subject: The Politics of Gender in Women's Autobiography*. Minneapolis: U of Minnesota P, 1992.

—, ed. *Interfaces: Women/Autobiography/Image/Performance*. Ann Arbor: U of Michigan P, 2005.

—, ed. *Women, Autobiography, Theory: A Reader*. Madison: U of Wisconsin P, 1998.

Spector, Janet. *What This Awl Means: Feminist Archaeology at Wahpeton Dakota Village*. St. Paul: Minnesota Historical Society, 1993.

Stasio, Frank. "Interview with Martha Hodes." Thursday, Sept. 28, 2006. *The State of Things*. North Carolina Public Radio 91.5 FM. <http://seacaptainswife.com/pages/all_author_appearances.php>

Stone, Albert. *Autobiographical Occasions and Original Acts: Versions of American Identity from Henry Adams to Nate Shaw*. Philadelphia: U of Pennsylvania P, 1982.

Swann-Wright, Dianne. *A Way Out of No Way: Claiming Family and Freedom in the New South*. Charlottesville: U of Virginia P, 2002.

Vlach, John Michael. *Back of the Big House: The Architecture of Plantation Slavery*. Chapel Hill: U of North Carolina P, 1993.

Walker, Alice. "In Search of Our Mothers' Gardens." *In Search of Our Mothers' Gardens: Womanist Prose*. New York: Harcourt, 1983: 231-243.

Whitney, Ann. Letter to Sarah Whitney. 17 April 1868. Ann Whitney Papers. Wellesley College Archives, Wellesley, MA.

Wilkie, Laurie A. *Creating Freedom: Material Culture and African American Identity at Oakley Plantation, Louisiana 1840-1950*. Baton Rouge: Louisiana State UP, 2000.

Yellin, Jean Fagan. "Introduction." Jacobs xiii-xxxiv.

"Labyrinthine Memories": Charles Chesnutt and Zitkala-Ša's Navigation of the Old and New in *The Conjure Woman* and *American Indian Stories*

Mary Frances Jiménez

In 1899, Charles Waddell Chesnutt published his first book, *The Conjure Woman*, through the major American publishing company Houghton Mifflin. A collection of short stories united by their narrators – John, a white northern entrepreneur who moves to North Carolina to capitalize on the post-Civil War economic vacuum in the South, and Julius McAdoo, a former slave and resident of the plantation John purchases – *The Conjure Woman* contains pieces Chesnutt published in *The Atlantic Monthly* between 1887 and 1899. In January 1900, "Impressions of an Indian Childhood," the first in a series of autobiographical sketches by Dakota Sioux writer Zitkala-Ša, appeared in that same magazine.[1] Appearing just a year after the *Atlantic* printed Chesnutt's "Hot-Foot Hannibal," the closing story in *The Conjure Woman*, Zitkala-Ša's sketches would become the the first pieces in one of her own book-length collections, *American Indian Stories*, published by Hayworth in 1921. At first glance, these two authors and their work have little in common: one, an African American man working as a stenographer in Ohio and publishing tales set on a ruined-but-reviving Southern plantation; the other, a young Native American woman known as a concert violinist and teacher who published recollections of her childhood in the West and education in the East. But, setting these apparent differences aside, Charles Chesnutt and Zitkala-Ša's juxtaposition across the pages of the *Atlantic* provides a point of entry to their more significant juxtaposition within the context of turn-of-the-century American literature and racial discourse.

Both Chesnutt's and Zitkala-Ša's lives seem to typify that of the "New" Negro or "New" Indian: a process of education in European and American masterworks and (apparent) adoption of middle-class values and professional life, which led each to prominence in the eyes of his or her own race and white society.[2] But unlike other participants in projects of racial uplift, such as Fannie Barrier Williams or Carlos Montezuma, whom some critics read as rejecting figures of the "Old" Negro or Indian in favor of a new identity for their races, Chesnutt's conjure tales and Zitkala-Ša's autobiographical sketches foreground characters that embody ancestral pasts and ways of knowledge. Using *The Atlantic Monthly*, a mainstream literary journal, as a forum that would lead to wide readership and subsequent publication of their book collections, Chesnutt and Zitkala-Ša circulated works that foreground folkloric tropes and characters who embody "Old" black and Native American identities as a means of resisting white supremacist racial discourse. In highlighting the tension between a past embodied in oral history and folk knowledge and a future that would confront the possibilities and problems of their races' new roles in American society, Chesnutt and Zitkala-Ša suggest that the integration of Old Negroes and Indians into the lives and work of the New generation is both necessary and inevitable.

Unfortunately, many twentieth- and twenty-first century literary critics have ignored not only the important resonances between Chesnutt's and Zitkala-Ša's life and works, but also the ways that, by juxtaposing African American and Native American history and literature, a fuller picture of the Reconstruction and post-Reconstruction periods emerges. By considering not just the Freedman's Bureau, but also the Bureau of Indian Affairs; not just the horrors of lynching in the South, but also the battle at Little Bighorn and the massacre at Wounded Knee (not to mention the nation's expansion of imperialist foreign policy following the Spanish-American War), one begins to understand that the kind of hegemonic discourse which Chesnutt subverted through his manipulation of the plantation genre and Zitkala-Ša through her invocation of American autobiography was a discourse whose logic necessitated more than just the attribution of a fixed, inherent inferiority to newly emancipated blacks. The private and public discourse of white supremacy which led to social segregation and Jim Crow laws for blacks also mandated that other minority groups in America participate in erasing their own racial and ethnic traditions in pursuit of an "assimilation" that (at least in the case of Indians) they would rarely be permitted to achieve: despite these marginalized groups' efforts to cast off the cultural practices that set them apart, whites would continue to inscribe lines of difference.

To illustrate this white investment in a discourse of difference, we might return to the pages of the *Atlantic*. Chesnutt and Zitkala-Ša's work appeared alongside that of writers as diverse as W.E.B. Du Bois, Sarah Orne Jewett, Finley Peter Dunne, Sui Sin Far, George Bird Grinnell, and John Muir. Though we can read this list today as evidence of an emerging multicultural, multiregional canon within American literature, the editors of *The Atlantic Monthly* hardly saw it as such. Against the backdrop of the Spanish-American War, the closure of the frontier, and new technologies that permitted increasing contact with the world beyond America's borders, this collection of regional and ethnic voices suggests white America's desire to scrutinize and gape at an exotic Other. As Cathy N. Davidson and Ada Norris point out, Zitkala-Ša's pieces appear in the same issues as Mary Johnston's *To Have and to Hold*, a serialized historical novel which "indulges in all the possible stereotypes of evil and devilish 'savages,'" the very stereotypes Zitkala-Ša's narrative works to subvert and turn back upon white "civilization" (xxxiv). The editors of the *Atlantic* apparently were not bothered by the incongruity between the two women's depiction of Indian life – nor were readers likely to notice that Chesnutt's tales undermined the white supremacist tradition of plantation fiction in which they appeared to participate. Charles Hannon has called the turn-of-the-century *Atlantic* "the recognized locus of nativist New England intellectuals," and this haphazard pairing of texts by black, Indian, Asian, and Irish writers with works that undermined those authors' very humanity attests to the blind illogic of nativist and white supremacist rhetoric: while mainstream journals' selections imply an interest in nonwhite cultures, that interest only extends as far as the selections can be read as counterpoints to notions of white superiority (Hannon 190).

For Charles Chesnutt and Zitkala-Ša, then, publication in *The Atlantic Monthly* marked their entrance into the prevailing literary world of upper- and middle-class white America, yet also exposed them to that audience's misreading. For example, a review of Chesnutt's stories (this time in their post-*Atlantic* collected form) in *The Bookman* calls Julius "a fine type of the old slave devoted to his master, never lacking in dignity and courage, but withal possessing an indifferent code of morals," and asserts the cumulative effect of the stories is that of "the blind superstition and duplicity of character fostered by the life of servility and cringing to the master" (Morgan 372). For Zitkala-Ša, the journal publication of her autobiographical pieces paved the way for publication of her own first book, *Old Indian Legends* (1901), a collection of folk tales which one reviewer would call proof that "the undeveloped minds of primitive peoples may have been as happily filled and as completely satisfied with these childish stories as is the omnivorous reader of to-day with the wealth of literature that crowds upon the new century" ("Book Reviews" 37).[3] Thus, for Chesnutt and Zitkala-Ša, the thrill of publication would be tempered by the realization that even as the fact and content of their work asserted their status as participants in an American literary tradition, audiences still read them as "quaint" at best, "primitive" at worst (Morgan 373; "Book Reviews" 36-37). I use the synecdochic figure of author-for-work here deliberately, for the judgments passed on their literary achievements correspond to the limits placed on Chesnutt and Zitkala-Ša as emerging representatives of the New Negro and New Indian.

Life as part of a "New" generation of their races gave Chesnutt and Zitkala-Ša access to many of the trappings but few of the real benefits of American citizenship. Judith N. Shklar describes how notions of citizenship in America have been shaped by a system in which "the disenfranchised and the excluded were members of a professedly democratic society that was actively and purposefully false to its own vaunted principles by refusing to accept these people or to recognize their right to be voters and free laborers" (14). As a black man and an Indian woman in post-Reconstruction America, Chesnutt and Zitkala-Ša belonged to groups whose claims to citizenship were constantly under attack from rapidly consolidating discourses of white supremacy. Jim Crow laws, discriminatory practices in employment and education, broken treaties, the reservation system, lynch law, and a host of other legal and social practices worked to systematically disfranchise nonwhites and ensure that citizenship in the nation would be determined strictly along a color line – the achievements of a few so-called "representative" individuals notwithstanding.

Cognizant of the tension between the social standing they sought and the standing the nation accorded to nonwhites, African American and Native American writers of the late nineteenth century produced works that challenge the white supremacist ideology of the very middle-class society whose models of success and progress they appropriated. For some, this meant espousing a program of racial uplift through civilizationism and acculturation and embracing what Alexander Crummell would call "the discipline of freedom." Crummell, a prominent African American preacher in the post-Reconstruction era, exhorted his congregation against "extravagance[s]" in dress, entertainment, and political activity and called for an abandonment of "our educational hallucinations" of classical training for all black children (252, 250). But we must not mistake Crummell's intentions: educated at Cambridge and leading a cosmopolitan life that included almost two decades working in Liberia, Crummell was not of the accommodationist school. Rather, he advocated a middle-class, Christian work ethic in which "trading in politics" (let alone "put[ting] culture upon a nin-compoop") becomes "a waste of powers," which, "if garnered up, and used for useful purposes, would found Savings Banks, would start worthy mechanics and tradesmen in lucrative businesses; would set agoing springs of action in divers departments of noble activity" (250, 251).

Crummell's focus on economic uplift achieved through self-control forms one part of a more complex discourse on what the post-Reconstruction generation of African Americans could achieve. In a 1988 article, Henry Louis Gates, Jr., outlines what he sees as the emergence during the late nineteenth century of a "trope" of a New Negro, a rhetorical figure "crafted" by African American intellectuals with a dual intention: to refute the public image of blacks propagated by white racist media and to "restructure the *race's* image of *itself*" (137, 140; Gates's emphasis). A New Negro, according to Gates, was figured variously in terms of "education, refinement, and money," physical and sartorial conformity to aspects of white middle-class appearance, and participation in a new literary "voice" (136, 143-44). For example, in *Progress of the Race*, Fannie Barrier Williams writes of the role of African American women's clubs in "represent[ing] the new Negro with new powers of self-help, with new capacities, and with an intelligent insight into her own condition" (203). This work of self-help would include not only Barrier Williams's own literary project of recording the emergence of female organizations within the black community, but also social and sanitation movements in which "hundreds of poor Negro homes have felt the cleansing and refining touch of the home department of these various clubs" (210). The capable, self-aware New Negro woman would be the instrument of refinement through which all women of her race would leave behind the degradation slavery caused.

Gates argues that this image of the race as progressive "depends fundamentally upon self-negation, a turning away from the 'Old Negro' and the labyrinthine memory of black enslavement and toward the register of a 'New Negro'" (132). In Gates's estimation, black intellectuals in this era viewed images of the "Old Negro" as inseparable from "the white figure of the black as Sambo," a figure which "served various generations of racists as a sign of lack, of degeneration, of a truly negated *absence*" (130; Gates's emphasis). Rejecting that image and replacing it with that of the New Negro was a surefire means for blacks to assert their position as a presence within the nation – to extract themselves from the disorienting labyrinths of the past in favor of a new orientation toward an American future.

Gates's point about the forward-looking trend of African American writing is important to keep in mind as we consider the singularity of Chesnutt's collection: no other African American author depicts the Old Negro as extensively as Chesnutt does in *The Conjure Woman*, and none so boldly adopts – and subverts – a genre associated with the kind of damage Gates attributes to the Sambo figure. Gates's own representation of the trope of the New Negro, however, does not fully account for nuance in the identity-shaping projects of post-Reconstruction African American intellectuals. Gates's contention that images of a New Negro came at the expense of the Old Negro seems to turn a blind eye to the many post-Reconstruction literary representations of Old Negro characters (such as Madam Frances in Pauline Hopkins's *Contending Forces* and Grandmother Harriet Johnson in Frances E.W. Harper's *Iola Leroy*). Nor does Gates's own mention of post-Reconstruction African American historians such as William Grant Still and George Washington Williams address the necessarily "old" concerns of historiography, an endeavor that acknowledges and reclaims the past rather than rejecting it. Thus, although most black intellectuals foregrounded a modern self-image through representations of a New Negro, the Old Negro's persistent presence contributes to turn-of-the-century African American racial discourse.

Carla L. Peterson, on the other hand, notes that novels of the African American Nadir engage in imaginative grappling with slavery's legacy through a process of invented tradition in which authors recognized a need "to face rather than suppress the past" (35). Representations of the Old Negro in the historical romances Peterson discusses signal the novels' sometimes-conflicted attempts both to commemorate the past and to envision a future for the community beyond slavery. While these Old characters "complicate" and provide nuance to white culture's stock representations of the "darky," they also tend to remain at the margins of the novels' familial plots (Peterson 49). If, as Peterson suggests, Chesnutt's later novels are "infused with ambivalence" about the Old Negro's viability in post-Reconstruction America, an examination of his first published pieces – the conjure tales – provides a look at what happens when an author situates the Old Negro at the center of his literary project (49). Even as Chesnutt's adoption of a white genre and publication venue limits his ability to confront the problems of racism head-on, through Uncle Julius Chesnutt nevertheless circulates an image of the Old Negro that celebrates African American ancestry and knowledge.

One can trace a similarly ambivalent discourse of what it meant to be a New or Old Indian in the works of Native American writers at the turn of the century. Though the situations of blacks and Indians during the nineteenth century are not exact analogues[4], the turn of the century saw both groups struggling for social standing in the face of white supremacist discourse which insisted on their inherent and characteristic barbarism, immorality, and intellectual inferiority[5]. For some Native Americans, becoming a New Indian meant rejecting the idea of tribal membership altogether and accepting the benefits of citizenship that assimilationist policies seemed to offer. Carlos Montezuma, a Mohave-Apache Indian and Zitkala-Ša's one-time fiancé, avidly supported off-reservation education for Native American children: "Away with the reservations schools! Send all children to the most civilized communities, not in large masses, but scatter them in small classes over the United States [...]. You can never civilize the Indian until you place him while yet young (and the younger the better) in direct relations with good civilization. When you do this with judgment, you will succeed and make him a useful citizen of the Republic" (qtd. in Spack 185)[6].

More so than Crummell and Fannie Barrier Williams, Montezuma seems to subscribe to the era's discourse of civilization. For Montezuma, overcoming the label of "savage" would occur not through an upsetting of binaries or a rejection of the ascription of "barbaric" qualities to his race[7], but through active excision – and even better, circumvention – of those learned barbarisms associated with tribal life. Montezuma aims to assert social standing for Indians through forced inculcation in the ways of the civilized nation: rejecting claims of Indians' inferiority along lines of racial characteristics, he vows that Indians *can* learn to be citizens, and they must. Unfortunately, Montezuma's hopes would fall prey to what Hannon characterizes as the fundamental contradiction in turn-of-the-twentieth-century cultural and political policy toward Indians: though the Dawes Act of 1887 insisted that Indians "give up their own cultures [and] assimilate to American society, and thereby 'become' Americans," they were "consistently excluded from the American polity by nativist rhetoric, which constructed American identity as something that could be achieved only by descendents of the 'original' colonial English" (Hannon 184). This rhetoric went hand in hand with the white supremacist rhetoric against blacks (as well as other racial minorities) to create a picture of the citizen as one who was culturally, politically, and racially Anglo-Saxon.

Surrounded by a national narrative of progress yet barred from participating in it, Chesnutt's and Zitkala-Ša's similarly complicated positions as representative "New" members of their groups translated, I will argue, into important similarities in their early works. Responding to the demands of an audience that expected the Other to conform linguistically and generically to white literature while simultaneously emphasizing their own cultural differenes, Chesnutt and Zitkala-Ša each produced works that foreground representations of Old Negroes, Old Indians, and traditional ways of life. But, rather than replicate the denigrating tropes of the genres they appeared to adopt, Chesnutt and Zitkala-Ša maneuver within those forms to produce works that undermine racial stereotypes. In so doing, they insist that the “Old” characters, who embody a past before the Civil War, before the reservation, have not vanished. By representing these characters in terms of their connection to the past, to the land, to the family, and through all these to collective memory, Chesnutt and Zitkala-Ša insist upon the integrity of blacks and Indians, an integrity that precedes white intervention and the imposition of middle-class values. The Old Negro and Old Indian, then, are not roles for the New Negro and Indian to cast off but rather to honor and integrate into their present lives of freedom, individual success, and racial uplift.

In *The Conjure Woman*, Chesnutt places the voice of the Old Negro at the center of a project to reclaim the past. Chesnutt positions a white Northerner, John, and his wife, Annie, as auditors of a series of tales concerning antebellum life in the neighborhood of their newly purchased North Carolina plantation. These tales are narrated by the former slave they blithely dub “Uncle Julius.” To John, whose narration frames each of Julius’s tales, the stories are at best “legend[s]” and at worst “absurdly impossible yarn[s]” (108, 61). As many critics have pointed out, John’s white perspective mediates between Julius’s African American voice and Chesnutt’s white readership. As an auditor who fails to see beyond the types of character and plot he expects from the plantation genre, John’s comments anticipate those of Chesnutt’s reviewer in *The Bookman*. The stories John’s cynical perspective dismiss as fiction in fact serve as an important record of black life in Patesville before emancipation and, in a larger sense, of the history of slavery itself. By presenting these stories through the voice of a former slave – an Old Negro – Chesnutt insists upon the existence of a rich oral history of African American life. This oral record of the community emerges from within the labyrinth of slavery and predates the mainstream, written histories produced by some of Chesnutt’s New Negro contemporaries.

Because his stories lack the kind of written documentation that white audiences require from conventional histories, Julius must constantly confront John’s skepticism about their authenticity. For example, after listening to the story of a white man transformed into a slave on his own plantation in “Mars Jeems’s Nightmare,” John asks Julius, “By the way, did you make that up all by yourself?” (101). Julius’s face “assumed an injured look, expressive more of sorrow than of anger, and shaking his head he replied: – ‘No, suh, I heared dat tale befo’ you er Mis’ Annie dere wuz bawn, suh. My mammy tol’ me dat tale w’en I wa’n’t mo’ d’n knee-high ter a hopper-grass’” (101). Julius insists that his tale is not merely a means to an end – the continued employment of Julius’s grandson, which John reads as the tale’s economic motivation – but rather part of his community’s oral history, and more specifically of his own cultural inheritance from his mother. The tale is older than John and Annie themselves, yet they refuse to acknowledge its veracity. This denial of the past constitutes a real injury against Julius and his community.

With his conjure tales, Chesnutt tries to alleviate the loss of an important source of black history – and the sorrow that loss causes. Publication in the *Atlantic* and later in book form puts Julius's stories of the Old Negro and of life under slavery on the record in a form whites will accept. Chesnutt's tales allow the always-masking Julius to share his real histories with a larger audience than John and Annie. Moreover, Chesnutt's use of the vernacular not only reproduces the oral quality of Julius's voice, it both translates and encodes his histories, packaging their message in a visibly "Negro" form and insisting that white characters do not interfere with its transmission. Though Julius offers various forms of alternative documentation for his stories, such as his offer "ter prove" the story of "The Goophered Grapevine" by "lead[ing] de way right ter Henry's grave ober yander in de plantation buryin'-groun'," Chesnutt's own representation of these histories – intact within a white framework – will have the better chance of establishing slavery's violence (33).

Julius also uses his community's connection to the land as a way to assert an alternative system of myth and history. Jeffery Myers explains that "Chesnutt's stories reveal how plantation owners literally carved [plantation] culture from both the bodies of slaves and the forests themselves" and more importantly how "African Americans and the land they have worked, as well as surviving tracts of uncultivated and undeveloped land, have a symbiosis that the slave-owning plantation owners – and the Northern capitalists who replaced them as land owners – lack" (6). Chesnutt implies that this symbiosis with the land belongs particularly to the Old Negro. In *The Conjure Woman*, the theme of black characters' link to the land is rendered literally through various results of conjure: Henry's hair and health, which wax and wane according to the state of the goophered grapevines; Dan and Mahaly's haunts, which "hang 'roun'" the woods after their tragic transformation into animals results in their deaths (192); and Sandy's body, which his wife conjures into a tree so that he "could stay on the plantation fer a w'ile" rather than being lent out to service repeatedly (45). Here again, Chesnutt exploits the generic expectations of his audience, using the plantation tradition popularized by white writers like Thomas Nelson Page to present starker truths about the relationship between the black community and the Southern land they worked for centuries. In contrast to Page's plantation fiction, which attributes the Old Negro's desire to remain on the plantation to his longing for the benevolent protection of a white master – his "Marse Chan" depicts a former slave nostalgic for the "good ole times" of slavery when "Niggers didn' hed nothin' 't all to do" (10) – Chesnutt reveals that the Old Negro experiences a profound connection to the land where his community's history is rooted. Unfortunately, when the master owns the land and everything on it, that connection is subject to severance with no notice or recourse, and that severance is often fatal, as the story "Po' Sandy proves" –

the master saws down Sandy's tree to build a new kitchen. Like the community's oral histories, the land becomes a record – this time physical – of collective memory, and John's plans to alter it threaten Julius' right to a land which bears not only the fruits of decades of unpaid labor, but also the echoes of black joy and trauma.

Like Charles Chesnutt, Zitkala-Ša blends truth and fiction and employs multiple frameworks and perspectives in her texts. Though the three sketches Zitkala-Ša published in the *Atlantic* rely on recollections of material from her life, they are not strictly autobiographical. Zitkala-Ša deliberately crafts details of her stories, eliding the identity of her white father, for instance, and selecting symbolically weighty images from the multiple communities among which she moves (her description of the American East as a tempting "Land of Red Apples" serves as a good example here). Her unnamed first-person narrator follows a *bildungsroman* pattern reflected in the titles of her three pieces: "Impressions of an Indian Childhood," "The School Days of an Indian Girl" and "An Indian Teacher Among Indians." This hybridity of genre allows Zitkala-Ša to challenge entrenched white traditions of autobiography even as it creates and exposes tensions for the author. Looking back on her childhood selves, the narrative voice in these pieces shifts between a limited perspective in the narrated moment and a more experienced consciousness. These shifts illustrate the incongruity of the old and new worlds the author describes even as the text works to reconcile them and insist on their inseparability.

Participation in literacy marks an important fissure between Old and New Indian identities. Zitkala-Ša depicts a rich storytelling practice as central to her community's transmission of history. As with Chesnutt, orality becomes a way to encode resistance. In "Impressions of an Indian Childhood," she writes that she "loved best the evening meal, for that was the time when old legends were told" (71). The child Zitkala-Ša recalls these evening gatherings of "old folks" thus: "I pillowed my head in my mother's lap; and, lying flat upon my back, I watched the stars as they peeped down upon me, one by one. The increasing interest of the tale aroused me, and I sat up eagerly listening to every word" (71-72). Some of these tales are the Iktomi trickster stories Zitkala-Ša would later collect and retell as *Old Indian Legends*, but one, in particular, differs. The child narrator asks an old woman "the meaning of the blue lines on her chin." Although the old woman calls her tattoos "signs – secret signs I dare not tell you," she relates a story about a woman "whose magic power lay hidden behind the marks upon her face." The old woman calls it "a wonderful story," but the young girl it is a "fearful" one: the tale leaves an "impression [...] so acute that the picture still remains vividly clear and pronounced" (72-73).

Despite this strong impression, Zitkala-Ša shares no details of the story with her reader. The disconnect between the old woman's wonder and the child's fear prefigures Zitkala-Ša's eventual disconnect from the community history the old woman transmits orally and bodily. Later, Zitkala-Ša describes how she and the other Indian children "delighted in impersonating our own mothers [...]. We imitated their various manners, even to the inflection of their voices [...]. [W]e rested our elbows on our knees and bent forward as old women were most accustomed to do" (75). At this early stage in their lives, the narrator and her peers understand and emulate an Old Indian transmission of collective memory. Not only the words, but the mannerisms of orality – movements of the body and inflections of voices – constitute aspects of this tradition, in which Zitkala-Ša participates freely before the intervention of white education and literacy. Denying the reader access to the matter of this collective memory, while still insisting upon its importance, Zitkala-Ša gestures toward her own secret signs – signs of community membership, of oral history, of resistance to white ways of knowing – which her stories hold at a distance from her white readers. Later, however, Zitkala-Ša exchanges this tradition for another, describing her studies in English as "weaving [...] the magic design which promised me the white man's respect" (101). Like the marks on the tattooed woman's face, the meaning of written English hides behind signs that are both "wonderful" and "fearful."

These important moments of transmission of an Indian oral tradition are implicitly juxtaposed with a scene in "The School Days of an Indian Girl" in which the narrator hears the "white man's legend" of "an insolent chieftain among the bad spirits" – the Christian devil (94). Here, Zitkala-Ša turns the othering logic of the Quaker missionaries who enticed her to attend the school back upon itself, calling Christianity a "legend." This word had no negative connotation when Zitkala-Ša used it to recall her own tribal stories, but she knows white culture uses it as a way to dismiss non-white religious practices and ways of knowing, just as John belittles Julius's conjure tales. However, Zitkala-Ša also recognizes the power of legends in a way whites do not. Unlike the missionaries, she extends this power to the stories of a different religious tradition. After hearing that "this terrible creature roamed loose in the world, and that little girls who disobeyed school regulations were to be tortured by him," the narrator dreams of the devil bursting into her mother's cottage (94):

> He looked exactly like the picture of him I had seen in the white man's papers. He did not speak to my mother, because he did not know the Indian language, but his glittering yellow eyes were fastened upon me. [...] I threw down my spools, and ran to my mother. He did not fear her, but followed closely after me. Then I ran round and round the stove, crying aloud for help. But my mother and the woman seemed not to know my danger. They sat still, looking quietly upon the devil's chase after me. [...] Beside my mother's chair I fell in a heap. Just as the devil stooped over me with outstretched claws my mother awoke from her quiet indifference, and lifted me on her lap. Whereupon the devil vanished, and I was awake. (95)

As with the legends of the narrator's people, the missionaries' legends have real power to create fear and inspire dreams. Not only does this dream manifest the narrator's anxieties over her loss of her mother, it also portrays language as the line along which that loss has occurred. Zitkala-Ša's education into the palefaces' language leaves her open to haunting by the devil of their legends and renders her mother – the Old Indian – silent, unable to help her until the end of the dream. Having lost her connection to oral history, the narrator strikes back against the assimilating forces of Christianity by wresting an even stronger weapon from the hands of white acculturation: "Stealing into the room where a wall of shelves was filled with books, I drew forth *The Stories of the Bible*. With a broken slate pencil I carried in my apron pocket, I began by scratching out his wicked eyes. A few moments later, when I was ready to leave the room, there was a ragged hole in the page where the picture of the devil had once been" (95). This moment, which Zitkala-Ša calls her "revenge upon the devil" begins her deployment of the tools of literacy against white supremacy (95). Zitkala-Ša learns, however, that participation in America's written tradition can cause distance and even alienation from the Indian community. For Zitkala-Ša, the pen will become a many-edged sword: a source of estrangement from her mother, a sign of membership in middle-class United States culture, and a means to question the legitimacy of that nation and its language.

Susan Bernadin explains how Zitkala-Ša subverts formal conventions to "present an ethnographic view of American culture – under the guise of sentimental autobiography – that forces non-Indian readers to view themselves from an outsider's oppositional perspective" (218). As with Chesnutt's Julius, whose orality is framed by John's literacy and whose vernacular works as a linguistic code readers must decipher to access his multiple intentions, Zitkala-Ša uses language simultaneously to invite the reader into her experience and to remind that reader of the marginalizing effect of literacy on minorities in America. By using the tools of her new American literacy to call the nation's master texts into question, Zitkala-Ša challenges the hegemony of Christianity and undermines white America's claim to exclusive rights of national myth-creation and history-keeping.

Old Indian identification – literal oneness – with the land functions centrally in Zitkala-Ša's recuperation of her community's history in a way that is similar to Chesnutt's use of the land in his conjure tales. As Chesnutt does in "Po' Sandy," Zitkala-Ša tells the story of a man linked to the land through a tree: her mother shows her a plum bush whose "roots are wrapped around an Indian's skeleton" (80). Buried with the seeds that were tokens in his favorite game, the dead Indian is now sustenance and substrate for the bush that grew from those seeds. Passing the bush with this new knowledge, the child narrator "grew sober with awe, and was alert to hear a long-drawn-out whistle rise from the roots of it. Though I had never heard with my own ears this strange whistle of departed spirits, yet I had listened so frequently to hear the old folks describe it that I knew I should recognize it at once. The lasting impression of that day, as I recall it now, is what my mother told me about the dead man's plum bush" (80-81). Thus, Zitkala-Ša unites the notion of connection to the land with collective memory and oral history: the story is significant not only because it evinces the Old Indian interdependence with the land, but also because it figures the transmission of that interdependence across generations. Both the physical presence of the dead man's plum bush and the spiritual presence of the story surrounding it provide potential links between the Old and the New Indian. The young Zitkala-Ša hopes to recognize the whistle of a departed ancestor, but the adult autobiographer finds something more "lasting" in the voices of her mother and other "old folks." For Zitkala-Ša, attention to elders is a crucial act for those who would maintain a connection to the land and through it to the voice of the past.

Later, however, after years of education in white schools and separation from Old Indian ways, Zitkala-Ša expresses her disconnection from her community in terms of her estrangement from the land:

> For the white man's papers I had given up my faith in the Great Spirit. For these same papers I had forgotten the healing in trees and brooks. On account of my mother's simple view of life, and my lack of any, I gave her up, also. I made no friends among the race of people I loathed. Like a slender tree, I had been uprooted from my mother, nature, and God. I was shorn of my branches, which had waved in sympathy and love for home and friends. The natural coat of bark which had protected my oversensitive nature was scraped off to the very quick.
>
> Now a cold bare pole I seemed to be, planted in a strange earth. Still, I seemed to hope a day would come when my mute aching head, reared upward to the sky, would flash a zigzag lightning across the heavens. (112)

Zitkala-Ša has become the tree which, if rooted to the land, could whistle and vibrate with the spirits, but yet again white literacy has rendered Indian orality mute. Severed from the Old Indian and transplanted into the foreign soil of a hated race, the New Indian is a tree without roots or branches – an individual with no past, no genealogy, to tie her to her community, and no desire to reach out to the community that uprooted her. Though her literacy allows her to circulate images of Indian identity to a mainstream audience, the act of writing only underscores the author's own separation from her ancestral land and traditions.

Both the New Negro and New Indian, then, look to the older generation's connections to the land and oral history for alternative documents of their communities' collective memories. But Chesnutt and Zitkala-Ša show that the place of the Old Negro and Indian is not just in the past. Both writers focus on family as means to show the Old generation's important connection to the future. Although Chesnutt and Zitkala-Ša's education and participation in the lives of the New generation may have inculcated them with values of (white) middle-class domesticity, as Laura Wexler's work on nineteenth-century sentimental benevolence suggests, their texts insist that readers recognize the presence of coherent families before the intervention of white benevolence[8]. In Julius's tales of slave life in the neighborhood of the McAdoo plantation and in Zitkala-Ša's recollection of her life before the "palefaces" arrived to escort her to "the Land of Red Apples," the family serves as a bulwark of Old Negro and

Old Indian culture that outside pressures threaten to erode. Chesnutt and Zitkala-Ša refute the logic of white supremacy by insisting that white interference, not the degeneracy of "inferior" races, poses the greatest threat to black and Indian families. The Old Negro and Old Indian, cognizant of the value of collective memory and family history in a way that the New generation is not, invest the most to ensure these families' continuation.

Almost all of the stories in *The Conjure Woman* involve black family members' separation from one another: Sis' Becky loses her husband and nearly loses her child; Mars Jeems sends Solomon's junesey away; Chloe's sweetheart Jeff is sold and drowns. Even the Guinea conjure man in "The Conjurer's Revenge" – a free black – has a family history to share, in which "his daddy wuz a king, er a guv'ner, er some sorter w'at-you-may-call-'em 'way ober yander in Affiky whar de niggers come fum, befo' he was stoled erway en sol' ter de spekilaters" (120-21). Reunion of families or lovers often provides the motivation for conjure. Though conjure's fantastic results take center stage, providing Chesnutt's white readers with diversionary "local color," Julius's stories also – and perhaps most importantly – function as a record of slavery's disruption of black genealogies. "Po' Sandy" serves not just as evidence of Old Negro connection to the land, but also as one of the most poignant examples of this dissolution of black families. In "Po' Sandy," Julius tells John the story of a slave who "wuz a monst'us good nigger, en could do so many things erbout a plantation," that he gains special notice among the family who owns him. Julius explains how "w'en mars Marrabo's chilluns growed up en married off, dey all un 'em wanted dey daddy fer ter gin 'em Sandy fer a weddin' present" (41). Mars Marrabo solves the problem by sending Sandy to live with each of his children for a few months in turn.

Sandy's transformation into a tree results from his desire to stay near his second wife – his first was traded away in his absence – and perpetuate his own family tree. Recognizing that his status as a Marrabo family heirloom precludes any stability within his own life, Sandy declares, "[I]t 'pears to me I ain' got no home, ner no marster, her no mistiss, ner no nuffin. I can't eben keep a wife [...]. I wisht I wuz a tree, er a stump, er a rock, er sump'n w'at could stay on de plantation fer a w'ile" (44-45). Sandy's claim to have no master or mistress is ironic, of course, given that he actually belongs to a series of owners – and it makes the outcome of his desire for a permanent tie to the plantation even more tragic. Although Sandy's new wife, Tenie – a former conjure woman linked to an African past and non-Christian religious practices – transforms him into a tree, the white master's destructive reach extends even into the couple's literal attempt to put down roots. When Mars Marrabo cuts down the Sandy-tree to build his new kitchen, he performs the economic script of slavery in which black bodies generate material for their white masters' estates. Further, Marrabo's actions enforce white codes of inheritance from one generation to the next, which interrupt and override blacks' attempts to establish family trees of their own.

"Po' Sandy" not only relates the physical fragmentation that Sandy's family suffers, it also grapples with the difficulty of recording and re-presenting these kinds of histories at all. After Tenie watches white men saw her husband into planks, she goes through a period in which she "'pear[s] ter be out'n her min' fer a long time" (56). But she gets "quiet' down," and her next act is to "up'n [tell] her marster all erbout Sandy en de pine-tree" (57). Mars Marrabo's rejects Tenie's attempt to tell the story of her loss, labeling her "de wuss 'stracted nigger he eber hearn of" (57). In Tenie's story, Mars Marrabo hears not an account of the traumatic experience that caused her "spells," but rather evidence of pre-existing, causeless insanity; he thinks that "de spekilater what he got Tenie fum had fooled him by wukkin' a crazy 'oman off on him" (56). Chesnutt's focus on Old Negro families highlights and critiques this refusal by whites to allow black voices to assert their own history, let alone participate in American historiography.

Haunting becomes one form of alternative history that the black community understands and can commemorate orally. Though Tenie's master forbids Tenie to share her story of Sandy's death with the other slaves, "somehow er 'nudder de niggers foun' out all erbout it, en dey all knowed de kitchen wuz ha'nted by Sandy's sperrit" (58). This haunting persists from the time of Tenie and Sandy to that of Julius in the present, recording trauma in a way that white history does not. Haunting, coupled with Julius's own act of conjuring as storyteller, also becomes a way to reclaim Sandy's material inheritance to his broader "family" in the community: after hearing the story of Sandy and Tenie, John's wife Annie declines to use the old kitchen/schoolhouse wood for a new kitchen, freeing the building to be used by Julius's church.

Julius's tales present a version of the past that counters plantation fiction's invented history of black-white relations, and Chesnutt's depiction of Julius's own life works to undermine this as well. Julius appears to relegate stories of disrupted families to his tales of the Old Negro as he was in slavery, but Chesnutt reminds his readers that the echoes of this disruption resonate into the present. Though "Marse Chan" ends with Page's black storyteller returning home to his waiting wife, perpetuating the myth that intact black families were the norm under slavery, Julius's own wife is notably missing. We might further note Julius's responsibility for his grandson, Tom – Chesnutt makes no mention of the boy's parents. The text makes this absence visible only to the reader who understands Julius's codes and moves beyond the entertainment value of the tales to acknowledge another collective wound: a lost generation of blacks, victims of slavery or the Civil War. But John, who employs Tom, merely finds him "trifling" and feels "much annoyed by his laziness, his carelessness, and his apparent lack of any sense of responsibility" (66). Tom, who likely has little or no recollection of slavery, represents one version of the New generation in the post-Reconstruction era, perhaps the version Alexander Crummell had in mind when he bemoaned the "nin-compoops" among the race. However, Tom may be an adequate worker who simply has not learned to play the part of the subservient Negro to John's satisfaction; his name, in fact, may be a play on Harriet Beecher Stowe's Uncle Tom, the archetypal "good servant" John (and Chesnutt's white audience) longs for as he attempts to recreate a nostalgic version of the plantation.

Only Julius's intervention, through storytelling, between his white employer and his grandson enables the New Negro's continued employment. That story is "Mars Jeems's Nightmare," in which a white master himself is transformed into the "noo nigger" on his own plantation (82). By thus reversing the definitions of black and white, master and slave, employer and employed, Julius, the Old Negro, performs a work of negotiation his grandson cannot. He reminds John and Annie to be patient with "po' ign'ant niggers w'at ain' had no chanst ter l'arn," for "dem w'at is kin' en good ter po' people is sho' ter prosper en git 'long in de worl'" (100). Julius's access to his community's history provides the material for this negotiation, and his reading of John's material motivations helps him translate that history into a language of prosperity and progress John can understand. It may be that by the end of the story Julius has also educated his grandson in the ways of masked resistance, for Annie rehires him and notices that "He seems so grateful, and so earnest in his promises of amendment" (102). The Old Negro strategy of "seem[ing]" one thing while meaning another becomes an important piece of knowledge Julius can pass on to the New generation. Similarly, Chesnutt uses what appears to be plantation fiction to present less-familiar stories about continuities in black family life and intergenerational exchanges that continue despite the ruptures of slavery and its aftermath.

Zitkala-Ša, in some ways, parallels Julius's grandson in her position as recipient of the Old generation's knowledge, transmitted through the ties of family. But, as with black families in the South, Indian families face the constant threat of dissolution from whites' destructive agency. Zitkala-Ša characterizes her childhood in terms of her constant proximity to her mother, who already models the domestic behaviors white reformers would later claim to "teach" Indian women – cooking, cleaning, and decoration of home and clothing through beadwork. But Zitkala-Ša senses sorrow in her mother: "Often she was sad and silent, at which times her full arched lips were compressed into hard and bitter lines, and shadows fell under her black eyes. Then I clung to her hand and begged to know what made the tears fall" (68). Zitkala-Ša asks her mother to include her, to educate her, in the history of her family's trauma, but it is a request her mother often denies, saying, "Hush; my little daughter must never talk about my tears" (68). Eventually, however, Zitkala-Ša learns the history of her tribe's forced removal to the reservation where she now lives. Her mother tells her how "[a]t last, when we reached this western country, on the first weary night your sister died. And soon your uncle died also [...]. Both your sister and uncle might have been happy with us today, had it not been for the heartless paleface" (70). The hill where they lay buried, to which Zitkala-

Ša's mother points during this story, serves as the only remaining connection to these lost family members.

Despite her initiation into the Old Indian's knowledge of whites' duplicity, the young narrator succumbs to the temptation of the "Land of Red Apples" promised by the missionaries who come to take Indian children to their boarding school (87). By riding the "iron horse" East, Zitkala-Ša perhaps subconsciously realizes how education will prepare her for changes she will face as a member of a New generation (87). However, she also endangers her connection not just to her mother but to an extended family of "grandfathers" and "grandmothers" – the Old Indians of her tribe who offered an education in legends and folk knowledge – without realizing the psychological costs of this separation from her community. In the passage I quoted at length earlier, the narrator bemoans this "uprooting" from her mother, home, and friends – and from the knowledge they offered of the "healing in trees and brooks" (112). Thus distanced from family and collective memory as well as the knowledge they possess, Zitkala-Ša must venture alone into life as a New Indian. Telling her story to what she knows is a skeptical, myopic audience, Zitkala-Ša does not mask her criticism as Chesnutt does, but rather ends her sketch by demanding the reader consider "whether real life or long-lasting death lies beneath this semblance of civilization" (113). Though this harsh question perhaps implies a thorough rejection of the dominant culture, it was the simultaneity of Zitkala-Ša's participation in Indian and American communities that would enable her future of activist work on behalf of Native peoples. Zitkala-Ša's constant shifting and maneuvering among these worlds make her life and work a fascinating study of the New generation's complicted navigations within and across communities often at odds with one another. Her early use of the pages of "civilized" publication to reach out to the Old Indian in her past, as well as her written representations of the orality that constitutes her literary and cultural ancestry, reveal the vexed choices Zitkala-Ša and other members of her generation faced as they created and circulated identities for white audiences and Native selves.

Charles Chesnutt and Zitkala-Ša's works conform neither to the official narrative of national belonging nor to their own races' alternative narratives of life as a "New" Negro or Indian. In *Constituting Americans*, Priscilla Wald invokes W.E.B. Du Bois's description of encountering "untold stories" in Georgia's Black Belt to explain how authors perplex and combat "official stories": narratives of nationhood and citizenship that "determine the status of an individual in the community," which "change in response to competing narratives of the nation that must be engaged, absorbed, and retold: the fashioning and endless refashioning of 'a people'" (1-2). Though apparently conventional in genre and regional in focus, Charles Chesnutt and Zitkala-Ša each uncover and manipulate loopholes in mainstream publication trends to participate in this refashioning of America. By showing that "already told" stories of plantation fiction and sentimental autobiography were actually untold, Chesnutt and Zitkala-Ša "confront" – and, I would argue, extend – "the limits of storytelling" (Wald 1). Chesnutt and Zitkala-Ša present the untold stories of Old Negroes and Old Indians as critical to a re-imagined story of the nation whose would-be progressive vision has blind spots and whose call to citizenship is insincere. The future representatives of their races must not, they insist, overlook the contributions of equally important representatives of the old ways. By exploring what Gates called the "labyrinthine memory" of their races' histories of slavery and dislocation, Chesnutt and Zitkala-Ša chart a path for the New generation to reclaim and retell the story of the past.

---

[1] Born Gertrude Simmons and later married to Raymond Ohiya Bonnin, whose surname she used in her activist work, Zitkala-Ša published under her self-chosen Indian name, sometimes translated as "Red Bird." As with her name, Zitkala-Ša's tribal affiliation comes in multiples: born on the Yankton Sioux reservation in South Dakota, Zitkala-Ša is also variously written of as Dakota or Lakota Sioux.

[2] Although he spent a few years as a student at the Howard School for Blacks, established by the Freedman's Bureau in Fayetteville, North Carolina, Chesnutt was largely self-educated; Zitkala-Ša began her education at White's Manual Labor Institute, an Indian boarding school in Wabash, Indiana established by Quaker missionaries. She continued her schooling at Indiana's Earlham College and the Boston Conservatory of Music. For more on Chesnutt's biography, see, for example, Andrews or McElrath et al. For more on the life of Zitkala-Ša, see, for example, Davidson and Norris or Fisher.

[3] This unsigned review of Zitkala-Ša's work appears in the *Southern Workman*, the official publication of the Hampton Normal and Agricultural Institute. Hampton, founded by Gen. Samuel Chapman Armstrong, was one of a few, as well as one of the earliest, post-Civil War trade and teacher education institutes to bring black and Indian students together. In addition to the magazine's function as an important post-Reconstruction publication venue for African American and Indian material—both newly-authored pieces (including several stories and essays by Charles Chesnutt) and collections of folklore recorded by Hampton students—Hampton's white administrators and trustees used the *Southern Workman* to promote and raise funds for their often-paternalistic educational and missionary goals. The mixed purposes of the magazine, as well as the probable editorial oversight of white staff, are evident in this condescending review. For more on the Hampton Institute, see Engs and Wexler.

[4] The seemingly contradictory government policies of forced assimilation for Indians and forced segregation for blacks mark just one division that shaped how the two groups differently navigated the denial of their national belonging.

[5] In *Iron Cages*, his expansive study of the way white male identity constructed itself by making Others of blacks, Indians, Mexicans, and Asians throughout the nineteenth century, Ronald Takaki outlines how white notions of "progress" simultaneously gave rise to and were shaped by "The Indian Question" and "The Negro Question." These debates laid the groundwork for suppressive actions against blacks and Indians, includ-

ing the Dawes Act of 1887, which gave the government authority, in the name of assimilation, to break up reservation land and allot it for individual Indian ownership – and to sell the excess parcels to white settlers. For blacks, the horrors of slavery were followed by the disappointments of the post-Reconstruction era and a "New South" whose industrial progress reproduced the old racial order of white paternalism under slavery (see Takaki 171-214). For further discussion of the relationship between African American and Native American racial uplift, see Gaines.

[6] This exhortation, along with additional biographical material on Montezuma and a discussion of his relationship with Zitkala-Ša, appears in Ruth Spack's article, "Dis/Engagement: Zitkala-Ša's letters to Carlos Montezuma, 1901-1902." The original she quotes is found in Montezuma's papers as "The Indian Problem from an Indian's Standpoint," an address given to the Fortnightly Club of Chicago on 10 Feb. 1898.

[7] At this point in the paper, I find it important to address the problems created by referring to Native Americans as a "race": for one, it erases Indians' tribal affiliation, a marker of collective identity that, at least at one point in the history of this continent, was far more important to Indians themselves than their membership in a shared "race." On a larger level, the idea of applying categories of race is biologically unfounded – it is just as inaccurate to speak of African Americans as belonging to a race of "blacks"; here, a cultural and experiential understanding of the notion of race is often invoked. But, more importantly, some Native Americans, Montezuma included, avoided this essentialist term, created and promulgated by whites and tied to a rigidly hierarchical system of race that insisted on Native Americans' innate inferiority. However, the fact remains that racial discourse shaped the world into which Zitkala-Ša wrote and was a term she used herself. "Race" is a useful shorthand for representing both the essentializing thought of the government and the founders of schools like Hampton and Carlisle and for discussing pan-Indian movements' attempts to create a unified cultural identity in the late nineteenth and early twentieth century.

[8] In *Tender Violence: Domestic Visions in an Age of U.S. Imperialism,* Laura Wexler examines the role of Hampton Institute, an important post-Reconstruction site of interaction between blacks and Indians, who were students in its "civilizing" project. She also discusses the all-Indian Carlisle Institute at which Zitkala-Ša taught. Wexler provides a compelling reading of the domesticating agenda of "before and after" photographs at those schools; however, she fails to read Zitkala-Ša's stories as a conscious and willful rejection of that same schooling. Reading Zitkala-Ša's work in the *Atlantic* as a sign that "Zitkala-Ša's self conception had been so effectively ensnared within the codes of sentiment that there is nothing Native American in them that is untouched by Western representations," Wexler discusses Zitkala-Ša's later activist work for Native American rights as a change in which she "suddenly rejected" Eastern ways, rather than a continuation of a work of subversion and resistance that her autobiographical publications began (120-21, 122). Of course, to say that Zitkala-Ša's late life was unmarked by participation in white middle-class values is as inaccurate as claims that her young adulthood was shaped by a complete usurpation of the Indian values of her childhood – Zitkala-Ša's constant shifting and maneuvering among these worlds are part of what makes her such a fascinating author and individual.

Works Cited

Andrews, William L. *The Literary Career of Charles W. Chesnutt*. Baton Rouge: Louisiana State UP, 1980.

Bernadin, Susan. "The Lessons of a Sentimental Education: Zitkala-Ša's Autobiographical Narratives." *Western American Literature* 32.3 (1997): 212-38.

"Book Reviews." *Southern Workman* 31.1 (1902): 35-37.

Chesnutt, Charles. *The Conjure Woman*. 1899. Intro Robert M. Farnsworth. Ann Arbor: U of Michigan P, 1969.

Crummell, Alexander. "The Discipline of Freedom" [Undated Thanksgiving Day sermon]. *Destiny and Race: Selected Writings 1840-1898*. Ed. Wilson Jeremiah Moses. Amherst: U Mass P, 1992. 245-53.

Davidson, Cathy N., and Ada Norris. Introduction. *Zitkala-Ša: American Indian Stories, Legends, and Other Writings*. New York: Penguin, 2003.

Engs, Robert F. *Educating the Disfranchised and Disinherited: Samuel Chapman Armstrong and Hampton Institute, 1839-1893*. Knoxville: U of Tennessee P, 1999.

—. *Freedom's First Generation: Black Hampton, Virginia, 1861-1890*. New York: Fordham UP, 2004.

Fisher, Dexter. "Zitkala-Ša: The Evolution of a Writer." *American Indian Quarterly* 5.3 (1979): 229-38. Reprinted as Foreward to *American Indian Stories* by Zitkala-Ša. Lincoln: U of Nebraska P, 1985. v-xx.

Gaines, Kevin. *Uplifting the Race: Black Leadership, Politics, and Culture in the Twentieth Century*. Chapel Hill: U of North Carolina P, 1996.

Gates, Henry Louis, Jr. "The Trope of a New Negro and the Reconstruction of the Image of the Black." *Representations* 24 (1988): 129-51.

Hannon, Charles. "Zitkala-Ša and the Commercial Magazine Apparatus." *"The Only Efficient Instrument": American Women Writers and the Periodical, 1837-1916*. Ed. Aleta Feinsod Cane and Susan Alves. Iowa City: U of Iowa P, 2001.

Harper, Frances Ellen Watkins. *Iola Leroy*. 1892. Ed. Hazel Carby. Boston: Beacon, 1987.

Hopkins, Pauline E. *Contending Forces: A Romance Illustrative of Negro Life North and South*. 1900. New York: Oxford UP, 1988.

McElrath, Joseph, Jr., Robert C. Leitz III and Jesse S. Crisler. Introduction. *Charles W. Chesnutt: Essays and Speeches*. Stanford: Stanford UP, 1999.

Morgan, Florence A.H. "Novel Notes: The Conjure Woman," *The Bookman* 9.3 (1899): 372-73.

Myers, Jeffery. "Other Nature: Resistance to Ecological Hegemony in Charles W. Chesnutt's *The Conjure Woman.*" *African American Review* 37.1 (2003): 5-20.

Page, Thomas Nelson. *In Ole Virginia, or Marse Chan and Other Stories*. New York: Scribner's 1887.

Shklar, Judith N. *American Citizenship: The Quest for Inclusion*. Cambridge: Harvard UP, 1991.

Spack, Ruth. "Dis/Engagement: Zitkala-Ša's Letters to Carlos Montezuma, 1901-1902." *MELUS* 26.1 (2001): 173-204.

Takaki, Ronald. *Iron Cages*. New York: Knopf, 1979.

Van Evrie, John H. *White Supremacy and Negro Subordination*. 1868. New York: Negro UP, 1969.

Wald, Priscilla. *Constituting Americans: Cultural Anxiety and Narrative Form*. Durham: Duke UP, 1998.

Wexler, Laura. *Tender Violence: Domestic Visions in an Age of U.S. Imperialism*. Chapel Hill: U of North Carolina P, 2000.

Williams, Fannie Barrier. "Club Movement Among Negro Women." *Progress of a Race*. Ed. John William Gibson and Wiliam Henry Crogman. Atlanta: Nichols, 1902. 197-231.

Zitkala-Ša. *American Indian Stories*. 1921. *Zitkala-Ša: American Indian Stories, Legends, and Other Writings*. New York: Penguin, 2003. 68-153.

"Shrinking at No Lofty Theme": The Race Literature of Victoria Earle Matthews, Gertrude Mossell, and Katherine Tillman

Hanna Wallinger

By speaking and writing about slavery and its aftermath, women's rights, white on black violence, and efforts to uplift the race, a generation of African American women intellectuals in the second half of the nineteenth century undertook the task of presenting the hardships faced by, and the injustices committed against their race.[1] During their lifetimes, Victoria Earle Matthews (1861-1907), Gertrude Bustill Mossell (1855-1948), and Katherine Davis Chapman Tillman (1870-?), as well as such contemporaries as Frances Ellen Watkins Harper (1825-1911), Fannie Barrier Williams (1855-1944), Anna Julia Cooper (1858-1964), Amelia E. Johnson (1858-1922), Pauline Elizabeth Hopkins (1859-1930), Ida B. Wells Barnett (1862-1931), and Mary Church Terrell (1863-1954), witnessed all or most of the following: the end of slavery, the Reconstruction and post-Reconstruction periods, the end of a century, World War I, women's suffrage, and the Harlem Renaissance. Although neglected and often suppressed, theirs were voices that needed to be heard. This essay focuses on essays, fiction, and poetry by the lesser-known figures Matthews, Mossell, and Tillman to illustrate the contributions of the larger chorus of women intellectuals, activists, and writers who were proponents of race literature.

These writers committed themselves to race literature, which is literature with a social and political function, its main goal being to record the past and offer a vision of the future. It was women's literature with a pronounced focus on racial issues, and it was race literature with a decidedly feminist point of view. They had not only to fight the general neglect of the female voice but also to refute the racist representations of black women in American culture. Matthews's, Mossell's, and Tillman's concern with race literature was twofold. They wrote and spoke about it eloquently and persuasively while, at the same time, they also produced this literature themselves. The function of literature was foremost in their minds because, as Elizabeth McHenry rightly contends in her study of African American literary societies, "literature resurfaced as one of the practical tools black Americans envisioned using not only to reflect but also in fact to redefine themselves and their roles in the larger community" (188). Race literature thus became a tool that served specific purposes, foremost among them, of course, the deep need of these women to express their concerns and those of other black women.

When her mother was forced to flee the South, Victoria Earle Matthews, who was born a slave in Georgia in 1861, was taken to New York where she became an active clubwoman, teacher, social welfare worker, short story writer, and journalist. Although she had very little formal education, she was well read and had learned the art of rhetoric and quickly mastered the intricacies of work at the various women's organizations. She was active in the National Association of Colored Women (NACW) and established the White Rose Mission in New York, a social center for community women and children, offering shelter and protection to young women coming from the South in search of employment (Cash 760). With the desire to do practical, useful work, Matthews began to deliver dramatic and forceful lectures on such subjects as the political and social responsibilities of self-improvement. She demanded respect for Black women, their work, and their accomplishments (see Cash).

Gertrude Bustill was born in 1855 into a family of black Quakers who later became Presbyterians. She received an excellent education, taught in the public schools of Philadelphia, Camden, New Jersey, and Frankford, Delaware, and contributed essays to numerous journals. After her marriage to Dr. Nathan F. Mossell, a founder of the Douglass Memorial Hospital in Philadelphia under whose initials she published some of her work, and the birth of two daughters, she continued her career as a feminist, social reformer, and journalist (see Braxton, Terborg-Penn, Tate, *Domestic Allegories*, 132-4). *The College Life or Practical Self-Educator: A Manual for Self-Improvement*, an 1896 publication about college-educated African Americans, describes her as follows: "Mrs. Mossell has selected journalism as her profession, believing [...] that the future of women, especially of Afro-American women, is in this line of literary work. In her writings she deals particularly with women and the Afro-American race as a whole. She is alive to all the interests of our race; and since journalism is her mission, she is ever on the alert to ascertain some way in which to make it a success" (Northrop et al. 103).

Biographical data about Katherine Davis Chapman Tillman are less abundant. She was born in 1870, published several essays in the *A.M.E. Church Review* and the *Voice of the Negro*, a number of individual poems in the *Christian Recorder*, a collection of poetry called *Recitations* (1902), several plays, and short fiction, including *Beryl Weston's Ambition: The Story of an Afro-American Girl's Life* (1893), "Miles the Conqueror" (1894), *Clancy Street* (1898-99), and "The Preacher at Hill Station" (1903). *The College Life or Practical Self-Educator* states that she wrote her first poem at the age of thirteen and that "She was educated in the public schools of Louisville and the State University of that city. She may be regarded as one of the most gifted women of her race, possessing rare mental endowments, fine imagination and an excellent command of language" (102).

In 1895 Matthews was invited to participate in the First Congress of Colored Women of the United States, in Boston, a meeting of intelligent, educated, eloquent, and mostly middle-class women organized by Josephine St. Pierre Ruffin to refute a notorious letter from John W. Jacks denigrating black women. Elizabeth McHenry identifies Jacks as the President of the Missouri

Press Club, who, in a letter to a white clubwoman, degrades colored women as "prostitutes" and "natural liars and thieves" (362, n. 6). He was by no means alone in propagating such stereotypes. In her *Primer of Facts*, Pauline E. Hopkins quotes extensively from Mrs. Jeannette Robinson Murphy's *Southern Thoughts for Northern Thinkers*, published in the *Presbyterian Standard* in 1903, in which she perpetuates the plantation school's view of slavery as a benevolent institution and asserts that slave mothers routinely asked their masters to sell their own no-account children away from them (see Wallinger 124-125 and 309). Another – albeit extreme – example will suffice to establish the overall negrophobic attitude that some white women took toward African American women. In an article titled "Experiences of the Race Problem," "A Southern White Woman,"[2] very similar to Murphy, portrays the racial hierarchy in the South as natural and unchanging: "Personally I never passed judgment upon them. So far as I knew God had done that when he made me white and them black. Naturally that fixed the basis of our relationship. I had an affection for them, but there was not the least conception of equality in it. I was not taught these race distinctions, I was born with them, and notice that they are intensified in each succeeding generation of white children" (592). The author elaborates in shocking terms her fear and hatred for colored men, regarding them as totally depraved and degenerate criminals but condemns African American women even more harshly, asserting that they "evidence more nearly the popular idea of total depravity than the men do. They are so nearly all lacking in virtue that the color of a negro woman's skin is generally taken (and quite correctly) as a guarantee of her immorality" (593). She elaborates on this point as follows:

> [Negro women] are evidently the chief instruments of the degradation of the men of their own race. When a man's mother, wife and daughters are all immoral women, there is no room in his fallen nature for the aspiration of honor and virtue. He is bereaved of hope and a pride that even the worst white man always has to stimulate him to decency. I sometimes read of virtuous negro women, hear of them, but the idea is absolutely inconceivable to me. I do not deny they exist, but after living in a section all my life that teems with negroes I cannot imagine such a creation as a virtuous black woman. (593)

Talking about colored students, the writer observes that most of them are mulattoes or octoroons "the offspring of negro women, but *not* of negro men" (594). Addressing further the issue of amalgamation, she observes: "Whatever this intimates of the Southern white man's morals, it teaches two things clearly – that negro men are rarely the fathers of those individuals in the race who develop to any marked degree intellectually, and that negro women who are prostitutes are the mothers of these ambitious sons and daughters" (594).

Given that this article is one that reflects the widely held but less frequently printed sentiment of much of the white population in the post-Reconstruction era, it is no wonder that writers of Matthews's, Mossell's, and Tillman's generation had to defend themselves and pronounce their standards and values. It is in this context that the term race literature entails race apology and feminist manifesto. African American women writers had to define their identities in outspoken and intelligent ways so that they could be heard. However, because not all white Americans subscribed to such wholesale denigration of the entire black population, African American women were able to find the space and means to organize conferences, establish women's clubs and missions, and publish their literary and journalistic writing in books and magazines.

At the 1895 conference, Matthews represented the Women's Loyal Union of New York and Brooklyn and was "arguably the most active" of the 104 delegates (Logan, *With Pen and Voice* 128). In her speech about "The Values of Race Literature," a text that McHenry calls "the manifesto of the black women's movement" (190), Matthews sees the production and dissemination of race literature as necessary to rebut the many negative stereotypes against African Americans in general and African American women in particular. She hails such writing as "the preserving of all the records of a Race," and for "saving from destruction and obliteration what is good, helpful and stimulating" (144-5). In doing so she supports the position of Booker T. Washington that African Americans should look to the future with "helpful and stimulating" writing rather than concentrate on past wrongs. She also opposes dialect writing because it often perpetuates the stereotype of African Americans as subordinate servants.

As for the content of race literature, Matthews thinks that writers must "win a place by the simplicity of the story, thrown into strong relief by the multiplicity of its dramatic situations; the spirit of romance, and even tragedy, shadowy and as yet ill-defined, but from which our race on this continent can never be dissociated" (131). Although she admits that there are as yet not too many distinctive texts, she offers a list of writers, including Phillis Wheatley, Frederick Douglass, William Wells Brown, and Frances Harper, who constitute a nascent African American literature. By pointing out the inherent worth, heroism, and nobility of their black and mixed-race protagonists, these writers seek to refute stereotypes and improve race conditions. At the same time, Matthews says, writers must meet certain standards and their writing requires modesty and judiciousness: "True culture in Race Literature will enable us to discriminate and not to write hasty thoughts and unjust and ungenerous criticism often of our superiors in knowledge and judgement" (145). Adhering to the general principles of the club movement, she sees the female sex playing an important part in this project: "When living up to her highest development, woman has done much to make lasting history, by her stimulating influence and there can be no greater responsibility than that, and this is the highest privilege granted to her by the Creator of the Universe" (146).

In addition to defining the character and subject of race literature, Matthews identifies it as distinctly American. The indisputable fact of the unequal treatment of the American Negro leads to a literature that "will of necessity be different in all essential points of greatness, true heroism and real Christianity" from mainstream American literature (129). Speaking not long before the *Plessy v. Ferguson* decision of 1896, Matthews designates blacks as "typical" Americans and yet separate from their white counterparts: "We are the only people most distinctive from those who have civilized and governed this country, who have become typical Americans, and we rank next to the Indians in originality of soil, and yet remain a distinct people" (130). For her, race literature is the vehicle to convey "the unnaturally suppressed inner lives which our people have been compelled to lead" (131). The questions of how and to what extent African American and mainstream American literature differ continue to engage critics of African American and ethnic literature to this day.

Matthews contrasts her conception of race literature with that implicit in texts that engage issues of race by white writers such as Washington Irving, Mark Twain, John Ridpath, William Dean Howells and Arthur Conan Doyle. She talks about Howells's "tortuous jugglery of words" (134) and questions his status as a "littérateur, diplomat, journalist, altruist" (135). She takes her lead here from an article in Anna Julia Cooper's *A Voice from the South*, in which Cooper terms Howells's novel *An Imperative Duty* "an insult to humanity and a sin against God" for its "sweeping generalizations of a race [based] on such meager and superficial information" (203). Nevertheless, Matthews's words were brave coming as they did in Howells's Boston at a well-publicized conference.

Matthews calls upon her generation of black women to produce their own literature and, as Shirely Wilson Logan puts it in *"We Are Coming,"* "demonstrate their own intellectual potential to skeptical readers" (137). At the same time, Matthews points out the unrecognized influence of African American topics, characters, and plots on white writing. In this effort to highlight the contributions of people of African descent to world literature, she is joined by Tillman who published an article about "The Negro Among Anglo-Saxon Poets," in which she reads Shakespeare's *Othello* and points out Africanist tropes in Elizabeth Barrett Browning, John Greenleaf Whittier, Henry Wadsworth Longfellow, and A.T. Worden as well as discussing Alexander Dumas, Père, and Alexander Sergeivich Pushkin as authors of African descent.

In "The Values of Race Literature," Matthews programmatically proposes that African American authors should intensify their "thoughtful, well-defined and intelligently placed efforts" to inform Americans in accurate terms about the lives of black people (136). Although her speech lacks a political call to action against wrongs committed, it acknowledges the need to subtly manipulate public sentiment in favor of a more nuanced picture of the African American through race literature.

The texts of most black writers of that period reflect tensions between accommodation and rebellion, racial solidarity and elitism, disapproval of negative stereotyping and celebration of black perseverance. Although Matthews rejects the denigrating "darkey" image, she praises the "happy, hopeful, enduring character" (128) of the African American and his profound sense of Christian forgiveness. Critics are tempted to group the intellectuals of that time into either the more conservative Booker T. Washington camp or the more politically radical group associated with W.E.B. Du Bois. But the distinctions are not always so clear-cut. Matthews, for example, has a strong sense of the proper role of women and sees the need to forgive the sins of the past, but she is definitely a politically active woman and a strong supporter of Ida B. Wells's anti-lynching campaigns.

In 1897 Matthews delivered a more optimistic speech, "The Awakening of the Afro-American Woman," at the Annual Convention of the Society of Christian Endeavor in San Francisco, which was a "Protestant, interdenominational young people's movement established in 1881" (Logan, *With Pen and Voice* 123). When seen in its proper context, what we now might be tempted to read as a rather conservative appeal to protect black women and keep them in their proper places was for its time a radical call to grant them the same rights as white women. Matthews addressed a mainly white group of young Christian men and women and this definitely tempered her tone and feminist and racial rhetoric. She sees the awakening of the African American woman as one of "the most promising facts in our national life" (154), asserting that progress has been made since emancipation: "The auction block of brutality has been changed into the forum of reason, the slave mart has been replaced by the schoolroom and the church" (150). Her metaphors of growth, of night and day, of homebuilding, and of salvation through Christianity are carefully chosen to address her white audience's lack of knowledge about slavery and prejudices about the morality of black women. Besides former slave women's achievements as breadwinners, church women, educators and clubwomen, Matthews emphasizes their great accomplishment in making "a home for [their] race, an abiding place for husband, and son, and daughter" (153). Her argumentative rhetoric culminates in a call for American society to abandon unjust marriage and divorce laws, end segregated transportation, establish homes for the elderly, the sick, the outcast, and the orphaned, and reform the prison system: "I appeal to the Christian sentiment which dominates this organization, to assist us in righting the wrongs growing out of these regulations, to the end that our womanhood may be sustained in its dignity and protected in its weakness" (155).

Despite the pivotal position she holds in this generation of eloquent women because of her advocacy of race literature, Matthews's own fiction is less well known and less readily available than that of her contemporaries. Under her pen name Victoria Earle, Matthews published several works of fiction, among them "Aunt Lindy: A Story Founded on Real Life."[3] It concerns an old black nurse, Aunt Lindy, into whose care is entrusted the victim of a great fire. She nurtures the man back to health even after she recognizes him as her former master who sold her children away from her. The desire for vengeance and bitter hatred, however, are seen as temptations that a true Christian spirit has to conquer. The faithfulness and loving care of the old woman might be difficult to accept from a modern point of view, but it was felt to be necessary at that time to demonstrate the race's potential for forgiveness and superior moral sentiment. "Aunt Lindy" exemplifies an ideal shared by Matthews's fellow black women intellectuals. Tillman singles it out in her "Afro-American Women and Their Work" (87). Comparing it to Harper's novel *Iola Leroy* and Anna Julia Cooper's collection of essays *A Voice from the South*, both published in 1892, Mossell praises it in "A Sketch of Afro-American Literature": "Only the race itself knows its own depth of love, its powers of forgiveness. In the heart of this race, if the American nation will only see it, they have the truest type on earth of forgiveness as taught by the Redeemer of the world" (64).

Written with compassion and pathos, Matthews's "Zelika – a Story," published in the *A.M.E. Church Review* in 1892, narrates the life and death of a cruel plantation owner, Robert Claiborne, whose granddaughter Valerie is given the beautiful slave Zelika "in much the same way as a Northern mother would give her child a doll" (73). Zelika is loved by a strong and faithful slave, known as "King George" because of his "reputed royal ancestry in the benighted fatherland," "proud bearing," and reputation for "native wisdom and resource" (873). The characters of this "legend" are larger than life: the giant and brave hero King George; the wicked, fearsome tyrant Claiborne; and the beautiful, soft, forbearing, and deeply Christian heroine Zelika, who is, at one point, compared to Penelope waiting for her Ulysses (76). As with many stories of this period, it turns out that Zelika is Claiborne's own daughter by his slave Miriam, who was killed protecting Claiborne from a bullet. On his death bed, when General Sherman is at the gates of Atlanta, Claiborne leaves a note for Zelika telling her where to find a buried treasure. With true Christian patience, Zelika suffers through the difficult end of the war and faithfully waits for King George's return before she opens this letter, whereupon they find the treasure and leave the South.

Another little-known story by Matthews, "Eugenie's Mistake," published in the *A.M.E. Church Review* in 1891, tells of a beautiful young heiress to a Southern estate who is found to possess a drop of black blood. She flees to France where she is educated and is joined there after five years by her husband who then reveals to her that he himself is also of African descent. While the story uses some of the predictable elements of passing literature, such as hinting at the color of the two protagonists and a series of misunderstandings and intrigues, it does not contain the usual melodramatic scene of revelation in which the hero or heroine laments belonging to the black race. Instead, when Eugenie finds out her ancestry, there is no word about the social consequences for herself; her only thought is how she can protect her young husband and spare him the supposed shame of her color.

Whereas Matthews's essays are sharp, well-informed, straightforward answers of a public speaker to the negative portrayal of black women, her lesser-known fiction displays a more private and intimate side of this outspoken defender of the rights of women. "Aunt Lindy," "Zelika," and "Eugenie's Mistake" concentrate on the resourcefulness and innate nobility of slaves, former slaves, and their descendants. They do not directly condemn white Southern slaveholders. Instead, they emphasize reversals of fortunes: the former master who depends on the good will of his former slave, the slave master who is abandoned by all his family except for the one daughter whom he has never acknowledged as such, and the cruel separation of a married couple because of anti-miscegenation laws. Although the theme of Christian forgiveness makes her fiction appropriate for church publications, the wrongs of slavery do not go unacknowledged. It is the cruelty of the slave system that bring about the reversals of fortunes.

In their articles and creative writing, Mossell and Tillman propagate ideas similar to those of Matthews. In "A Sketch of Afro-American Literature," published in 1894 as part of *The Work of the Afro-American Woman*, Gertrude Mossell raises some fundamental questions about the nature of Afro-American literature: "The intellectual history of a people or nation constitutes to a great degree the very heart of its life. To find this history, we search the fountainhead of its language, its customs, its religion, and its politics expressed by tongue or pen, its folklore and its songs" (48). Because for a long time the African American could make no law nor write his own history, Mossell contends, "he could only protest against the injustice of his oppressors in his heart, in his song, and in his whispered consolations to the suffering and dying" (49). Oral history is thus a reliable source of information. At the same time, literature is history and reflects the three great happenings in the African American past: the middle passage, which is described by Mossell as "the separation from native land and friends, and later arrival in this land of forced adoption" (48); slavery, a period Mossell calls "two hundred years of bondage and oppression mitigated only through the hope thrown upon life's pathway by the presence of hundreds of freemen of the race eking out an existence hampered on all sides by caste prejudice" (48-9); and life after emancipation, which she calls freedom and citizenship "defrauded of its substance by every means that human ingenuity could devise" (49). Mossell's tone here is by no means conciliatory. She sees race literature as useful for not only the writers, but present and future readers because it offers a distinctively African American version of history.

As Joanne Braxton points out in her introduction to the Schomburg edition of *The Work of the Afro-American Woman*, Mossell replaces the ideal of the true woman as pious, obedient, and subservient, with the concept of a "noble womanhood" that includes the humble workers and housewives as well as the more public orators and clubwomen such as Ida B. Wells (47). Mossell is of the firm opinion that women writers of her time and race should assume the role of pioneers as to their subject matter and be self-consciously feminist. It is this latter idea that makes Mossell of particular interest to the modern critic. For example, in "The Opposite Point of View" she offers an early criticism of the idea that the care and responsibility for a happy home relies solely on women and in "A Lofty Study" she anticipates Virginia Woolf by asserting that a woman writer needs to have a room of her own.

The Work of the Afro-American Woman includes a number of poems, most of which feature end-stopped, four-stress quatrains and are full of anaphora and alliteration, much in the style of Longfellow and Whittier. They typically concern love between mother and child, married bliss, Christian love earned and dearly gained, the failure of love, the death of a beloved person, and the cycle of life ending in loss. These poems provide readers with a reassuring message of divine justice. They are less feminist than Mossell's prose works, their chief aim being to refute the black women's reputed deficiency in personal character and moral values. Without being explicitly feminist, a few poems are nevertheless outspoken and overtly political, such as "Tell the North That We Are Raising" and "Child of the Southland." Although the bosom of the child of the latter is "Reeking with venom" (4), his (or her) bright future will entail access to "the promised land" (22). These poems demonstrate the tension between Mossell's need to foster a sense of solidarity among African Americans and her belief that African Americans should take combative action in order to obtain equality. The two aforementioned politically engaged poems also hint that white America can not rely on the ever-lasting meekness of the former slaves.

Like her contemporaries, Katherine Davis Chapman Tillman undertakes a revisionist history with the aim of firmly establishing the valuable, resourceful, intelligent, and artistic contributions of African American women. She begins her essay "Afro-American Women and Their Work," originally published in the *A.M.E. Church Review* in 1895, by stating "Woman has always had a mission in the world" (70). After enumerating women of historical significance, such as Cleopatra, Heloise, and Joan of Arc, she shifts swiftly – and logically – to the African American slave women, whom she calls heroic and worthy. Tillman describes the hard work of field and house slaves and their suffering at the hands of cruel masters and mistresses and points out their spiritual distress due to a lack of Christian training. She cites the example of Stowe's Uncle Tom to illustrate that an innate sense of Christian forbearance and spirituality comes naturally to slaves and they have the ability and longing to accept religion. Tillman then lists the accomplishments of particular African American women in the fields of religion, art, medicine, elocution, journalism, writing, domestic service, and homemaking. She praises every group because black women's achievements in each of these fields disprove those who "are continually on the outlook for the darkest side of life" (89). Tillman ends with plea for uplifting the race through the work of women: "Let us Afro-American women pledge ourselves to the elevation of our home. Let us war against intemperance, against infidelity, against gambling in saloons and parlors, against bad literature and immorality of all kind, for these are the demons that destroy our homes" (92).

As Claudia Tate states in her introduction to the *Works of Katherine Davis Chapman Tillman*, a reader schooled in the rhetoric of twentieth-century racial protest fiction will find "that complex issues of race (such as alienation, the extensiveness of institutionalized racism, and intraracial discrimination) are either unrealistically depicted or missing altogether" (53) from Tillman's texts. Much like her contemporaries, Tillman, who mainly published in the *A.M.E. Church Review* and the *Christian Recorder*, had to reconcile the spirit of Christian patience expected by and from the readers of these church magazines and the call to arms against racial discrimination that she knew was needed. Similar to Amelia E. Johnson she chose a partly sentimental mode to address her readers. Tate describes Tillman's novellas as "female narratives of domestic ideality" that "outline ideal patterns of male and female ego formation as well as racial individuation and socialization through the configuration of a black female protest" (54). It would be wrong, however, to assume, in the light of the more outspokenly racialized novels of her male contemporaries Charles W. Chesnutt and Sutton E. Griggs, that this is simply and only the result of a gender predilection for domestic rather than political issues. Chesnutt and Griggs also concentrate on the family as the background of inter- and intraracial strife. Two exemplary tales of self-help through good behavior and education as well as several poems about a mythologized South and the hardships of women demonstrate Tillman's strategy of disguising her political and social agenda.

Published in the *A.M.E. Church Review* in two installments (July and October 1893), *Beryl Weston's Ambition: The Story of an Afro-American Girl's Life* chronicles the development of bright and ambitious Beryl, who wants to become a teacher of modern languages and higher mathematics. When her mother suddenly dies, she has to abandon her college career and stay at home to work not only for her family but also for her friends and the community. In her work she is supported by Dr. Warren, a physician who has been reunited with his mother – the village nurse – from whom he was separated as a slave child. Beryl also finds religion with the help of the young minister Harold Griswold. The encounter between these two admirable male characters leads to a discussion of the race problem, a stock ingredient in much fiction of that time. This exchange functions, as Claudia Tate says in *Domestic Allegories of Political Desire*, as "discursive displacement" enabling a writer to avoid direct criticism of racism by putting criticism into the mouth of fictional characters (200).

The gender issue at the heart of this novella is Beryl's refusal to marry the minister because life with him would limit her ambition to become a writer. Her eventual marriage to Dr. Warren has to be read as her reward for an exemplary life in the service of her family and friends because it enables her to travel extensively and even serve as a teacher for some time, which suggests that virtuous role models for future generations of young women, such as Beryl, will be rewarded with a fulfilling life despite the limited opportunities available to them.

As it is for Beryl, education serves as the key to success for the hero in Tillman's story "Miles the Conqueror" (1894). In tone and mood this story is typical of much writing of this period. Its message is that an African American, however poor and uneducated he may be, needs to strive for education and gain the respect of his peers by exceptional dedication to his studies, sweetness of mind and exemplary behavior. The eponymous hero of this tale – in true Booker T. Washington fashion – begs for admission into a college and works his way through school, eventually winning the affection of one of the most racist and race-conscious white students by nursing him through a dangerous illness. His reward is respect, friendship, and honor. Like Matthews's Aunt Lindy and Zelika, Miles is deeply religious, and like Beryl he is determined to be educated. The message in these tales and poems by Matthews, Mossell, and Tillman is not simply that religious forbearance and faith will bring social and professional success, but that an inherent nobility of mind and character will win respect despite racial difference and a general climate of prejudice and discrimination. These stories and poems offer the vision of a better future, highlight the greatness, heroism, and true Christianity of African Americans, and win their place through the spirit of romance and tragedy that Matthews, as shown above, designates as key ingredients of race literature.

Tillman's poetry covers themes ranging from the slave past, notable black men and women, everyday family life, and the academic and religious education of young people. Most of them were collected in *Recitations*, originally published by the A.M.E. Book concern in Philadelphia in 1902.[4] Dickson D. Bruce cites *Recitations* as a collection typical of its time because it contains dialect poems "hand-in-hand with verse that deal[s] with black heroism and that bitterly excoriate[s] American prejudice" (111). The juxtaposition of poems in various registers enables Tillman to express an understanding of the need of the former slaves to see meaning in their past suffering and at the same time to place that need in a critical context.

Protest against injustice and wrongdoing permeates Tillman's poetry. A typical example is "America's First Cargo of Slaves," in which slave transportation is called "America's dark shame" (195). In "Clotelle – A Tale of Florida," a young fair-skinned slave woman is in love with a dark and stately "prince of olden days" (156), but her master, predictably, forbids this union because he himself lusts after the beautiful slave: "You love Pierre, you say – my servant; / You prefer my slave to me, / Your love will but prove his ruin; / Never thou his bride wilt be" (157). Pierre is hanged and Clotelle, the "sweet maiden," drowns herself and thus demonstrates the depth of feeling that was so often reputed to be lacking in slave women. In "Our Cause" Tillman laments white people's lack of support for African American causes. In other poems she honors the courage and contributions of Phillis Wheatley, Ida B. Wells, African American religious leaders, and black soldiers.

Tillman's dialect poems stress a mythologized past, praise the admirable qualities of the men and women she depicts, and thus work against the image of savage black males and immoral black women (see Sherman 12-13). They are memorable because of the loving tribute they pay to the common heroes and heroines of black history and contemporary life. “Uncle Ned’s Story” concerns an old farm slave, Uncle Ned, whose slave wife Chloe refused to leave the plantation after emancipation. In bitterness and scorn Uncle Ned reports about her staying back while he went off fighting and how, when he came home, he found her dead, buried beside her mistress. “Seeking the Lost” is a moving recollection of an old former slave searching for his family. In “Sen’ Me Back to de Souf,” an old father asks his daughter, with whom he lives in the North, to let him spend his Christmas holidays in the warm South with his folks: “You’ve tried quite hard since I’ve been heah / To mek me feel young lak an’ gay, / But nothin’ meks it seem lak home” (173). In “When Mandy Combs Her Head” (reminiscent of Dunbar’s more famous “When Malindy Sings”), a young African American girl gives very careful attention to her hair. A very intelligent young person, “And she’s got her books down fine; / She can figure like a lawyer, / And read Latin, line for line” (160), she nevertheless exaggerates her efforts to straighten out her hair and despairs about its unruliness. Tillman beautifully handles the black vernacular in these poems. Her voice is one of understanding and loving care. She does not ridicule the father who wants to go home South nor the bright girl who does not know what to do with her hair nor the deeply felt faith of former slaves in such poems as “Uncle Ike’s Testimony.” Her aim is to demonstrate the needs and virtues of the common people, giving them the grace and dignity of finely turned verse.

From a modern perspective, arguably her most memorable poems are those written to and about women because they reflect a remarkable awareness of gender solidarity among women of all classes. In “She Who Never Had a Chance,” a female speaker looks back on her life of shame, need, and lovelessness. Driven into a sinful mode of living through poverty and deprivation, she awaits an early death at the age of forty-three. She asks for tolerance from women, such as “[t]e heartless coquette, the unfaithful wife” (177), who are spared an existence such as hers even though they have not lead exemplary lives themselves. When she concludes that “They’d never think of helping a woman like me” (177), this is a plea to the leading women of the race not to disdain the so-called fallen members of their sex.

“Bashy” addresses the subject of intraracial prejudice. It is about a young black girl who has no opportunities in life because she is too dark and is looked down upon not only by white but also by black people. Even the man she loves does not marry her because of her dark skin. Bashy dies, an all too common fate, causing the speaker to ask: “Oh, women and men of the Negro Race, / Can we not raise above color of face? / Teach our girls that the worst disgrace / Is blackness of life, not blackness of face!” (175). More than the other poems, this poem spells out the ideals of the women’s club movement: “Lift the women up and the race ascends; / Let the women go down, and our progress ends” (175). Mixed with her dialect poems and those about heroism, “She Who Never Had a

Chance" and "Bashy" subtly express a radical political and social message and add to the wide array of topics the author addresses. In her writing Tillman carefully balances content and topic, moving between uplift rhetoric in her essays and plays and an outspoken and personal voice in her poetry.

The black women intellectuals and writers of the post-Reconstruction era answered Matthews's call "to form habits of observation and commence to build a plan for posterity by synthesis, analysis, [...] aiming and striving after the highest" ("Value" 144). Despite African Americans' growing hardships, for Matthews "the outlook for Race Literature" (146) was never brighter. Matthews, Mossell, and Tillman exemplified their generation's race consciousness. "Shrinking at no lofty theme, shirking no serious duty, aiming at every possible excellence, and determined to do their part in the future uplift of the race" (145), as Matthews herself puts it, these women and others of their ilk embraced race literature as a mode of self-definition and thereby provided inspiring models for coming generations.

I would like to thank John Gruesser for his very helpful comments on this essay and his unfailing eye for the better phrase. I would like to thank Mary Frances Jiménez for providing me with a copy of Matthews's "Eugenie's Mistake." Thanks are due to my colleagues Linda Reschen and derek de-silva for their support and good advice.

[1] See Shirley Wilson Logan's summary in *"We Are Coming": The Persuasive Discourse of Nineteenth-Century Black Women*, 3.

[2] This was part of a series of articles published in *The Independent* in 1904, comprising "The Race Problem – An Autobiography" by a Southern Colored Woman, "Experiences of the Race Problem" by a Southern White Woman, "Observations of the Southern Race Feeling" by a Northern Woman, and "A Northern Negro's Autobiography" signed by Fannie Barrier Williams. All of them are were republished in Leo Stein's *Fragments of Autobiography*.

[3] This story was first printed in *The A.M.E. Church Review* 5 (January 1889), 246-50. It was printed in hard cover as a separate volume in 1893 by J.J. Little & Company, Astor Place, New York City (see Tate, *Domestic Allegories*, n 18, 260). It is available as a hypertext at http://www.facstaff.bucknell.edu/gcarr/19cUSWW/VEM/AL.html

[4] The following poems are from *Recitations*. They are identified by the page numbers in the Schomburg edition. For detailed interpretations, see Tate, Introduction 34-42.

Works Cited

Braxton, Joanne. Introduction. Mossell xxvii-xlii.

Bruce, Dickson D., Jr. *Black American Writing from the Nadir: The Evolution of a Literary Tradition 1877-1915*. Baton Rouge: Lousiana State UP, 1989.

Cash, Floris Barnett. "Matthews, Victoria Earle." *Black Women in White America: An Historical Encyclopedia*. Ed. Darlene Clark Hine, et al. Bloomington: Indiana UP, 1993. 759-761.

Cooper, Anna Julia. *A Voice from the South*. 1892. New York: Oxford UP, 1988.

"Experiences of the Race Problem." Stein 590-594.

Hopkins, Pauline Elizabeth. *A Primer of Facts Pertaining to the Early Greatness of the African American Race and the Possibility of Restoration by Its Descendants – with Epilogue*. 1905. In Wallinger 291-314.

Logan, Shirley Wilson. *"We Are Coming": The Persuasive Discourse of Nineteenth-Century Black Women*. Carbondale: Southern Illinois UP, 1999.

—, ed. *With Pen and Voice: A Critical Anthology of Nineteenth-Century African-American Women*. Carbondale: Southern Illinois UP, 1995.

Matthews, Victoria Earle. "Aunt Lindy: A Story Found on Real Life." 1893. Designed by Jennifer L. Ciotta. The Online Archive of Nineteenth-Century U.S. Women's Writings. Ed. Glynis Carr. Online. Internet. Posted: Summer 2000. 17 January 2008. http://www.facstaff.bucknell.edu/gcarr/19cUSWW/VEM/AL.html

—. "The Awakening of the Afro-American Woman." 1897. Logan, *With Pen and Voice* 149-155.

—. "Eugenie's Mistake." *A.M.E. Church Review* 8 (1891): 256-68.

—. "The Value of Race Literature: An Address Delivered at the First Congress of Colored Women of the United States." 1895. Logan, *With Pen and-Voice* 126-148.

—-. "Zelika – A Story." *A.M.E. Church Review* 9 (July 1892): 72-78.

McHenry, Elizabeth. *Forgotten Readers: Recovering the Lost History of African American Literary Societies*. Durham: Duke UP, 2002.

Mossell, Mrs. N.F. *The Work of the Afro-American Woman*. 1894. Schomburg Library of Nineteenth-Century Black Women Writers. New York: Oxford UP, 1988.

—. "A Sketch of Afro-American Literature." Mossell 48-66.

Northrop, Henry Davenport, Joseph R. Gay, and I. Garland Penn. *The College Life or Practical Self Educator: A Manual of Self-Improvement for the Colored Race*. Chicago: Chicago Publication and Lithograph, 1896.

Sherman, Joan R. *African-American Poetry of the Nineteenth Century*. Urbana: U of Illinois P, 1992.

Stein, Leo, ed. *Fragments of Autobiography: An Original Anthology*. New York: Arno, 1974.

Tate, Claudia. *Domestic Allegories of Political Desire: The Black Heroine's Text at the Turn of the Century*. New York: Oxford UP, 1992.

—. Introduction. Tillman, *The Works of Katherine Davis Chapman Tillman* 3-62.

Terborg-Penn, Rosalyn. "Mossell, Gertrude E.H. Bustill." *Black Women in White America: An Historical Encyclopedia*. Ed. Darlene Clark Hine, et al. Bloomington: Indiana UP, 1993. 820-821.

Tillman, Katherine Davis Chapman. "Afro-American Women and Their Work." Tillman 70-92.

—. *Beryl Weston's Ambition: The Story of an Afro-American Girl's Life*. Tillman 207- 46.

—. "Miles the Conqueror." Tillman 247-50.

—. *Recitations*. Tillman 152-203.

—. *The Works of Katherine Davis Chapman Tillman*. Schomburg Library of Nineteenth-Century Black Women Writers. New York: Oxford UP, 1991.

Wallinger, Hanna. *Pauline E. Hopkins: A Literary Biography*. Athens: U of Georgia P, 2005.

Notes on the Contributors

Shanna Greene Benjamin is Assistant Professor of English at Grinnell College, Iowa. A specialist in African American literature and culture, her current projects include "Race, Faces and False Fronts: Shakespearean Signifying in the *Colored American Magazine*," "Does it Matter if They're Black or White: Racial Ambiguity in Frances Ellen Watkins Harper's 'The Two Offers' and Toni Morrison's 'Recitatif'," and *The Ananse Aesthetic: Transformations of the Trickster Spider in African American Folklore, Fiction, and Fiber Art.*

Monique-Adelle Callahan is a doctoral student in Comparative Literature at Harvard University. Her current work focuses on the literary transnationalism of black literatures in the Americas, specifically the poetic narratives of slavery and "inventions" of freedom in early afrodescendente literatures.

Sarah Clere is a doctoral student at the University of North Carolina at Chapel Hill. Her areas of specialization are nineteenth and twentieth-century American literature, and she is writing a dissertation on the role of the body in Willa Cather's fiction.

John Cullen Gruesser is the author, most recently, of *Confluences: Postcolonialism, African American Literary Studies, and the Black Atlantic*, and the editor of *The Unruly Voice: Rediscovering Pauline Elizabeth Hopkins*, and *The Black Sleuth* by John Edward Bruce.

Mary Frances Jiménez is a doctoral candidate in nineteenth-century American literature at the University of Maryland, College Park. Her research and teaching interests include empire studies and African American literature; an interview she conducted with Cyrus Cassells is forthcoming in *African American Review.*

Alisha R. Knight is an Assistant Professor of English and American Studies at Washington College in Chestertown, Maryland, where she teaches courses in African American literature and American print culture. Her essays have been published in the *Oxford Companion to African American Literature* and *American Periodicals*. She is currently working on two projects: one is a critical study of Pauline Hopkins entitled *Debunking the American Dream*, and the second is a study of African American book publishing practices at the turn of the twentieth century, tentatively titled *Racing into the Publishing Marketplace.*

Jennifer Larson earned her PhD in English from the University of North Carolina at Chapel Hill. She is the assistant editor of *Reading Contemporary African American Drama: Fragments of History, Fragments of Self* (Peter Lang, 2007) and the editor of the David Walker section in *The North Carolina Roots of African American Literature* (University of North Carolina Press, 2006).

Jessica Metzler is a doctoral candidate in English at Cornell University. Her dissertation concerns questions of narrative temporality, affect, and performance in twentieth-century American literature.

DoVeanna S. Fulton Minor is an Associate Professor and Chair of the Women's Studies department and Director of African American Studies and at the University of Alabama. Her research interests are Black feminist criticism and African American oral traditions. Her research has concentrated on African American literature and manifestations of oral traditions by Black women. Her books, *Speaking Power: Black Feminist Orality in Women's Narratives of Slavery*, (SUNY Press, 2006) and *Speaking to Write/Right: Three African American Women's Oral Slave Narratives* (SUNY Press, forthcoming) examine written and oral traditions in African American women's writing. She has published articles in such distinguished journals as *Legacy: A Journal of American Women Writers* and the *Journal of American Folklore.* Her current research project, *Radical Prohibition: African Americans Writing Race and the Anti-Drink Movement, 1860-1919*, is on African American activism in the Temperance Movement. To complete this project, Dr. Fulton Minor received a grant from the National Endowment for the Humanities and the American Association of University Women Educational Foundation Postdoctoral Fellowship.

Angelita Reyes is a professor of African and African American Studies and English and an affiliate faculty of Women and Gender Studies at Arizona State University. She is the author of *Mothering ACROSS Cultures: Postcolonial Representations* (2002) and was a faculty curator of the multi-media exhibition, *Dynamic Journey: Transformations of Slavery-Era Spaces, Routes and Sounds* (2007). Her current research focuses on Sarah Parker Remond's Italian years, 1866-1894, which is part of a forthcoming monograph on Remond. Her interest in vernacular architecture and sustainability led to the naming of an antebellum log cabin to the National Register of Historic Places and to scholarship, which highlights Vicey Skipwith as an autobiographical paradigm.

Isabel Soto teaches at the Universidad Nacional de Educación a Distancia in Madrid. She has been Visiting Scholar at Vassar College and Honorary Fellow of The Schomburg Institute for Research and Black Culture. In 2000 she co-founded the independent scholarly publisher *The Gateway Press* devoted to publishing work on liminality and text. Her interests lie in liminality theory and African American studies. She has published and lectured widely on Langston

Hughes's relationship with Spain and is preparing a book on that subject. Her most recent publication, the essay "The Empowerment of Displacement," appeared in *Montage of a Dream: The Art and Life of Langston Hughes* (Columbia and London: University of Missouri Press, 2007).

Hanna Wallinger is Associate Professor of American Studies at Salzburg University in Austria. She is author of *Pauline E. Hopkins: A Literary Biography* (2005), editor of *Transitions: Race, Culture, and the Dynamics of Race* (2006) and has published essays on Hopkins, Alice Walker, Gloria Naylor, Sutton E. Griggs, W.E.B. Du Bois, Alice Moore Dunbar-Nelson, and others. She is secretary of the Collegium for African American Research.

FORECAAST

(Forum for European Contributions to African American Studies)
edited by Prof. Dr. Sabine Broeck, Prof. Dr. Maria I. Diedrich, and Prof. Dr. Christopher Mulvey

Fritz Gysin; Cynthia S. Hamilton (Eds.)
Complexions of Race
The African Atlantic
Complexions of Race: The African Atlantic reveals the ways in which conceptions of race have informed – and sometimes over-determined – readings of American experience. The first section is concerned with the geography of racial identity, with race, place, and with mapping. The second explores the way racial identities are constructed, reconstructed, or enforced through performance. The final section explores the way literary forms, generic constructions, linguistic strategies, and critical practices construct, re-construct, or reposition identities assigned or claimed on the basis of race.
Bd. 15, 2005, 264 S., 24,90 €, br., ISBN 3-8258-9030-9

LIT Verlag GmbH & Co. KG Wien – Zürich

Auslieferung Österreich: Medienlogistik Pichler-ÖBZ GmbH & Co KG
IZ-NÖ Süd, Straße 1, Objekt 34, A-2355 Wiener Neudorf, Postfach 133
Tel. +43 (0) 2236 / 63 535 - 236, Fax +43 (0) 2236 / 63 535 - 243, e-Mail: bestellen@medien-logistik.at

Auslieferung Deutschland: Fresnostr. 2 48159 Münster
Tel.: 0251 / 620 32 22 – Fax 0251 / 922 60 99
e-Mail: vertrieb@lit-verlag.de – http://www.lit-verlag.de